KRAZY & IGNATZ.

by George Herriman.

"A Wild Warmth of Chromatic Gravy."

Coalescing the Complete Full-Page Comic Strips,
with the usual extra Rarities.

1935-36.

Edited by Bill Blackbeard.

Fantagraphics Books, SEATTLE.

Published by Fantagraphics Books.
7563 Lake City Way North East,
Seattle, Washington, 98115, United States of America.

Edited and annotated by Bill Blackbeard.
Except where noted, all research materials appear courtesy of the San Francisco Academy of Cartoon Art.
Design, decoration, and some cutlines by Chris Ware.
Production assistance and scanning by Paul Baresh.
Promoted by Eric Reynolds.
Published by Gary Groth and Kim Thompson.

First Fantagraphics Books edition: July 2005.

ISBN 1-56097-690-X.

Printed in Korea through Print Vision.

Special thanks to Mr. Bob Beerbohm, Mr. Chris Boensh,
Mr. Alex Star, Ms. Marlene Shore,
Mr. Peter Merolo of Kokonino Kollectibles,
Ms. Laurie Sims of the Sheldon Memorial Art Gallery,
and Mr. John Fawcett of the Fawcett Toy Museum.

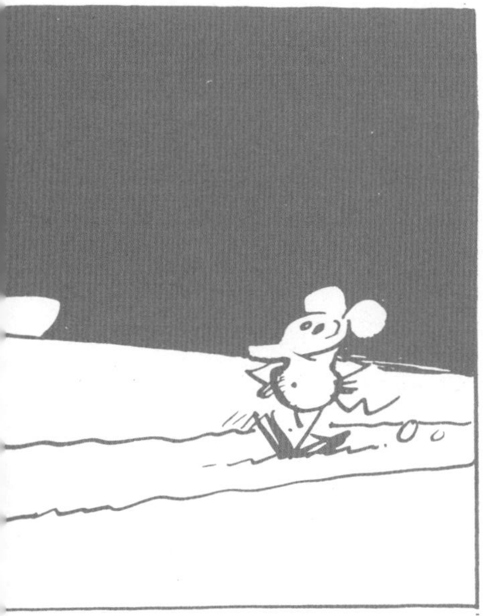

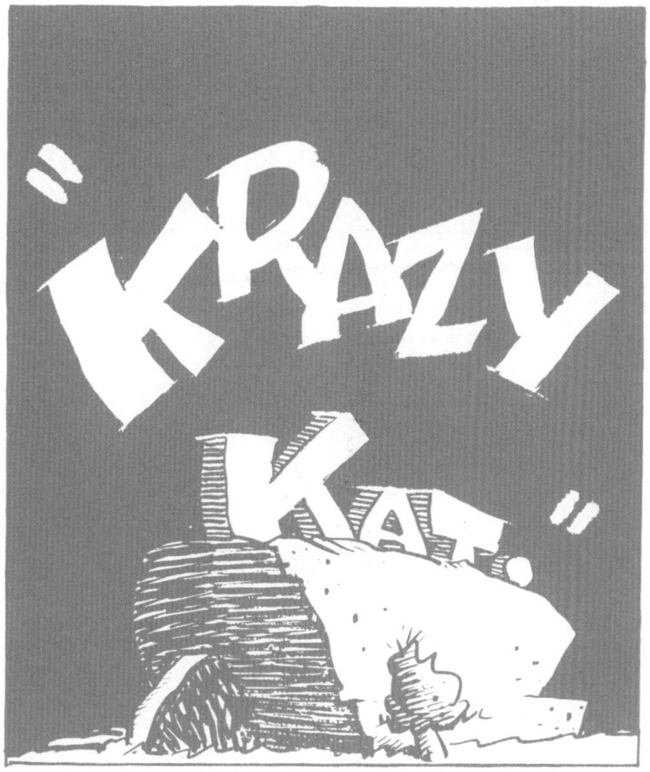
"KRAZY KAT."

KRAZY & IGNATZ.

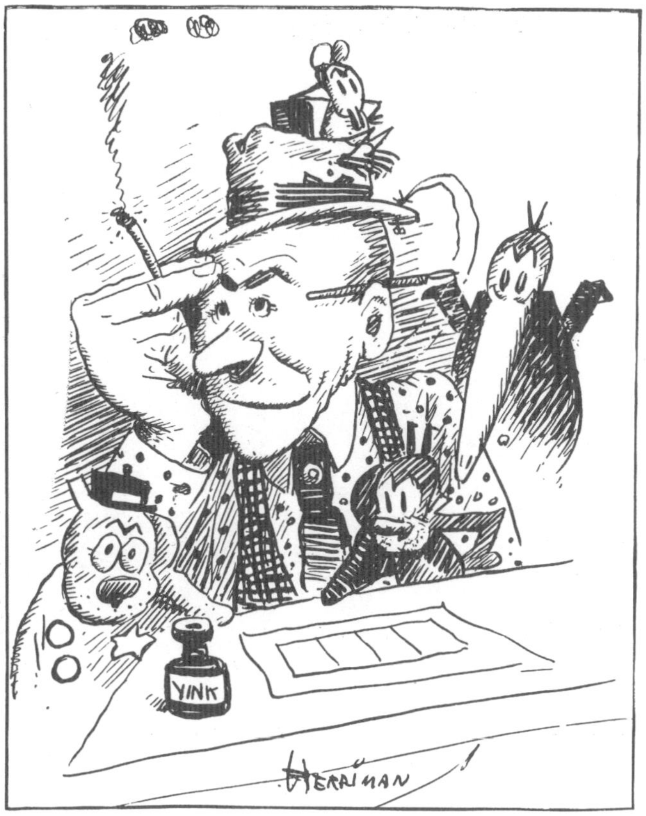
YINK
Herriman

Episode of 7/2/16, watercolored by Herriman. Courtesy of Peter Merolo.

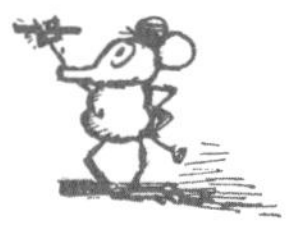

Autumn Leaves:

Herriman's Klosing Kat Pages Revel in Fine Syndicate Kolor (But With a Briefly Blue Ignatz.)

Introduction by Bill Blackbeard.

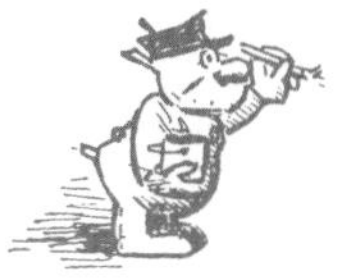

There are just over four hundred and fifty of them, and each one a masterpiece of graphic comedy. The marvelous product of the last nine years of Garge's richly fruitful life, these weekly color *Krazy Kat* pages, stunning as they are, almost failed to physically survive the editorial and institutional rigors of their time. We are, in fact, damned lucky to have them on hand at all as source material for this series. There were, you see, just two newspapers — six day a week sports and crime news afternoon newspapers, throwaway rubbish — that printed virtually all of the color Kat pages from start to finish. Neither the *New York Journal* nor the *Chicago American,* sensational Hearst papers, had any referential status at all, and most libraries in their sales areas shunned them — two papers that virtually no one of any artistic or literary taste and judgment ever saw from the strip's 1935 start to its 1944 conclusion. Two tombs for the foremost comic strip of all time.

Luckily there was a single dedicated comic strip buff, August Derleth of Sauk City, Wisconsin, founder of Arkham House in 1939, who clipped and saved every color Kat page, donating his run to the Wisconsin State Historical Society, where it served as the basis for two excellent reprint collections edited by Rick Marschall and published by Kitchen Sink Press fifteen years ago. Unfortunately, the Derleth file was from the *Chicago American*, which used a color press markedly inferior to that of the *New York Journal*, which called for an artificial jazzing up of the color in the Marschall volumes. By great good fortune, however, a fine, crisp file of the *Journal* pages (apparently the only one in existence) was obtained by your present editor, which will be used for this and the remaining Fantagraphics *Krazy and Ignatz* volumes. (This unique file will be deposited in the Cartoon Art Library at Ohio State University for permanent reference on the completion of the Fantagraphics series.)

When Hearst decided to move Herriman's weekly black and white Kat page into full color as a feature of the publisher's new Saturday color tabloid *Journal* and *American* 16-page comic section, he instructed his King Features comic strip coloring department to spruce up the Herriman page with appropriate hues. There is no evidence that Herriman was asked to touch up a page as a chromatic guide to the Hearst colorists — in fact, extant evidence indicates that the color department found itself more or less on its own, which is why we find an extraordinarily blue Ignatz Mouse romping through the first few color Kat pages. (Later, too, the colorists once failed to complete the tinting of Offisa Pupp's regalia, leaving the legal minion's left arm bone white, as is noted in the Debaffler commentary in this volume.) It is little wonder the Hollywood cartoonist relished watercoloring his gift originals whenever possible. (See facing page for a sumptuous sample.) Still, on the whole, the King Features coloring is deftly done, and when coupled with Herriman's deliciously imaginative art, gives us the inimitable feast that follows.

The important essay by Jeet Heer featured in this volume is, I feel, the definitive work on the controversial matter of Herriman's racial mix. A great read, Heer's painstaking analysis of the factors that lead to his conclusions will serve as the referential basis for all future commentary in this area. For me, a passing reference in Herriman's *Family Upstairs* daily strip of 1911 closed the issue. Mr. Dingbat, in discussing the current stage entertainment in New York, refers with evident relish to the comedy of Bert Williams, a brilliant black humorist of the time, of whom W. C. Fields memorably said, "He was the funniest man I ever saw, and the saddest man I ever knew." Williams' professional life was tragic. He could not eat or drink with his fellow Ziegfeld comedians, or stay in the hotels that housed them. To show the grim idiocy of his position, Williams could not have purchased a seat for a Ziegfeld performance to watch himself on stage. Herriman knew this, and picked Williams from the whole extant crew of New York comics to boost with a very uncommon reference to show business in his strip. Now go and enjoy Mr. Heer, to freshen up for the comic glory of the brickbat Kat to follow.

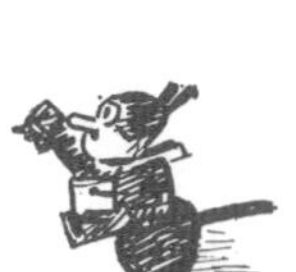

The Kolors of Krazy Kat.

By Jeet Heer.

Cartoon characters are often defined by their mysterious origins, secret identities, and colorful costumes. Sometimes these traits can be found in cartoonists no less than superheroes. Consider the case of George Herriman, the great cartoonist whose full-page *Krazy Kat* strips are collected in this series.

Herriman was a rare artist who bridged the gap between high culture and low. His surrealistic strip was admired by popular entertainers like Walt Disney and Frank Capra yet also had a highbrow fan club that included e.e. cummings, William de Kooning, Joan Miro and Umberto Eco. Almost uniquely, Herriman combined the aesthetics of modernism with a jazzy American voice: in the polymorphous polyglot world of *Krazy Kat*, the main character frequently switches gender while talking in a mixture of many tongues including Yiddish, Spanish, French and Brooklyn-ese.

The sweet oddness of *Krazy Kat* is matched by the biographical mystery surrounding his/her creator. All his adult life, Herriman's ethnicity was a subject of conjecture among his peers. He was variously described as German, French, or Greek. "He looked like a cross between Omar the tent maker and Nervy Nat," wrote fellow cartoonist Tad Dorgan in the early 1920s. "We didn't know what he was, so I named him the Greek." In time, Dorgan's friendly jest hardened into a biographical factoid: obituaries and reference books often described Herriman as the son of a Greek baker.

Dorgan went on to note that Herriman also had a trademark costume: "He always wears a hat. Like Chaplin and his cane, [Herriman] is never

Herriman's "Hidden" Hair Heralded in Hued Work. This revelatory piece of autobiographical art, watercolored on a typewritten sheet repeating part of Tad Dorgan's famed précis on Garge, was purchased in a lot of miscellaneous art and comics years ago, and I have no further information on the source. At least it's dated and signed from the Herriman house, possibly added by the Master to a typed copy of the Dorgan piece prepared for an admirer. Offisa Pupp might have captioned this, with a nod to Dr Seuss, "The Rat in the Hat." — B.B.

without his skimmer. [Cartoonist Harry] Hirshfield says that he sleeps in it." Many photographs attest to Herriman's love of hats: most often he appears with a modest Stetson but he also occasionally donned a Chaplinesque bowler, a Buster Keaton-style pancake hat and even an awe-inspiringly large sombrero.

In 1971, more than quarter century after Herriman's death in 1944, sociologist Arthur Asa Berger of San Francisco State University made a discovery which shed light on Herriman's cloudy background and relentless hat-wearing. Ordering Herriman's birth certificate, Berger was surprised to find that the cartoonist had been described as "colored" by the New Orleans Board of Health in 1880. Further biographical research revealed that Herriman's parents were listed as "mulatto" on the 1880 census. More recently, a close friend of Herriman told biographers that the cartoonist once confided that he was "a creole" possibly with "Negro blood" and wore his hat to hide his "kinky" hair.

The idea that Herriman was an African-American quickly won acceptance among some fans of *Krazy Kat*. In 1972, the novelist Ishmael Reed dedicated his novel *Mumbo Jumbo* to "George Herriman, Afro-American, who created *Krazy Kat*." Yet other cartoon Herriman-buffs have remained skeptical of this radical revision of the cartoonist's ethnicity biography. In 1996, after reading an academic article on *Krazy Kat* in the journal *Inks*, the late Karl Hubenthal, a sports cartoonist who knew Herriman in the 1930s, wrote that "I never saw any indication in pigmentation, facial structure or speech inflection that indicated anything Negroid about George Herriman."

The view of friends such as Hubenthal might be dismissed as a product of old-fashioned rigidity on race: the belief that only those with "Negroid" features are African American. Thomas Inge of Randolph-Mason College, who wrote the article that offended Hubenthal, says "I don't want to call these people racists, but there is clearly something disturbing to them about the notion of Herriman being black."

Yet Inge himself, while firmly believing that Herriman had African ancestors, is not sure whether the cartoonist can accurately be described as an African-American artist. A moment's thought should make clear that race and ethnicity are more a matter of culture and history rather than simple biology: there are people who are considered mixed in Brazil who would simply be classified as white or black in the United States. Given the cultural dimension of race, what are we to do with an artist who seems to have identified all his life with white culture and was thought of as white by his family and friends? While some scholars have searched for a "black aesthetic" within *Krazy Kat*, others believe that the cartoonist was as successful at passing as he was at cartooning. They believe he had no real cultural connection to the African-American experience.

A quick review of the arguments shows that virtually everything about Herriman and *Krazy Kat* is still being debated. Consider the seemingly undisputable factual evidence of Herriman's birth certificate being marked "colored." In an e-mail Bill Blackbeard of the San Francisco Academy of Comics Art states that Arthur Asa Berger was simply "unaware that this was a reference code used by highly prejudiced back country clerks of the time to 'inform' later file searchers of the newborn's like racial status, which was attributed to virtually all dark-skinned furriners such as southern Italians, Greeks, etc. Berger trumpeted his delightfully p.c. finding far and wide." (Blackbeard is of course a scholar who commands respect: more than anyone else he saved the comic strips of the 20th century from the dustbins that thoughtless librarians had confined them to. Aside from his absolutely essential archival work, he's also a prolific writer and editor with scores of books under his belt, including this one).

But even if Blackbeard is right about the term "colored," there is still the fact that the 1880 census listed Herriman's parents as "mulatto." "If both parents were mulatto, then how could the son be Greek?" asks Berger gleefully.

What about the hat that Herriman wore so often? According to Karl Hubenthal, "Herriman had a growth on the back of his skull. He referred to it as a 'wen' and was embarrassed to expose it in public." On the other hand cartoon collector Robert Beerbohm, who has been "accumulating photos of George Herriman without his hat" is convinced that these photos show the "waves" in his hair "which only comes thru a black person's 'kinky' hair all slicked down." In his correspondence, Herriman self-consciously referred to his "kinky" hair.

To outsiders, this debate about hair and hats might seem silly, yet it reveals a deep fissure in comic strip studies between fans and academics. Attuned by the contemporary academy to issues of identity, scholars tend to be fascinated by the problem of Herriman's ethnicity. Fans, by contrast, want to win a wider audience and aesthetic respectability for their beloved art form. Amid the welter of biographical disagreement, is there some way to satisfy both the fans and the profs, so that Herriman's ambiguous identity and aesthetic achievements can both be acknowledged and perhaps linked together?

George Herriman was born in 1880 in New Orleans, a city where a distinct creole community known as "free persons of color" had managed to carve out a unique space between black and white. This mixed-race community not only included Herriman but also his entire family. Digging through the New Orleans Public Library's genealogy department, comic strip fan Brian Nelson has discovered that "in the 1890 census that Herriman's paternal grandmother was born in Havana and that all family members were listed as mulatto." As Thomas Inge suggests, growing up with relatives of varying shades Herriman initially might not even have been aware of his own "race."

Yet Herriman's childhood also coincided with the rise of Jim Crow, which made the position of New Orleans' "free persons of color" precarious. Significantly, Plessy Vs. Ferguson (1896), the Supreme Court decision enshrining the doctrine of "separate but equal," upheld a Louisiana law enacted during Herriman's youth: in this new climate, the mulatto community would have to choose whether they were black or white. A decade before the Supreme Court affirmed Jim Crow, the Herriman family moved to California around 1886. The Herrimans were neither the first nor last "mulatto" family who found that simply by changing address they could become white. With its large Hispanic population, Los Angeles, where the family settled, was an ideal place for passing. In L.A., Herriman's father made for himself a middling existence as a baker and barber, which might have been impossible in racially polarized New Orleans.

Herriman became a cartoonist in 1897 and moved to New York three years later. It was an auspicious time: the city was still caught up in a now legendary newspaper war between William Randolph Hearst and Joseph Pulitzer. Both Hearst and Pulitzer used cartoonists such as Herriman to attract readers. In 1905 Herriman returned to Los Angeles but he came back to New York in 1910.

The newspaper bull-pens where Herriman learned his craft were open to immigrants but not to blacks. As Karl Hubenthal notes, one of Herriman's friends from his early newspaper days was Ralph "Pinky" Springer, "a thoroughly bigoted racist if there ever was one." Herriman's

early work reflected the larger trend in both cartooning and American racial politics. As Bill Blackbeard notes, Herriman, like white cartoonists of his day, did work "replete with extreme black caricatures." During the heyday of Jim Crow, white cartoonists almost invariably portrayed African-Americans as dim-witted, thick lipped, and child-like. Africans were also shown to be ooga-booga natives with a strong taste for cannibalism.

Such images, which make old "funnies" truly disturbing, can be found in Herriman's work and they may suggest that he identified himself with white culture. Yet even here, the evidence is ambiguous: in 1902 Herriman created a short-lived strip entitled *Musical Mose* about a black man who tries, comically and unsuccessfully, to "impussanate" white men. [*see page 12.*] "I wish mah color would fade," Mose says at one point. Was Herriman mocking Mose or his own life? Further, as Library of Congress Assistant Curator Sara Duke notes, the type of stereotypes found in Herriman's work were widely used by popular artists of all sorts, including African-American cartoonists such as E. Simms Campbell.

As an artist, Herriman made a quantum leap with the creation of *Krazy Kat* as a daily strip in 1913. Unlike the broad slap-stick humor of *Musical Mose* and other early Herriman strips, *Krazy Kat* was gentle, fey and whimsical. At the center of the strip is an inter-species love triangle: Krazy, the black cat, loves Ignatz, the white mouse. Ignatz, however, hates Krazy and takes delight in boping him/her with a brick. Krazy, with a charming naïveté, interprets these bricks as symbols of love. Offisa Bull Pupp, the white police dog who is secretly in love with Krazy, has a clearer

Two photographs of George Herriman, from the sunrise and twilight of his career, left, 1902, and right, in a photograph sent to Louise Swinnerton, c. 1940. Both images courtesy of Mr. Robert Beerbohm.

view of the matter and tries to jail Ignatz. Krazy of course is perfectly indifferent to Pupp but enjoys the way "like lil innisint childrens they [Ignatz and Pupp] play togeda."

With its playful ambiguity, *Krazy Kat* represented a break from the stereotype-laden conventions of comic strips. For the most part, cartooning is a profoundly conservative art form: popular strips such as *Peanuts*, *Blondie*, and *Dilbert* all deal in the stoic comedy of defeat and resignation. However much Charlie Brown, Dagwood Bumstead or Dilbert might grumble about childhood, the family, or work, by the last panel they come to accept their lot in life. *Musical Mose* was an early example of the comedy of resignation: the defeat of Mose at the end of the strip re-affirmed the idea that the color line was a solid wall.

Krazy Kat, although it also had a repetitive formula, took place in an absurdist universe that mocked both rebellion and society's rules. In the topsy-turvy universe of *Krazy Kat*, everyone won when the formula was enacted: Ignatz enjoys the thrill of brick throwing, Krazy the pleasure of being bricked, and Offisa Pupp the satisfaction of jailing the mouse. Of course, the dog and the mouse have to suffer each other's existence, so the greatest happiness is reserved for the cat. "It is a very nice universe for Krazy," Robert Warshow once noted. "He loves to be hit by the brick; but he respects Offissa Pupp's motives."

As a work of popular art, *Krazy Kat* had a curious fate: initially it was extremely popular with a mass audience but after a few years it grew too esoteric for the comic strip reading audience. However, by the time that *Krazy Kat* lost its mass reader-

ship, it had won a place in the heart of one important fan, William Randolph Hearst, who declared that so long as Herriman wanted to work on the strip he would be paid for it. In addition to his own affection for Herriman's work, Hearst was perhaps motivated by the fact that *Krazy Kat* was widely praised by intellectuals, hence a source of prestige for a newspaper chain often mocked for its tabloid practices.

With its highbrow admirers, *Krazy Kat* has attracted numerous competing interpretations over the years, many of which are avowedly allegorical. For poet e.e. cummings the strip was about how democracy (Krazy) existed as a balancing act between individualism (Ignatz) and society (Offisa Pupp). The radical critic Franklin Rosemont finds in *Krazy Kat* the proletarian militancy of the Industrial Workers of the World: the black cat was the Wobbly symbol for industrial sabotage. More pastorally, *New Yorker* writer Adam Gopnik sees Herriman's universe as a vision of Eden

before the fall: Krazy bisexually is both Adam and Eve, while Ignatz is the serpent and Offisa Pupp is the Archangel Michael. In a parallel argument, Ken Barker, a retired Presbyterian minister and comics fan, has written about how the sinner Ignatz is redeemed by grace (Krazy) even as he is condemned by the law (Offisa Pupp).

In a more secular vein, philosopher David Carrier describes *Krazy Kat* as a "posthistorical" work of art telling us what life will be like after "the end of history." "Whatever happens in this narrative is preordaned — nothing new can ever happen. History is not over so much as not yet started."

One of the most frequently used words to describe *Krazy Kat* is playful, a quality found not just in the art and language of the strip but also in the strange internal logic of the world Herriman created: we never ask why a cat should love a mouse, or a dog love a cat, since it seems natural. And this, perhaps, is where race becomes relevant. In his book *Comic Strips and Consumer Culture, 1890-1945*, Ian Lewis Gordon of the University of Singapore argues that the playful universe of Krazy Kat can be linked to Herriman's life as a mixed race individual living in world where people were forced to be either black or white.

"I think the problem is that Americans see things in terms of black or white," Gordon writes in an e-mail. "The complexities and diversities of society and culture in places such as New Orleans was reduced to black or white....On the other hand strips like *Krazy Kat* offered something different. The whole funny animal comics tradition could be seen as an effort to retain some sense of play in identity."

Bill Blackbeard suggests that as Herriman traveled in the circle of intellectuals and artists in the early 1920s, his attitude to race might have changed. In contrast to the deeply segregated newsrooms where Herriman drew his strip, Herriman's new friends moved in a more relaxed atmosphere. One of those friends was Gilbert Seldes, a pioneering critic in the study of popular culture, who praised *Krazy Kat* as "the most amusing and fantastic and satisfactory work of art produced in America today." Seldes took a missionary delight in sharing *Krazy Kat* with such acquaintances as Edmund Wilson, F. Scott Fitzgerald and James Joyce. (*Finnegans Wake*, which is filled with references to comic strips like *Mutt and Jeff*, might have been influenced by *Krazy Kat's* verbal antics and dream universe.) But Seldes was also an early white patron of black popular culture, especially jazz and theatre. Perhaps for the first time in his adult life, Herriman encountered an integrated cultural environment where African-American art was respected.

Throughout his *Krazy Kat* work, Herriman made use of racial themes and subthemes in a complex and interesting way. In one early strip, Krazy and Ignatz argue about evolutionary theory. Krazy is taken with Darwin's idea "that we all sprang from the same source." Ignatz rejects this idea and prefers the "polygeneric theory" that "you kats were always kats and we mouses always mouses." This argument between Krazy and Ignatz exactly mirrors post-Darwin debates over race, with virulent racists preferring the "polygeneric" theory that humanity does not share a common source.

In later strips, the racial implications become more plain: Krazy is not just a cat with black fur but also, in a profound way, an African-American cat. Krazy is revealed to have an uncle named Tom who lives in cotton (or kotton) patch and sings the blues. "Bugs in the taties—/Weevils in the kootin—/Weasels in the hen koop—/Honey, times is rotten—," Uncle Tom laments while strumming the banjo. (Uncle Tom is only one of many Herriman allusions to Harriet Beecher Stowe's anti-slavery novel.) With the introduction of Uncle Tom, some features of Krazy look slightly different: we can see for example that his/her banjo is part of the minstrel tradition. The songs Krazy sings come from a variety of traditions, including church hymns and the dance hall, but there is an undeniable African-American lilt in there as well. As Judith O'Sullivan noted in her 1971 book *On Comics*, Krazy's sing-song rhythm is evocative of the "dozens," the black oral art form was precursor to hip-hop and rap.

In an essay recently published in the interdisciplinary literary journal *Mosaic*, Eyal Amiran of Michigan State University argues that the presence of characters like Uncle Tom is evidence of Herriman's obsession with questions of genealogy and kinship. Amiran further notes that Herriman's racial concerns in Krazy Kat were intertwined with his formalist experiments into the nature of

cartooning. The division between black and white is embedded deeply both in American social life but also in the very fabric of cartooning: Herriman often had fun with the inescapable fact that his characters were merely black ink on white paper (except for its last decade, *Krazy Kat* was

Kat: even though black and white can and often are played with, the fundamental division remains because, in the comics page no less than in social life, the opposition between black and white can be redefined but not abolished. *Krazy Kat* doesn't upturn the division between black and white, but gives us a fresh ironic perspective on it.

Herriman's color play also shapes the strip's love triangle (which can be seen in general as a comically thwarted fantasy of miscegenation). The white Ignatz loves to hate Krazy, but only so long as he/she is black. Conversely, black Krazy loves Ignatz only so long as he's white. When Uncle Tom becomes a full-blown character in 1932, the love-hate triangle is subtly inverted. Uncle Tom hates all the mice, but he has a soft spot for one white rodent, Ignatz's wife.

We can see the racial comedy of passing played out in some of the strips reprinted in this volume. In the June 22, 1935 strip, Ignatz is blackened after hiding in a dirty pipe. Meanwhile, Krazy is thinking about her lover-mouse. "L'il blondish beautiful – so pink – so fair," Krazy sighs. Krazy is annoyed by the black-face Ignatz, mistaking him for "a l'il eethiopium mice." Only when Ignatz is washed clean does Krazy's happiness return.

In the strip from October 6th, 1935, the racial passing moves in the opposite direction. Krazy goes to a beauty salon and comes out all white. Ignatz suddenly falls in love with this pale cat until a dropped handkerchief reveals that his/her initials are "K.K." Then Ignatz reaches again for the brick. As Krazy reflects: "Lil Tutsi-Wutsi thinks because I change my kimplection I should change my name."

Like Krazy, George Herriman didn't change his name but somehow changed his complexion: born "colored" in 1880 he was listed as "Caucasian" on his death certificate in 1944.

Part of the difficulty with discussing Herriman's racial identity is that the phenomenon of passing makes people uneasy: passing suggests that race can be transcended on an individual level but only through the betrayal of group identity. An air of duplicity and rumor hangs over passing which Amiran has suggestively linked to the anxiety over genealogy which is a recurring theme in Krazy Kat.

Philip Roth's recent novel *The Human Stain* illustrates how morally complex passing is. Coleman Silk, the African-American hero of the novel,

always in black and white, even on Sundays). In Amiran's reading, Herriman becomes a profound poet of the paradox that identity is only created through difference, almost a Derrida of the funny pages.

In his/her earliest incarnation, Krazy Kat was little more than a smudge, almost looking like a bug squashed on the page. In later strips, Krazy and the other characters would often switch between black and white with delightful abandon. In an 1931 strip, an art critic visits Coconino County (home of Herriman's imaginary animal kingdom) and describes Krazy and Ignatz as "a study in black & white." Krazy catches his meaning ("He means us – me bleck. You white") and suggests to Ignatz that they "fool him. You be bleck and I'll be white." Ignatz agrees and in the next panel, Krazy is white and Ignatz is black. The art critic gets the last laugh, though, by describing the transfigured cat and mouse as "another study in black & white." Here we see a recurring irony in *Krazy*

is at times celebrated as an heroic American individualist who, like the Great Gatsby, re-makes himself. At other points in the novel, we are acutely aware that Silk's family believes he is "a traitor to his race." In Roth's novel, these two judgments stand in permanent tension.

Can a similarly complex assessment be made about George Herriman? Despite all the biographical bickering, a few clear statements can be hazarded: George Herriman had African-American ancestors and was aware of this fact. As an adult he adopted different strategies to deal with what his society taught him was an embarrassing ancestry. At times he hid his background and adopted the contempt his white friends had for black people. On the other hand, through his art Herriman tried to grapple with issues of identity and create a playful utopia, where different cultures could meet on equal ground.

In the early 1920s Herriman returned to California with his wife and two daughters. George Herriman came to love the landscape of the west and the culture of the Navajo Indians. He incorporated elements of both into his already multicultural strip and told Gilbert Seldes that he wanted to be re-incarnated as an Indian. Once again, he dreamed of escaping the world of black and white.

Jeet Heer, a writer based in Toronto, is the co-editor of Arguing Comics: Literary Masters on a Popular Medium (*University of Mississippi Press*). *He is also writing the introductions for the new collections of Frank King's strip "Gasoline Alley," issued under the series title* Walt and Skeezix, *co-edited and designed by Chris Ware (Drawn and Quarterly). This article originally appeared in slightly different form in* Lingua Franca *in September, 2001.*

A soaring watercolor work devised by GH for his son-in-law, Ernest Pascal, in 1932. From the collection of Dee Cox, Tucson, Arizona.

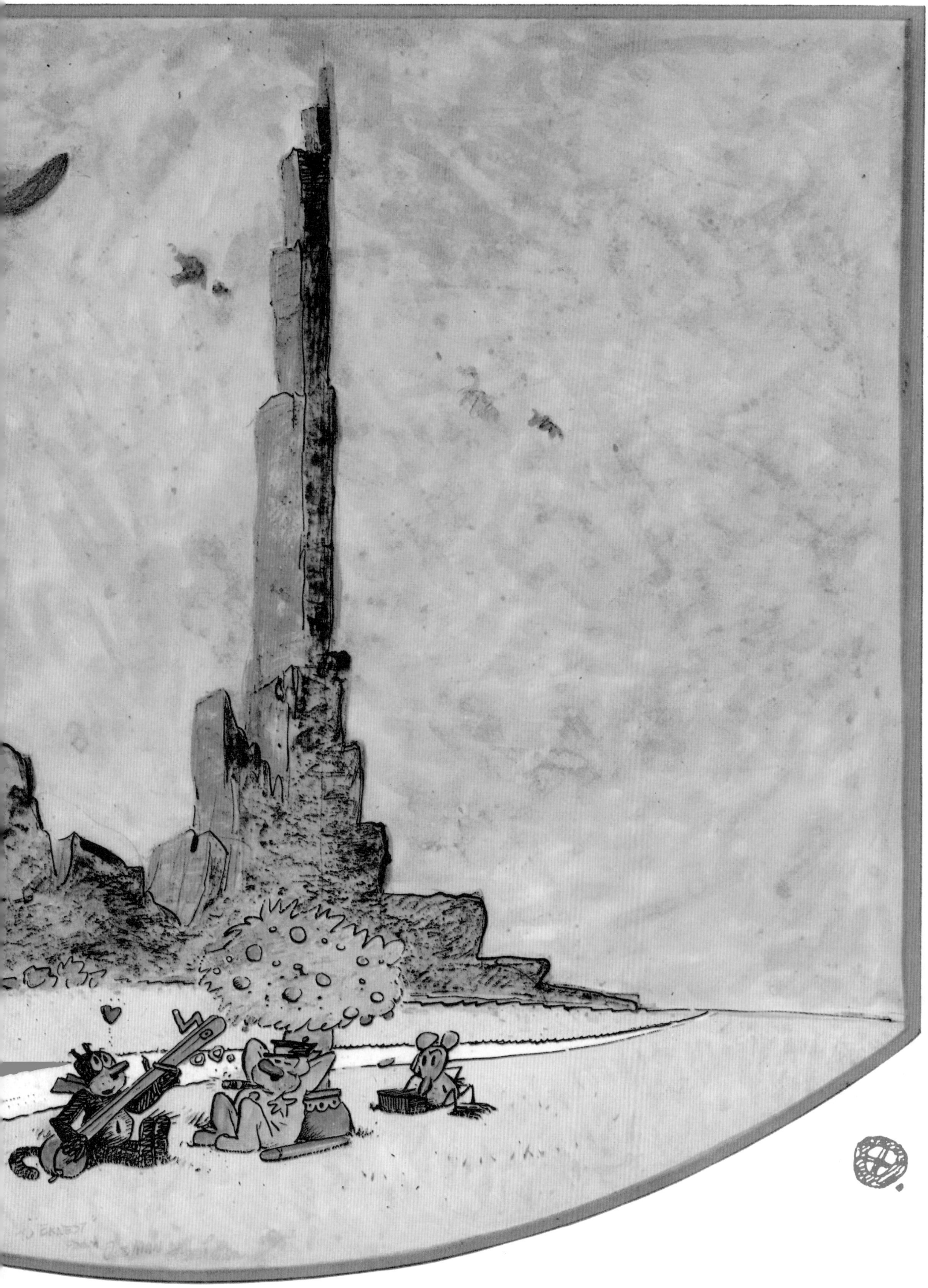

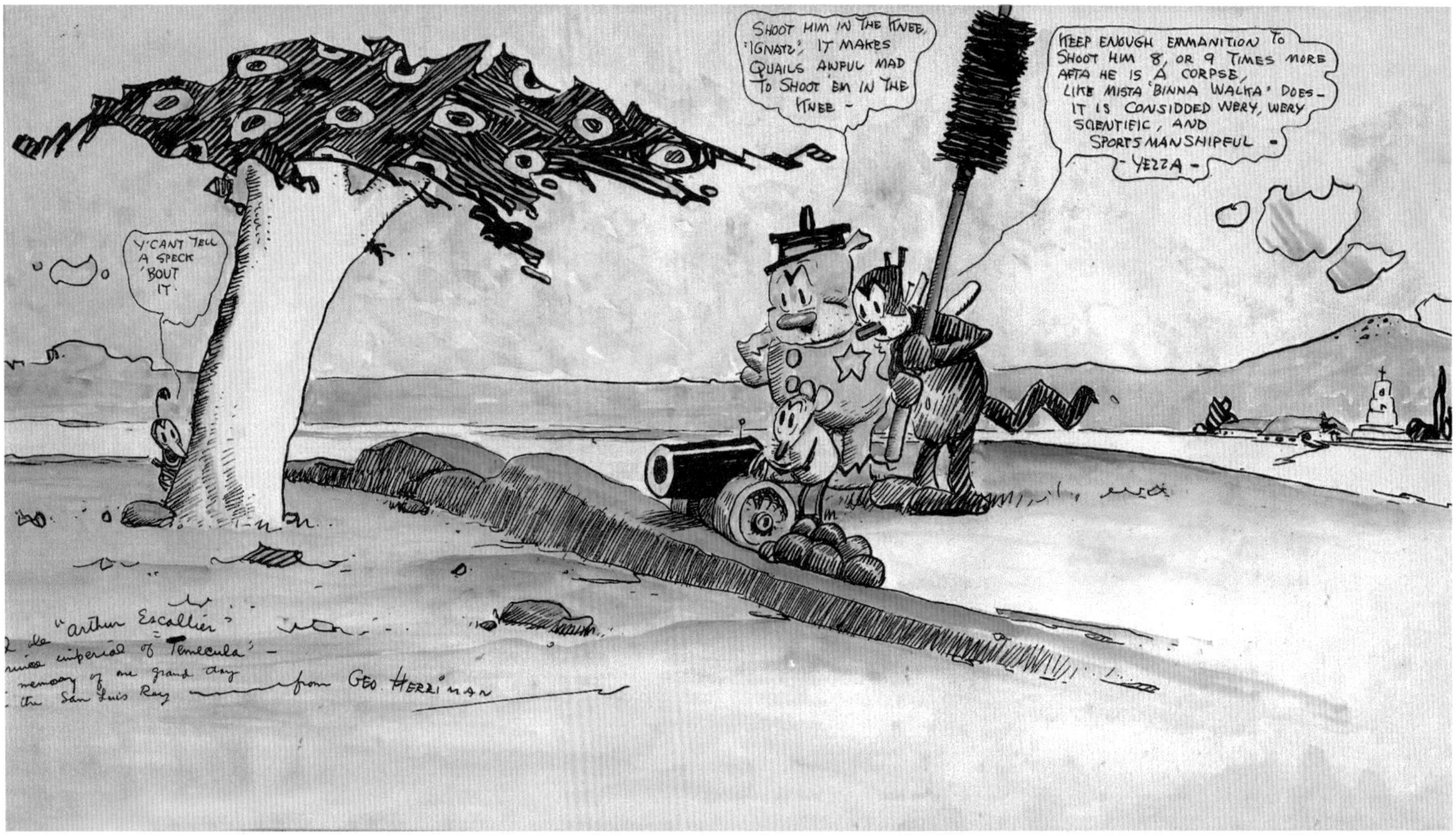
Y'CAN'T TELL A SPECK 'BOUT IT.
SHOOT HIM IN THE KNEE, "IGNATZ" IT MAKES QUAILS AWFUL MAD TO SHOOT 'EM IN THE KNEE –
KEEP ENOUGH EMMANITION TO SHOOT HIM 8, OR 9 TIMES MORE AFTA HE IS A CORPSE, LIKE MISTA 'BINNA WALKA' DOES – IT IS CONSIDDED WERY, WERY SCIENTIFIC, AND SPORTSMANSHIPFUL – – YEZZA –
de "arthur Escallier"
imperial of "Temecula" –
memory of one grand day
the San Luis Ray —— from GEO. HERRIMAN

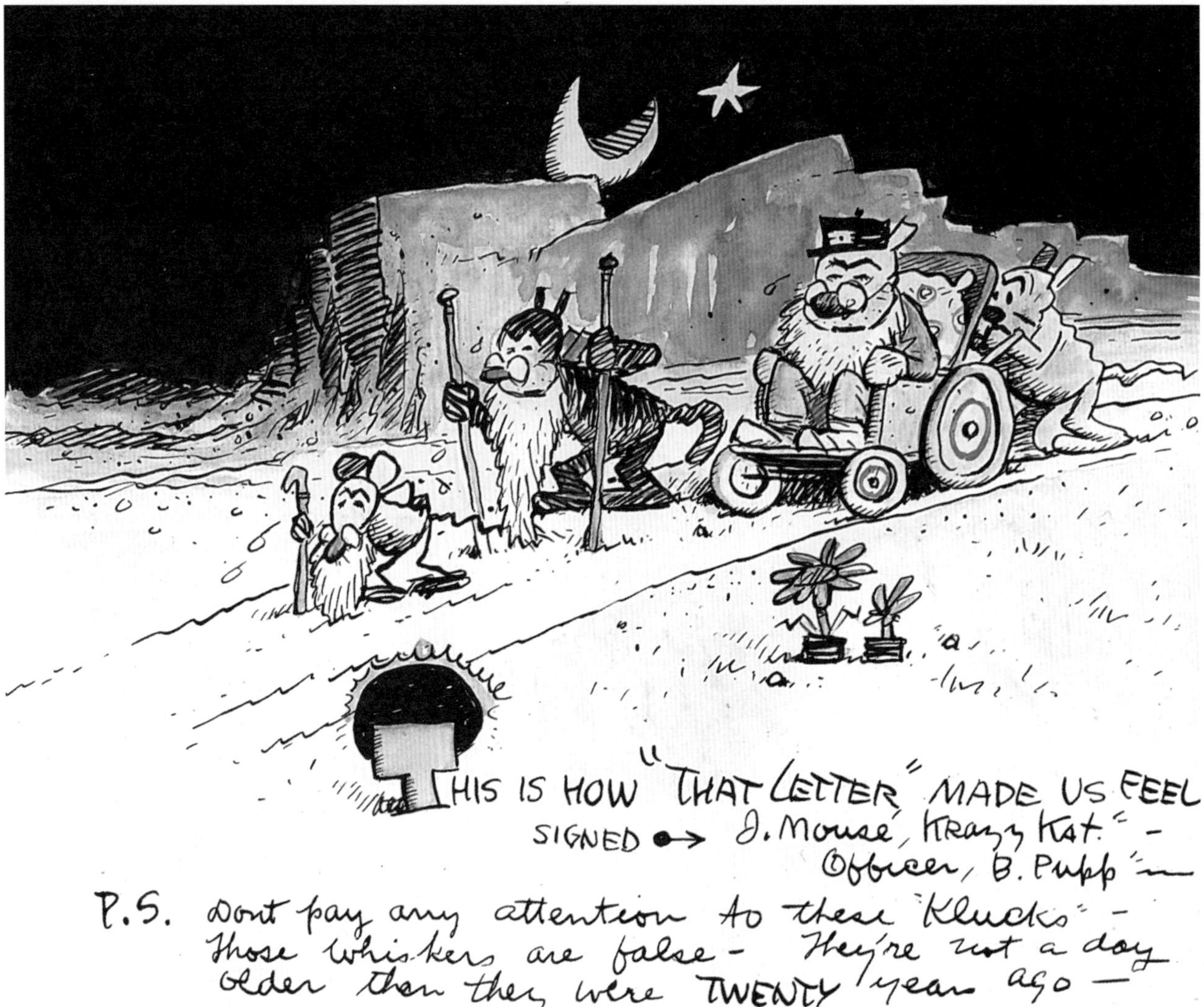
THIS IS HOW "THAT LETTER" MADE US FEEL
SIGNED → I. Mouse, Krazy Kat, – Officer, B. Pupp –
P.S. Dont pay any attention to these "Klucks" – Those whiskers are false – They're not a day older than they were TWENTY years ago –
"HERRIMAN" –

Above: A Herriman original for his *Embarrassing Moments* daily panel for 10/9/30. Courtesy of Heritage Comics.

Opposite Page, top: Typical of the dozens (perhaps hundreds) of original watercolors Herriman prepared for friends over the years, reflecting shared personal memories, is this cannonical work done for Arthur Escallier, apparently recalling a hunting trip of sorts they shared wth a maniacal overkiller of birds in San Luis Rey. Unfortuately undated. Courtesy of Heritage Comics. Bottom: These vintage denizens of Coconino County were limned by Garge in a watercolor sketch sent with a letter to a fan in the thirties. Gifted to the San Francisco Academy of Comic Art decades ago without provenance, this work is apparently reproduced here for the first time.

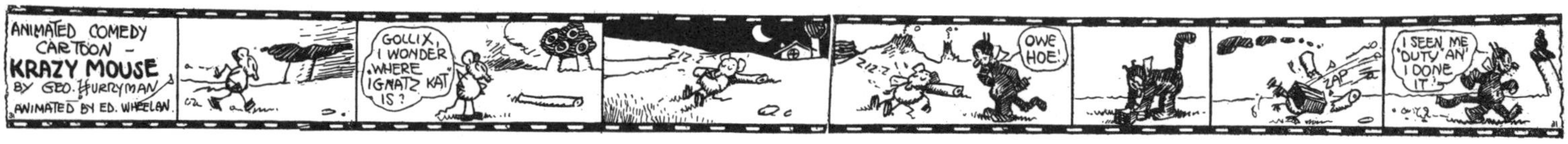
ANIMATED COMEDY CARTOON - KRAZY MOUSE
BY GEO. HURRYMAN
ANIMATED BY ED. WHEELAN
GOLLIX, I WONDER WHERE IGNATZ KAT IS?
OWE HOE!
ZAP
I SEEN ME DUTY AN' I DONE IT

Comics—And Their Creators

George Herriman, who draws the delirious comic "Krazy Kat" for King Features Syndicate, Inc., and hundreds of thousands of enthusiastic readers, is a slight, gray-eyed, quiet man who always wears a hat, and never gets into the limelight if he can help it. On one occasion, after refusing to pose for a picture, on the ground that "the public doesn't care about my face," he was finally maneuvered to a drawing-board. Then he graciously surrendered, complied with all requests, took off his coat, rolled up his sleeves, even sketched several large pictures of *Krazy Kat.* But he refused to pose without his hat. He did remove it for a moment "just to prove I have hair."

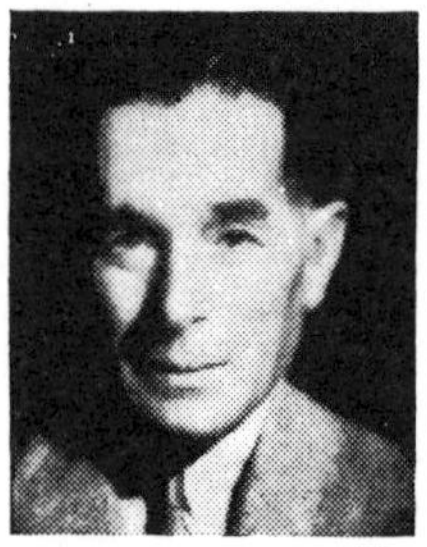

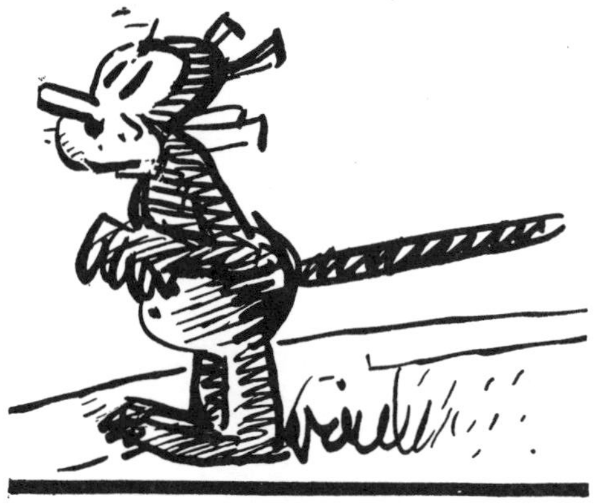

Krazy Kat

Herriman and the late "Tad," sports-cartoonist, were close friends, and Tad revealed this about him:

"His first name is George, but the boys call him *Garge*, because that's the way he pronounces it himself.

"No matter what happens *Garge* is always the same. You can steal his pens, but he only smiles. You can knock California, but he merely smiles. You can cut up rubber in his tobacco-pouch, and he'll smoke it just to give you a laugh. He brags about his favorites, *Garge* does, but never about himself. The violet imitated *Garge* when it assumed that attitude of shyness."

Above, top: A redikilus spoof of the Krazy Kat strip drawn by *Minute Movies'* Ed Wheelan for the Hearst papers' sports pages on 7/31/17. Above, middle: An entry and snapshot of Herriman for the weekly feature on comic strippers fielded by the old *Literary Digest* in the thirties, for 4/20/35.
Right: Perhaps the most bizarre rendering of Krazy to come from Garge's pen is this cut from the New York *Journal* for 6/22/12, apparently a comment on a convention at the Chicago Coliseum. Why Krazy's tail forms a question mark, what the minuscule inscription on Krazys tummy was meant to read, and what the convention heralded are matters for further research.

Opposite page, middle two strips: Herriman's bizarre *Family Upstairs* format was imitated in other daily strips, of which these two episodes (one from W. A. Aliman's *The Doings of the Duffs* for 11/20/14 and the other from Pop's *Keeping Up With The Joneses* for 6/18/19) are typical. Note the dog yclept Felix by the Momand cat! Bottom: In 1954, King Features experimented with a Sunday reprint feature called *Comics Museum,* which ran for only four weeks and featured restructured vintage color pages for *Happy Hooligan, Buster Brown, Jimmy,* and *Krazy Kat*. Apparently some KFS reader survey found no great interest in the series, and it was promptly dropped. This reprint is from the early forties and may feature the only mention of zoot suits in the Kat archives.
(Note also that the logo, page composition, and lettering have been completely redone by a "third party" — though the drawings are by Herriman. — C. W.)

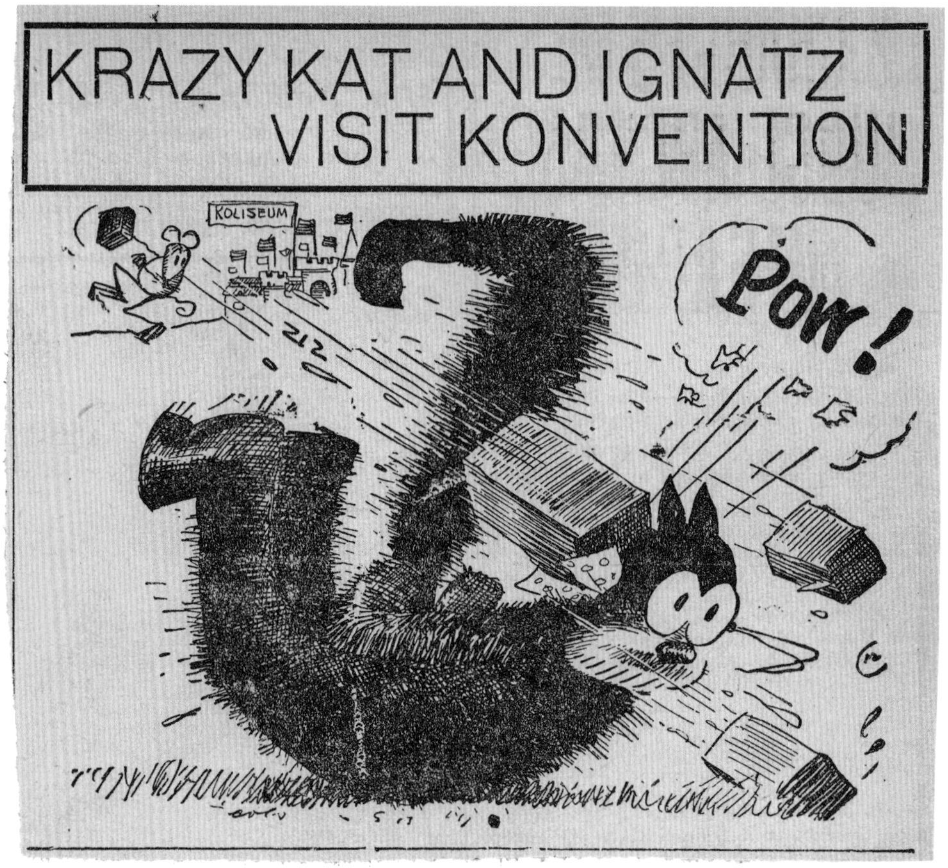
KRAZY KAT AND IGNATZ VISIT KONVENTION
KOLISEUM
POW!

KEEPING UP WITH THE JONESES—It's a Cruel World.   —By POP.

CAT TALES.   —By POP.

Right and below: A Herriman-illustrated menu for the "Mission Indian Grill" in the Hotel Alexandria in Los Angeles, California; one wonders if the gags about fraternal organizations come from Herriman's direct experience as a member. Undated, but judging from the drawing style, it appears to have been limned sometime around 1910 — or even earlier, as it is rather close to the "look" of Herriman's pre-*Krazy* work like *Major Ozone*. At least it's at least a safe bet it dates from before the 1930s, when the swastika had become much more than simply a mysterious symbol that looked neat on menu covers and carpeting. Collection of C. Ware.

Opposite: Never-before-seen images from an errant shadow-puppet performance of the John Alden Carpenter *Krazy Kat* ballet at the Denison University Conservatory of Music in Granville, Ohio, reproduced in the *Musical Courier*. Again, undated, but likely from the mid-1920s. Courtesty of and many thanks to Mr. Chris Boensch. — *C. W.*

 Anchovies 60   Fresh Astrach
Caviar 60   Peach Mangoes 3
Bismarck Herrings 30

BROTH IN CUPS   Hot or Cold
Clear Turtle 40

HOT   Crab Meat Royal 80
Filet Mignon Alexandria 7
Sweetbread En Brochette 60
Broiled Chicken, 75-1 5
Welsh Rarebit 40

A

Crab Flakes, Mornay 75
Crab Flakes, Creole 75

COLD   Boned Turkey with Truff
Ham 40   Westphalia 60
Pate de foie gras 75

SANDWICHES   Club 40
Chicken 35

SALADS   Chicken 60   Crab
Romaine 35   Tomato 40   Chiff
Asparagus Tips 50   Germ

SWEETS   Petits Fours 25
Meringue Panache 30

ICE CREAM, Etc.   Nesselrode P
Peach Melba 35   Vanilla 20
Coffee or Chocolate Parfait 30
Sorbet, Roma

FRUIT IN SEASON

CHEESE   Imported Camembert
Roquefort 15-25   Edam 15-25
Oregon Cream 20
Pot Chocolate or Cocoa (1) 20 (2)

Room S

DRAUGHT BEER   **Domesti**
Imported Pilsner Hoffbrau Gl

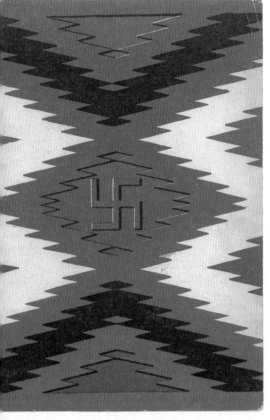

ar 80-150   Sweet Cucumber Chips 35
  Orange Mangoes 40   Spiced Pineapples 40
            Marinirter Herring 30

nme 25   Chicken 25   Bellevue 30
     Clam Broth 25

Flakes au Gratin 60   Terrapin, Maryland 1 50
     Sweetbread Broiled or Fried 60
                    Poulette 75
          Fried 75-1 50   Squab 70
Golden Buck 50   Scotch Woodcock 60

ria Specialties
  Newburg 75   Crab Flakes, Alexandria 75
     Eastern Oysters, Alexandria 75

          Assorted Meat 60   Roast Beef 40
hia 50   Tongue 40   Turkey 60
ab, Mayonnaise 50   Kalter Aufschnit 60

r 40   Ham 25   Tongue 25
  Beef 30   Swiss Cheese 20

  Lobster 60   Shrimp 60   Lettuce 25
0   Potato 30   Cucumber 40   Grapefruit 50
en Spargel 1 25   American Asparagus 40

ate Eclairs (1) 15 (2) 25   Charlotte Russe 25
Jelly 20   Bar Le Duc 40

35   Biscuit Tortoni 30   Biscuit Glace 30
awberry 20   Coffee 20   Chocolate 20
  Lemon Water Ice 20   Orange Water Ice 20
schino 20, Lalla Rookh 30

e Noir 10   Cafe Special 25

     Imported Stilton 25   Sierra 15-25
onzola 30   American 15   Imported Swiss 15-25
chatel 25   McLaren's Club Cheese 25
               Pot Tea or Coffee (1) 15 (2) 25

e Milk 10

5c per person extra.

Glass 10, Stein 20,
Stein 25   Wurzburger Glass 15, Stein 25

KRAZY KAT WITH KARPENTER MUSICAL KOMMENTS

THESE are photographs of a performance recently given at the Denison University Conservatory of Music, Granville, O., of John Alden Carpenter's ballet, Krazy Kat. The presentation was with marionette silhouettes with the permission of the composer. Such shadow puppets are well known in Java and the East Indies but are new to this country. Denison University has given several performances of operettas with marionettes: Mozart's Bastien and Bastienne, and Gay's Beggar's Opera. Further plans include Carl von Dittersdorf's Doctor and Apothecary, and Humperdinck's Haensel and Gretel.

The silhouettes for the characters in Krazy Kat were made by Stephen Tuttle. On the program with Krazy Kat was the Daniel Gregory Mason sonata for clarinet and piano, op. 14, and other American music. The Krazy Kat pictures to which John Alden Carpenter wrote his music are by George Harriman, who also made illustrations for the Schirmer publication of the score with special permission of the International Feature Service, Inc., and the New York Evening Journal, holders of the copyright.

EVEN THE MOON LAUGHS AT THIS ONE.

AT THE EXTREME LEFT—IT MAY BE A MUSHROOM.

SOMEBODY BELIEVES IN THE STORK.

Above: A bookstore knockout is this Herriman dust jacket for Don Marquis' *Archy Does His Part*, the last of the three volumes that made up the author's bestselling *archy and mehitabel* series, all illustrated by the Garge drawer.

Right: Apparently, the field of Herriman-related stage productions is ripe for study, as this previously unknown c. 1912 sheet music surfaced recently and — who knew? Possibly it was a complete violation of copyright, as Herriman's name is not even spelled correctly. One also wonders: did the production possibly feature a sidebar "cat and mouse" story? (This cover art is also obviously not by "Herrman.") Courtesy of and many thanks to Mr. Robert L. Beerbohm. — C. W.

Opposite: Easily the saddest aspect of Herriman's *Kat* Sunday page was its structural adaption to the general strip format featured by the *St. Louis Post-Dispatch* in the early thirties. After running the page for years in the newspaper's Sunday rotogravure section, where it often appeared in a special *Post-Dispatch* layout that altered Herriman's, but retained the integral Garge art itself, the Depression-addled editors abandoned the costly rotogavure section in 1931 and moved the Kat strip to the paper's color comic section, where alien hands completely redrew the strip to fit it into a half page format. The example reproduced here, for 7/6/31, sez it all — but to gauge the full degree of mutilation, refer back to the original (printed on page 44 of *Krazy + Ignatz 1925-1926*), where, among other things, the bewilderingly pointless explosion of crosshatching in this version's first panel makes graphic sense, as Herriman is trying to suggest a painterly texture (as if that panel were a painting) using just black and white lines — an effect ruined by the re-framing and colorization here.

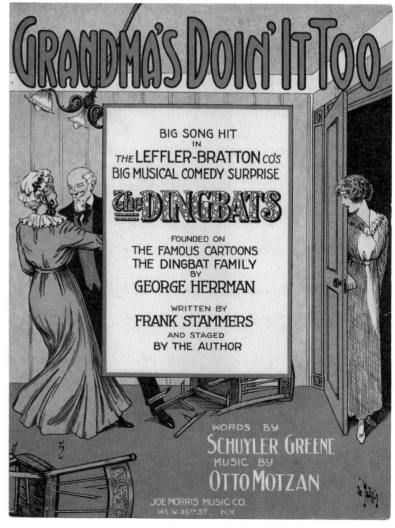

KRAZY KAT
By HERRIMAN
HERE'S YOUR FRAME AS ORDERED, MR MOUSE I DO HOPE YOU WILL PUT A GOOD PICTURE IN IT
YOU'RE DERN TOOTIN I AM
FIRST, I SAW A ROUND HOLE IN THE WALL
THEN, I PAINT A LINE, OR TWO ABOUT THE APERTURE
THEN, I PLACE THE FRAME OVER THE ORIFICE
A 'BRICK' VERY HANDY
NOW TO ROUND OUT MY SCHEME
NOW, LET COME THE PATRONS OF 'ART' - LET COME ESPECIALLY, THAT 'KRAZY KAT' - 'IGNATZ MOUSE' THE KEEN WIT IS READY TO RECEIVE
and yet - there is this
BUM BILL BEE, WHO WITH A TRUE "SELDESIAN" SENSE OF THE SELECTIVE, CHOOSES THOSE OF THE ARTS WHICH ARE WITHOUT PATRON. THE WHY, NOR WHOM OF WHICH MEANING NOTHING TO HIM - A WORRY THAT FILLS HIS WHOLE LIFE WITH NOTHING OF SOMETHING LESS, AND SOMETHING OF NOTHING MORE - A TRIUMPH IN EQUILIBRITY - THE SCALES SO DELIGHTFULLY DENOTE THE BEAUTIFUL BALANCE - AN EQUAL NUMBER OF UPS ON ONE SIDE TO A SIMILAR AMOUNT OF DOWNS ON THE OTHER - YES - OF COURSE NOT
OY, A BEAUTIFIL PITCHA - OY, A PRIDDY PITCHA - SO ARTISTICAL, AND SUCH
"OFFISSA PUPP" IF THERE IS A SPARTIL OF 'ART' AMONG YOUR SOUL, YOU MUST COME IN, AND LOOK AT THE NICE PITCHA OF 'IGNATZ' - ITS LOVELY ART
IT AIN'T GONNA DO MY EYE ANY GOOD BUT TO PLEASE YOU, KRAZY, I'LL STEP IN A MOMENT
WELL, WUDDA Y THINK FROM IT, 'OFFISSA PUPP' ?
M-M-M MMM
HUH I UNDERSTAND THAT 'IGNATZ' IS NOW EXHIBITING A PICTURE OF HIMSELF - I'LL GO IN AND LET ONE EYE SUFFER
I. MOUSE
DAGNAB THAT KOP, I WISH HE'D GO AWAY, SO I CAN CREASE THAT KAT'S NOODLE WITH THIS 'BRICK'
SO, THIS IS 'ART' ?
OWYOW" OW "OW" OOH-H -YOW WOW I'M STABBED OW
OOY-HOW RILLISTICAL-
OHO-
WOULD YOU BILLIV IT, MR BEE, OFFISSA PUPP WAS SO PLIZZED WITH THE PITCHA THAT HE'S GONNA SHOW IT TO A JUDGE AND A JURY, AND EVER BODY AIN'T THAT NICE
THIS 'LL BE A GREAT TREAT TO THE BOYS IN THE KLINK THEY LOVE ART SO MUCH - YOU WIFFIN
HERRIMAN

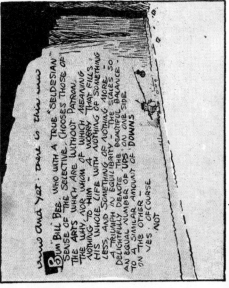

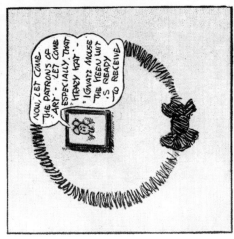

This page, like the one opposite, is printed in magic inks. To bring out their colors, take an ordinary brush or piece of cotton on a toothpick, dip in plain water and paint. Wash out brush or cotton frequently.

This odd gallery of color tinted Krazy Kat pages from circa 1919 was printed in the Games Sunday sections of the Hearst paper chain for a few weeks in 1922. Most were "colorized" by the addition of lightly dabbed moisture to pre-printed water-based inks, as instructed in the page indicia. As virtually the only tab-sized color Kat episodes published before the 1935 start of full color reproduction of the Sunday pages, they are included here "for the record." Those interested can check out the 1919 era black and white originals for comparison.

This picture is printed in magic inks. To see Krazy Kat's kolors, take an ordinary brush or piece of cotton, dip in plain water and paint with it. In painting every magic ink page be sure to wash out brush or cotton frequently.

Well! Well Well! Here's our little friend Krazy Kat and Ignatz Mouse up to their tricks again.

Take a brush or piece of cotton wrapped on a toothpick, dip in plain water and paint carefully to see the Krazy Kolored Krowd.

Be sure to wash out brush or cotton frequently

Here is a page of magic colors. Krazy Kat and his little friend Ignatz the Mouse found 'em very magical. To learn what puzzled them so take a brush or piece of cotton, dip in plain water and paint between the outlines. Do not run brush or cotton over the outlines. Wash brush or cotton frequently.

Krazy Kat's Krazy Kolors are in magic ink. To see just how strange everything looked in Krazy's place moisten the page with plain water. Use an ordinary brush, a piece of cotton or a toothpick and frequently wash out whichever you use.

Here again are our little friends, Krazy Kat and Ignatz Mouse and some of their friends.

Paint them with plain water, using an ordinary brush or a piece of cotton wrapped around a toothpick. Wash out brush or cotton frequently.

Coconino's Great Mystery.

It looks very black here   But paint the pictures between the outlines with a brush or piece of cotton dipped in plain water and see how bright their world will turn around Krazy Kat and Ignatz Mice.

WARNING!—Do not paint or cut out pages until you have looked over the whole book.   There may be something on the other side of a page you will like better.

Readers, please note: an Ignatz "dingbat" placed below a strip indicates a relevant or related footnote at the volume's end for that particular selection, all to be found in the "Ignatz Debaffler" section.

1935.

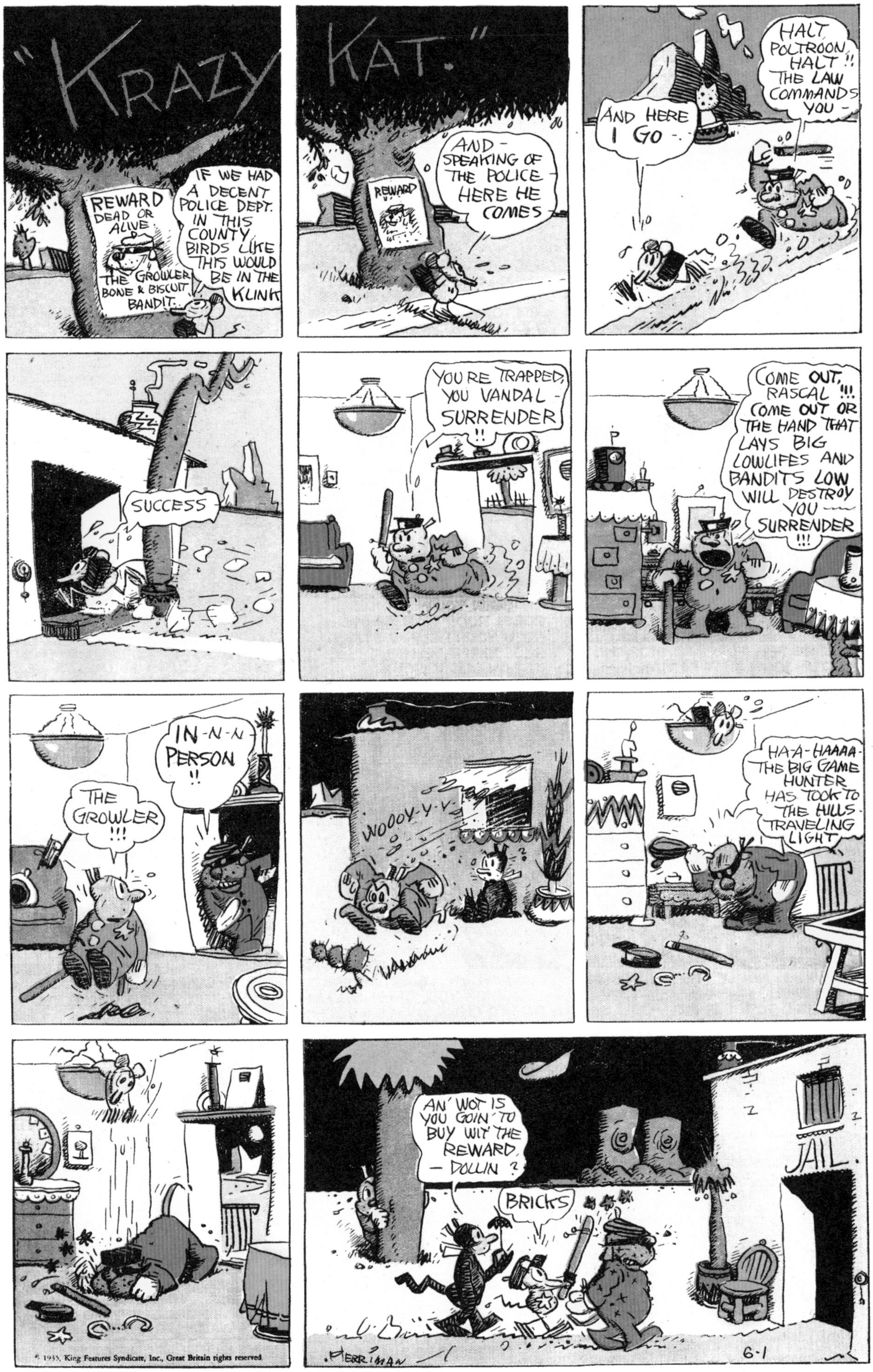

"KRAZY KAT."
REWARD DEAD OR ALIVE THE GROWLER BONE & BISCUIT BANDIT
IF WE HAD A DECENT POLICE DEPT. IN THIS COUNTY BIRDS LIKE THIS WOULD BE IN THE KLINK
REWARD
AND - SPEAKING OF THE POLICE HERE HE COMES
HALT POLTROON HALT !! THE LAW COMMANDS YOU -
AND HERE I GO -
SUCCESS
YOU'RE TRAPPED, YOU VANDAL - SURRENDER
COME OUT, RASCAL !!! COME OUT OR THE HAND THAT LAYS BIG LOWLIFES AND BANDITS LOW WILL DESTROY YOU - SURRENDER !!!
THE GROWLER !!!
IN-N-N PERSON !!
WOOOV-V-V
HA-A-HAAAA - THE BIG GAME HUNTER HAS TOOK TO THE HILLS - TRAVELING LIGHT -
© 1935, King Features Syndicate, Inc., Great Britain rights reserved
AN' WOT IS YOU GOIN' TO BUY WIT THE REWARD, - DOLLIN ?
BRICKS
JAIL.
HERRIMAN
6-1

June 1st, 1935.

"KRAZY KAT."
SOME DAY I WILL HAVE FREED COCONINO COUNTY OF SIN -
GLUE
NOT YET.
Z
HOWEVER, THIS WILL BE A STEP FORWARD FOR GOOD.
AND A STEP BACKWARD FOR SIN -
GLUE
AND FOR THAT SINNER - TOO -
GLUE
Z
SUCCESS, IT'S STUCK AS TIGHT AS A WAD OF GUM IN A GNU'S GOATEE - AND THE TRIUMPH OF GOOD OVER SIN IS COMPLETE.
GLUE
Z
AH, GOING TO VISIT YOUR LITTLE FRIEND, MY DEAR KRAZY ? - WELL - YOU'LL FIND HIM SAFE - SAFE AS AN EAGLE'S BABY.
OH - IF COURSE
WELL, I HAVE DONE A GREAT DEED - MY CLEVERNESS IMPROVES - IT WAXES - WHILE THAT MOUSE'S SLYNESS WANES.
AND NOW FOR THE RESPITE I HAVE SO WELL EARNED - A NAP - A PRETTY PASTIME SO SWEET TO A KOP'S HEART.
POW.
VINO TINTO
CANTINA
TRES FLORES
OUR WISIT WAS WERRA WERRA SIX SESSFIL OFFISSA PUPP - IGNATZ INTITAMED IN A BIG AN' IRIGINIL STYLE TIDDAY
OH-H HE DID - HEH ?
6-8
© 1935, King Features Syndicate, Inc., Great Britain rights reserved.
HERRIMAN

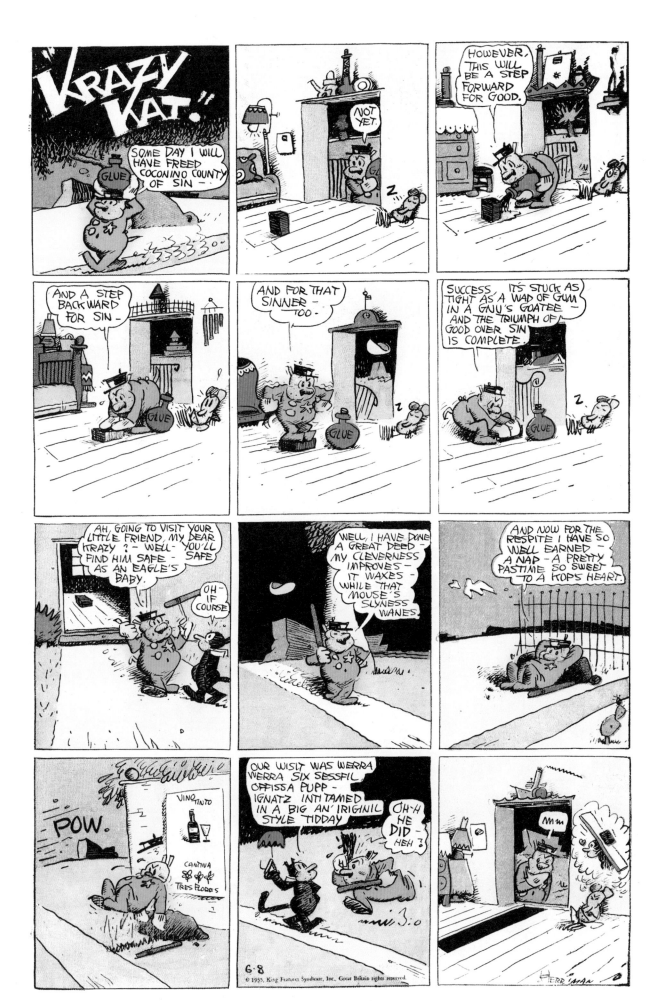

June 8th, 1935.

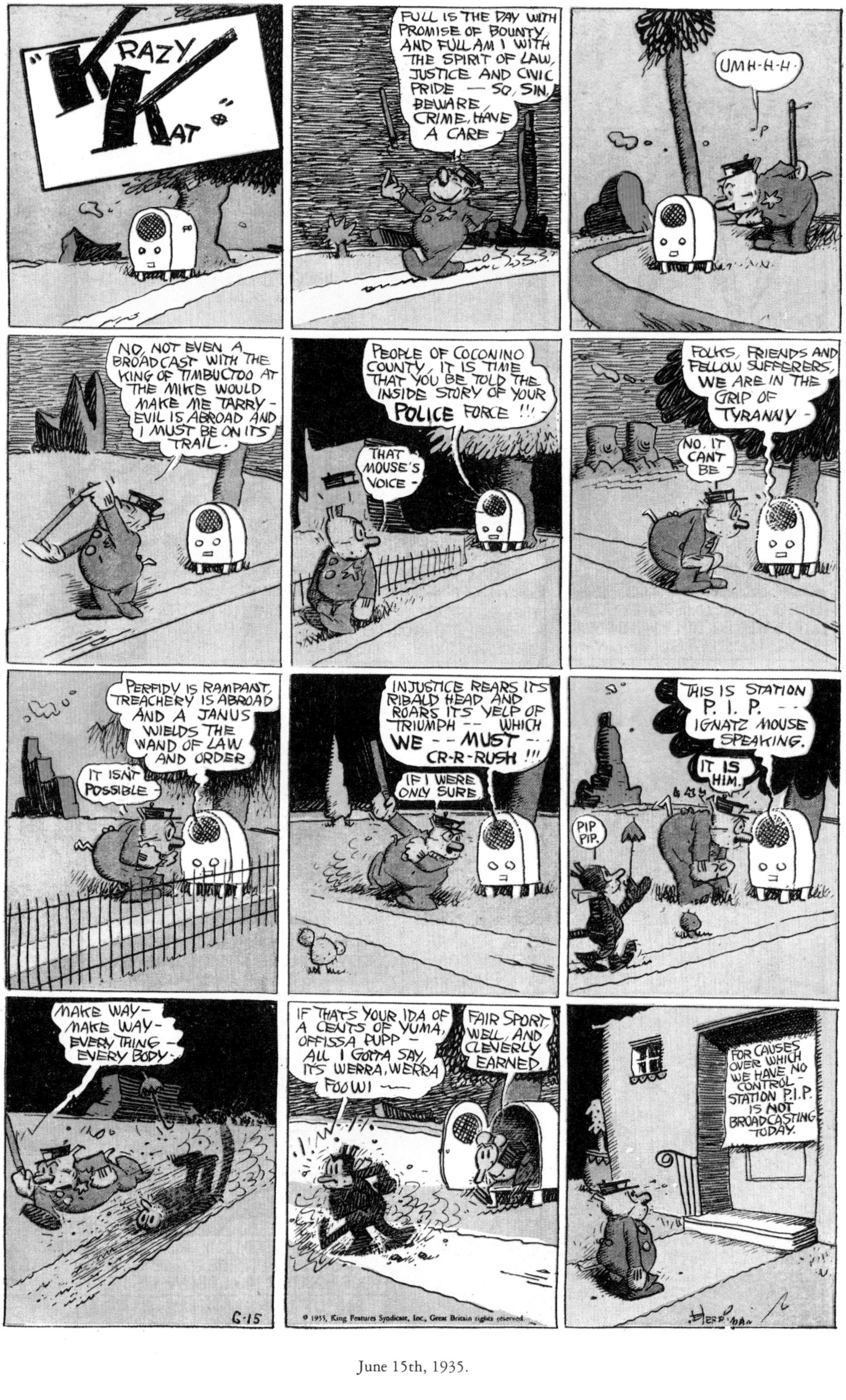
"KRAZY KAT"
FULL IS THE DAY WITH PROMISE OF BOUNTY, AND FULL AM I WITH THE SPIRIT OF LAW, JUSTICE AND CIVIC PRIDE — SO, SIN, BEWARE, CRIME, HAVE A CARE -
UMH-H-H-
NO, NOT EVEN A BROADCAST WITH THE KING OF TIMBUCTOO AT THE MIKE WOULD MAKE ME TARRY - EVIL IS ABROAD AND I MUST BE ON ITS TRAIL.
PEOPLE OF COCONINO COUNTY, IT IS TIME THAT YOU BE TOLD THE INSIDE STORY OF YOUR POLICE FORCE !!! -
THAT MOUSE'S VOICE -
FOLKS, FRIENDS AND FELLOW SUFFERERS, WE ARE IN THE GRIP OF TYRANNY -
NO, IT CANT BE
PERFIDY IS RAMPANT, TREACHERY IS ABROAD AND A JANUS WIELDS THE WAND OF LAW AND ORDER
IT ISN'T POSSIBLE -
INJUSTICE REARS ITS RIBALD HEAD AND ROARS ITS YELP OF TRIUMPH -- WHICH WE -- MUST -- CR-R-RUSH !!!
IF I WERE ONLY SURE
THIS IS STATION P. I. P. - - IGNATZ MOUSE SPEAKING.
IT IS HIM.
PIP PIP.
MAKE WAY - MAKE WAY - EVERY THING - EVERY BODY -
IF THAT'S YOUR IDA OF A CENTS OF YUMA, OFFISSA PUPP - ALL I GOTTA SAY, ITS WERRA, WERRA FOOWI —
FAIR SPORT, WELL AND CLEVERLY EARNED
FOR CAUSES OVER WHICH WE HAVE NO CONTROL - STATION P.I.P. IS NOT BROADCASTING TODAY.
6-15
© 1935, King Features Syndicate, Inc., Great Britain rights reserved.
HERRIMAN

June 15th, 1935.

KRAZY KAT
YES.
NO.
SUCCESS -
HEH-HEH-H-H- AS IF - AS- IF -
GRAN BAILE
ESTA NOCHE
BAA, WHY WASTE TIME, STOVE PIPE, MOUSE, BRICK - EVERY THING, EVERY BODY - OVER?!!!
TEATRO DE LAS PULGAS
TIC
L'IL BLONDISH BEAUTIFIL - SO PINK - SO FAIR - SO LIKE A PRIMP ROSE, WHERE IS HE AT NOW?
AI AI
JOSE CUERVO
BLAP!
HAA - A L'IL EETIOPIUM MICE, BLECK LIKE A MONTH FROM MIDNIGHTS - FUWI -
OH - YES?
OOY-Y-Y - SOTCH A NOIVE -
POW
ZIP
I GOT A GREAT CARE WHO I ISSOCIATE WIT' - Y- Y- Y' SUN BOINT KOFFA KAKE -
THIS WILL TITCH SOITIN PIPPILS TO KEEP IN THEIR OWN SOCIAL SPEARS - FRESH MOGG.
© 1935, King Features Syndicate, Inc.
Great Britain rights reserved.
HYE - THIS TIME I'LL !!!
POW
ZIP
IGNATZ - DOLLIN -
HAPPY AS A TREE FULL OF LARKS - THANKS TO MY EFFORTS IN KEEPING THAT MOUSE OUT OF HIS WAY.
6-22
Herriman

June 22nd, 1935.

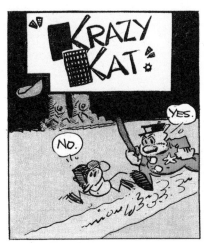

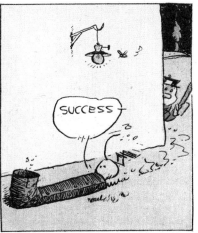

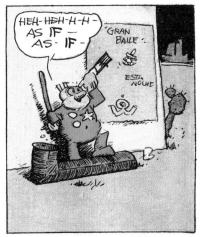

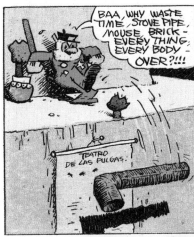

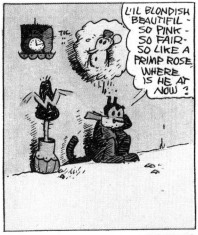

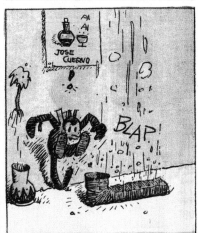

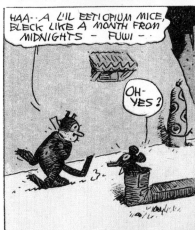

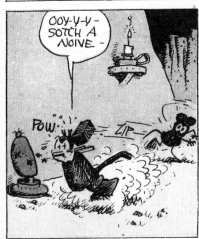

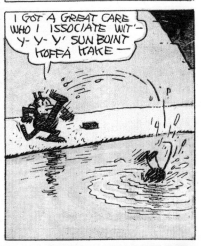

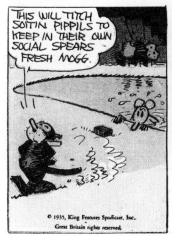

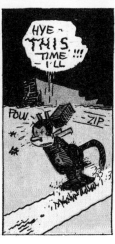

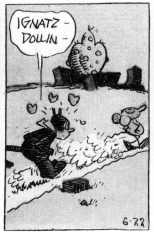

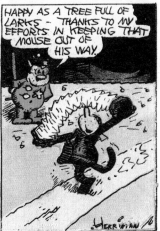

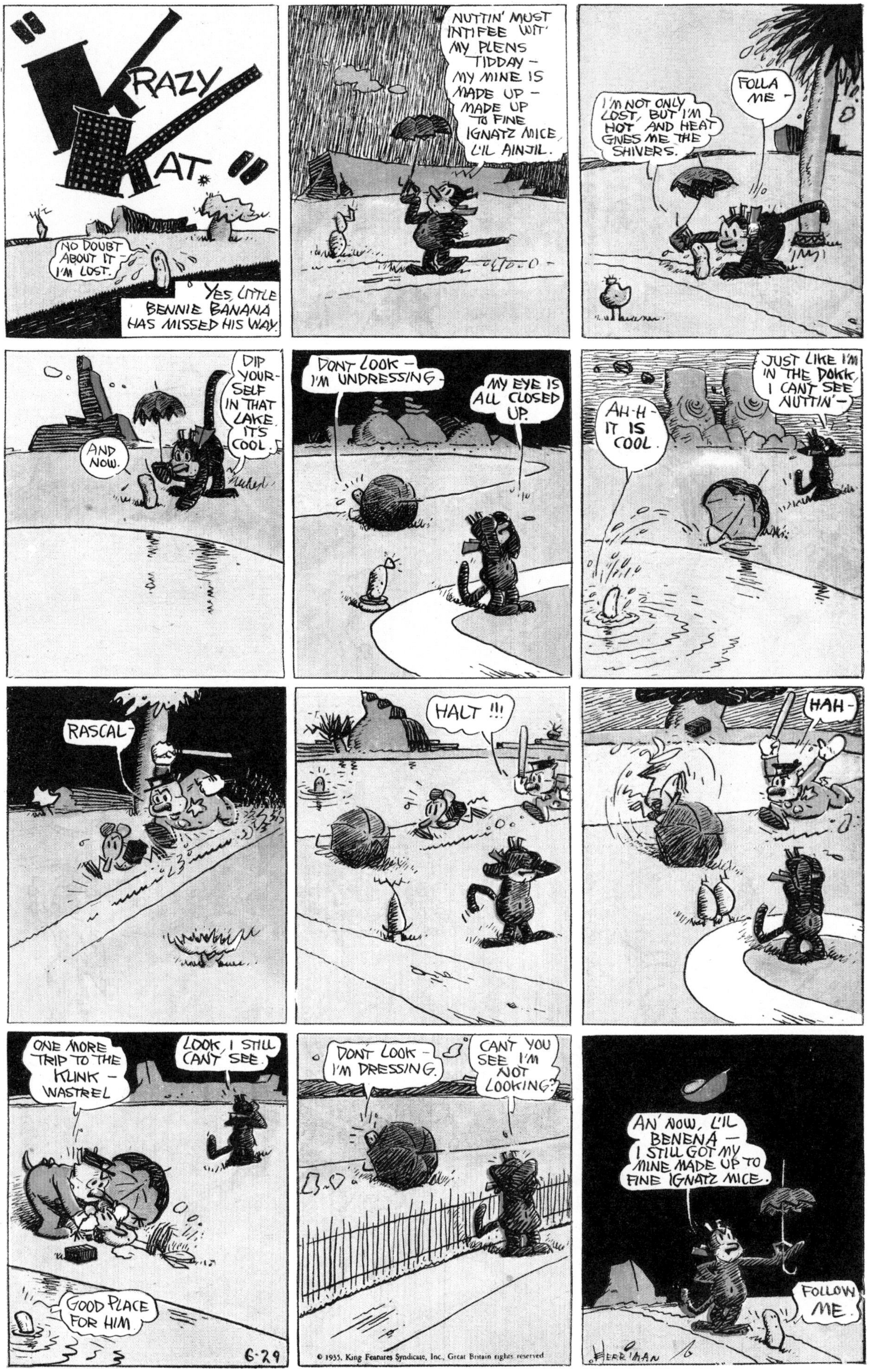
"KRAZY KAT"
NO DOUBT ABOUT IT - I'M LOST.
YES, LITTLE BENNIE BANANA HAS MISSED HIS WAY.
NUTTIN' MUST INTIFEE WIT' MY PLENS TIDDAY - MY MINE IS MADE UP - MADE UP TO FINE IGNATZ MICE, L'IL AINJIL.
I'M NOT ONLY LOST, BUT I'M HOT AND HEAT GIVES ME THE SHIVERS.
FOLLA ME -
AND NOW.
DIP YOURSELF IN THAT LAKE. ITS COOL.
DONT LOOK - I'M UNDRESSING -
MY EYE IS ALL CLOSED UP.
AH-H IT IS COOL.
JUST LIKE I'M IN THE DOKK, I CANT SEE NUTTIN' -
RASCAL -
HALT !!!
HAH -
ONE MORE TRIP TO THE KLINK - WASTREL
LOOK, I STILL CANT SEE.
GOOD PLACE FOR HIM.
6-29
DONT LOOK - I'M DRESSING.
CANT YOU SEE I'M NOT LOOKING?
© 1935, King Features Syndicate, Inc., Great Britain rights reserved.
AN' NOW, L'IL BENENA - I STILL GOT MY MINE MADE UP TO FINE IGNATZ MICE.
FOLLOW ME.
HERRIMAN

June 29th, 1935.

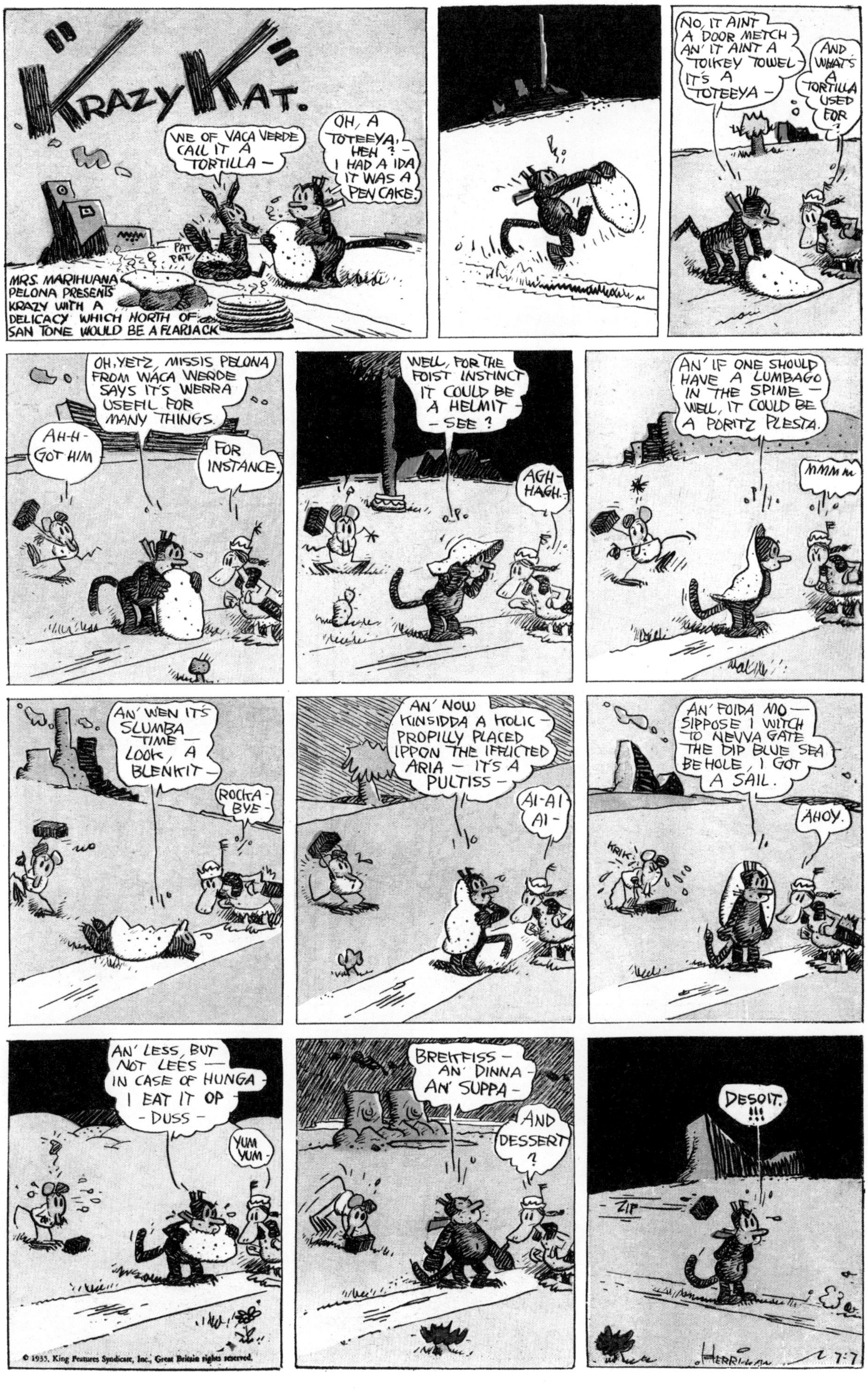
"Krazy Kat."
WE OF VACA VERDE CALL IT A TORTILLA —
OH, A TOTEEYA, HEH ? — I HAD A IDA IT WAS A PEN CAKE.
PAT PAT
MRS. MARIHUANA PELONA PRESENTS KRAZY WITH A DELICACY WHICH NORTH OF SAN TONE WOULD BE A FLAPJACK
NO, IT AINT A DOOR METCH — AN' IT AINT A TOIKEY TOWEL — IT'S A TOTEEYA —
AND WHAT'S A TORTILLA USED FOR ?
OH, YETZ, MISSIS PELONA FROM WACA WERDE SAYS IT'S WERRA USEFIL FOR MANY THINGS.
AH-H GOT HIM
FOR INSTANCE.
WELL, FOR THE FOIST INSTINCT IT COULD BE A HELMIT — SEE ?
AGH-HAGH.
AN' IF ONE SHOULD HAVE A LUMBAGO IN THE SPIME — WELL, IT COULD BE A PORITZ PLESTA.
MMMM
AN' WEN IT'S SLUMBA TIME — LOOK, A BLENKIT —
ROCKA-BYE
AN' NOW KINSIDDA A HOLIC PROPILLY PLACED IPPON THE IFFLICTED ARIA — IT'S A PULTISS —
AI-AI AI —
AN' FOIDA MO — SIPPOSE I WITCH TO NEVVA GATE THE DIP BLUE SEA BE HOLE, I GOT A SAIL.
AHOY.
KRIK
AN' LESS, BUT NOT LEES — IN CASE OF HUNGA — I EAT IT OP — DUSS —
YUM YUM
BREKFISS — AN' DINNA — AN' SUPPA —
AND DESSERT ?
DESOIT.
ZIP
HERRIMAN 7-7

July 7th, 1935.

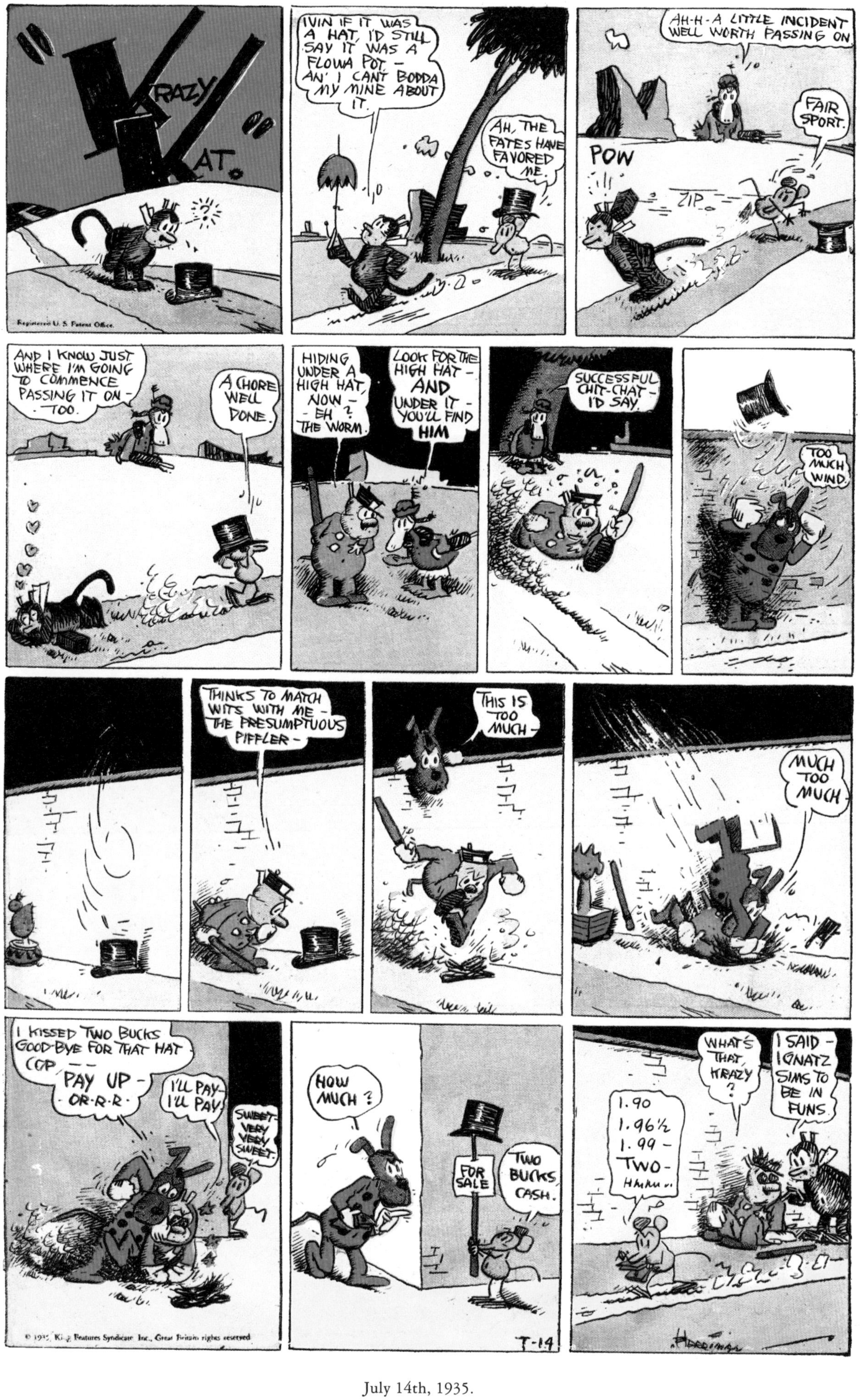

"KRAZY KAT."
Registered U. S. Patent Office.
IVIN IF IT WAS A HAT, I'D STILL SAY IT WAS A FLOWA POT, - AN' I CAN'T BODDA MY MINE ABOUT IT.
AH, THE FATES HAVE FAVORED ME.
AH-H-A LITTLE INCIDENT WELL WORTH PASSING ON.
FAIR SPORT.
POW
ZIP
AND I KNOW JUST WHERE I'M GOING TO COMMENCE PASSING IT ON - - TOO.
A CHORE WELL DONE.
HIDING UNDER A HIGH HAT, NOW - - EH ? THE WORM.
LOOK FOR THE HIGH HAT - AND UNDER IT - YOU'LL FIND HIM
SUCCESSFUL CHIT-CHAT - I'D SAY.
TOO MUCH WIND.
THINKS TO MATCH WITS WITH ME - THE PRESUMPTUOUS PIFFLER -
THIS IS TOO MUCH -
MUCH TOO MUCH -
I KISSED TWO BUCKS GOOD-BYE FOR THAT HAT COP - -
PAY UP - OR-R-R
I'LL PAY - I'LL PAY
SWEET - VERY VERY SWEET.
© 1935, King Features Syndicate, Inc., Great Britain rights reserved
HOW MUCH ?
FOR SALE
TWO BUCKS CASH.
T-14
WHAT'S THAT, KRAZY ?
I SAID - IGNATZ SIMS TO BE IN FUNS.
1.90
1.96½
1.99 -
TWO -
Herriman

July 14th, 1935.

"KRAZY KAT."
LOOK !!!
?
SAY YES, LOBELIA, SAY YES, YES - -YES -
THAT'S ALL I WUNT TO KNOW.
YES.
IT'S MY DUTY.
ENCHANTED MESA
ARE YOU SURE KAT ?
IF COARSE
JOE STORK
SEE ?
I SEE
YOU HAVE MADE ME SO HAPPY, LOBELIA - SO HAPPY
THAT KAT SURE KNOWS THINGS.
WELL CHIEF HOW WAS THAT FOR A LOVE SCENE ?
IT WAS GREAT LET'S TRY IT ONCE MORE -
TRAITOR !!! WAIT TILL I GET HIM
ZZ
© 1935, King Features Syndicate, Inc., Great Britain rights reserved.
HERRIMAN 7-21

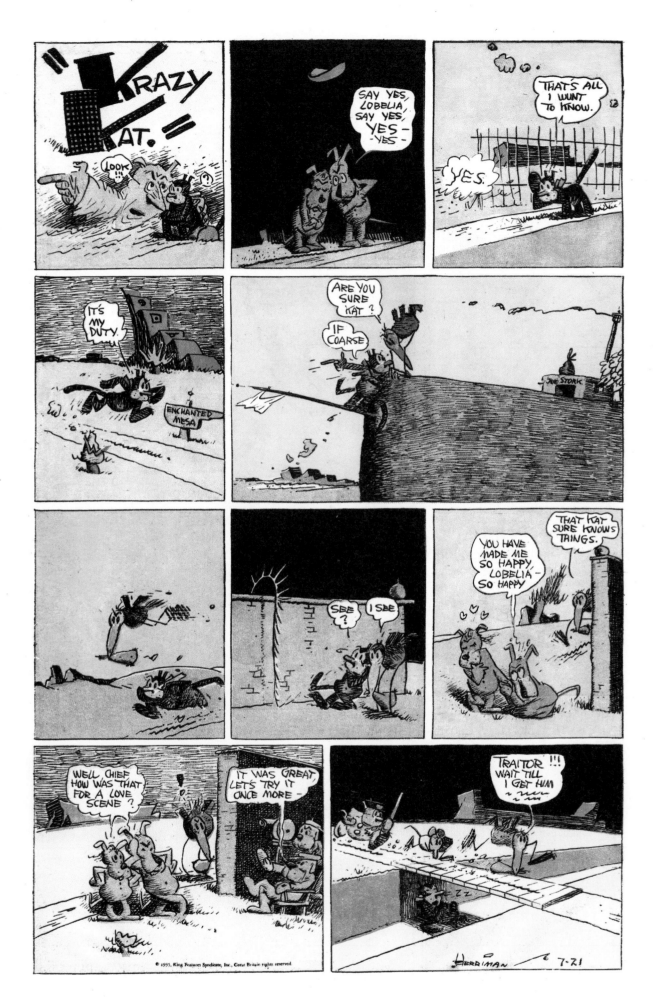

July 21st, 1935.

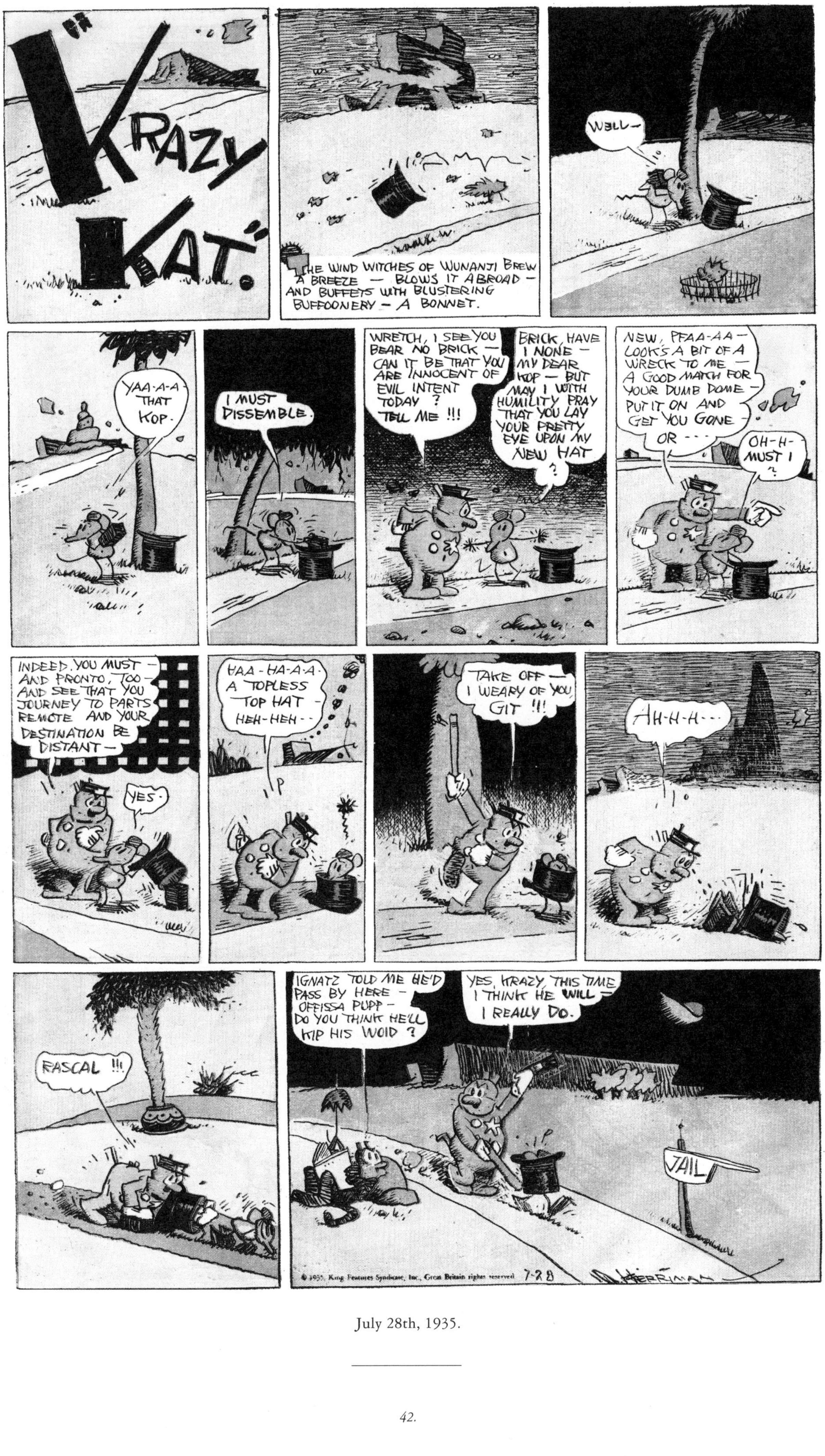
Krazy Kat
The wind witches of Wunanji brew a breeze — blows it abroad — and buffets with blustering buffoonery — a bonnet.
Well —
Yaa-a-a that Kop.
I must dissemble.
Wretch, I see you bear no brick — can it be that you are innocent of evil intent today? Tell me !!!
Brick, have I none — my dear Kop — but may I with humility pray that you lay your pretty eye upon my new hat?
New, pfaa-aa — look's a bit of a wreck to me — a good match for your dumb dome — put it on and get you gone or - - -
Oh-h — must I?
Indeed, you must — and pronto, too — and see that you journey to parts remote and your destination be distant —
Yes.
Haa-ha-a-a a topless top hat heh-heh - -
Take off — I weary of you. Git !!!
Ah-h-h - - -
Rascal !!!
Ignatz told me he'd pass by here — Offissa Pupp — do you think he'll kip his woid?
Yes, Krazy, this time I think he will — I really do.
Jail
© 1935, King Features Syndicate, Inc., Great Britain rights reserved.
7-28
Herriman

July 28th, 1935.

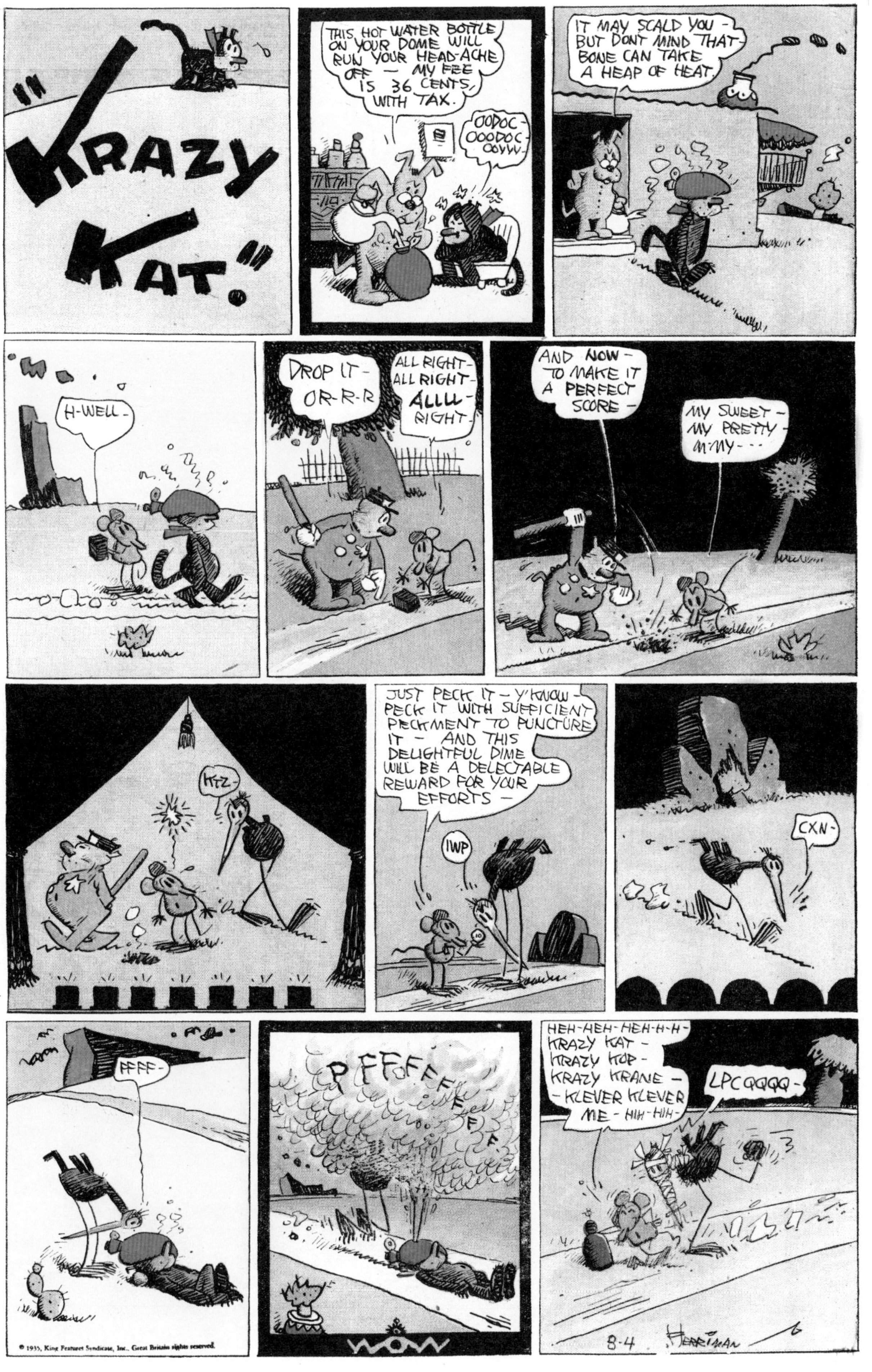
"KRAZY KAT."
THIS HOT WATER BOTTLE ON YOUR DOME WILL RUN YOUR HEAD-ACHE OFF — MY FEE IS 36 CENTS, WITH TAX.
OODOC-OOODOC-OOYW
IT MAY SCALD YOU - BUT DON'T MIND THAT - BONE CAN TAKE A HEAP OF HEAT.
H-WELL-
DROP IT - OR-R-R
ALL RIGHT - ALL RIGHT - ALLLL - RIGHT -
AND NOW - TO MAKE IT A PERFECT SCORE -
MY SWEET - MY PRETTY - M-MY - - -
KTZ-
JUST PECK IT - Y'KNOW - PECK IT WITH SUFFICIENT PECKMENT TO PUNCTURE IT - AND THIS DELIGHTFUL DIME WILL BE A DELECTABLE REWARD FOR YOUR EFFORTS -
IWP
CXN-
FFFF-
PFFOFFFFFF
HEH-HEH-HEH-H-H KRAZY KAT - KRAZY KOP - KRAZY KRANE - - KLEVER KLEVER ME - HIH-HIH-
LPCQQQQ-
8-4 HERRIMAN
WOW
© 1935, King Features Syndicate, Inc., Great Britain rights reserved.

August 4th, 1935.

"KRAZY KAT"
WOOOOO
HAH HAH - HAH
IT'S A GOATS - OFFISSA PUPP - A-AN' IT WENT W-WOOOOOO AT ME.
I-I-IT DID ?
WOOOO.
GET OUT BEE.
MOVE OVER - I WISH SHELTER.
REFUSE BUM-BILL BEE SANCTUARY - HEH ?
© 1935, King Features Syndicate, Inc., Great Britain rights reserved.
8-11
JAIL
Herriman

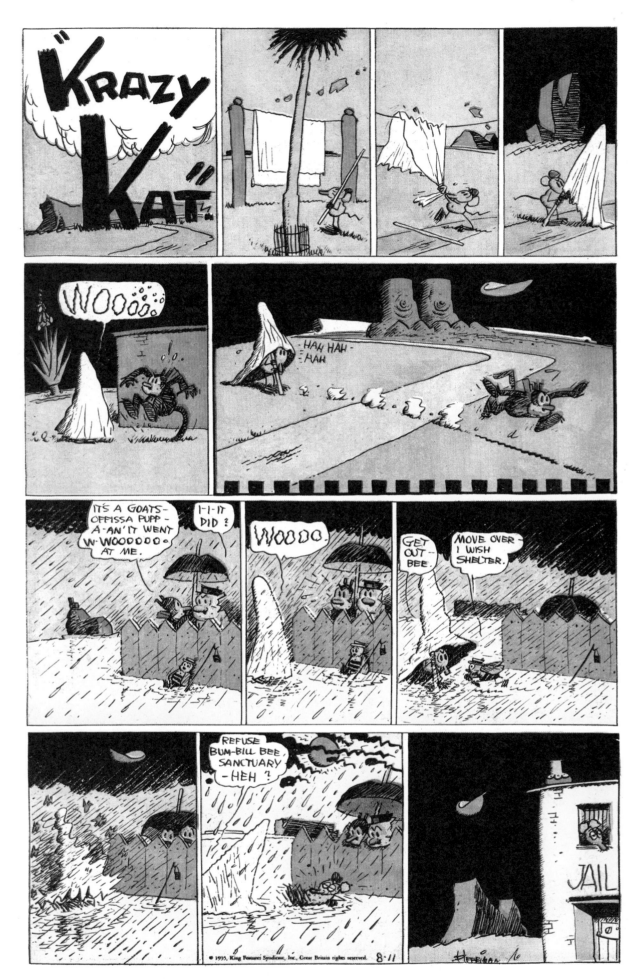

August 11th, 1935.

KRAZY KAT
WILL THIS STUFF GROW FUR ? HOHOHO - WILL IT GROW FUR ? IT'LL GROW FUR ON A DOOR-KNOB - AND THAT'S SOME DISH FOR A DIME -
GIVE IT TO ME.
THAT KOP WILL NEVER KNOW ME WITH FUR ON - I WILL TOSS BRICKS AT THAT KAT WITH IMPUNITY - AND WITHOUT FEAR OF APPREHENSION.
I SAID, WHAT HAVE YOU IN THAT BOTTLE ? HAND IT OVER - I WISH TO INSPECT IT.
HUH -
LIQUOR - S'WHAT I THOUGHT.
PFOOO.... - SMELLS AWFUL WICKED -
YOUR DOOM IS NIGH - MOUSE - AND ....
EXCUSE ME - I HAVE BUSINESS ELSEWHERE -
IMPORTANT BUSINESS.
I-I-I KNOW OF ONLY ONE WAY OUT OF THIS ---- - MOTHS -
WY - IF COURSE
AND WHO IS THE NEW PRESIDENT OF THE MOTHS' UNION WHO WON'T LET YOU TAKE THIS JOB ?
IGNATZ MOUSE
© 1935, King Features Syndicate, Inc., Great Britain rights reserved.
8-18
HERRIMAN

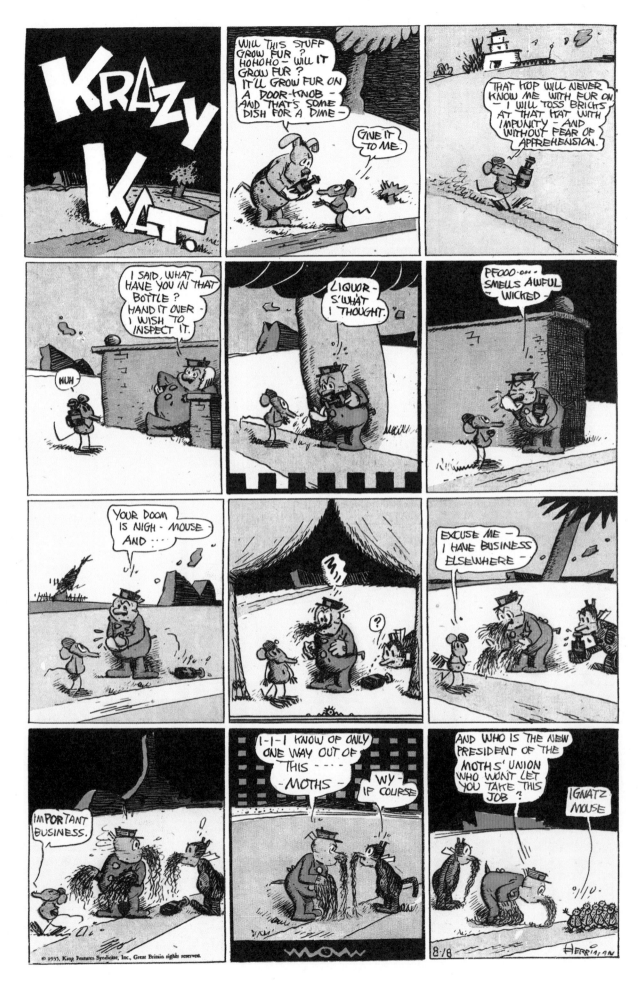

August 18th, 1935.

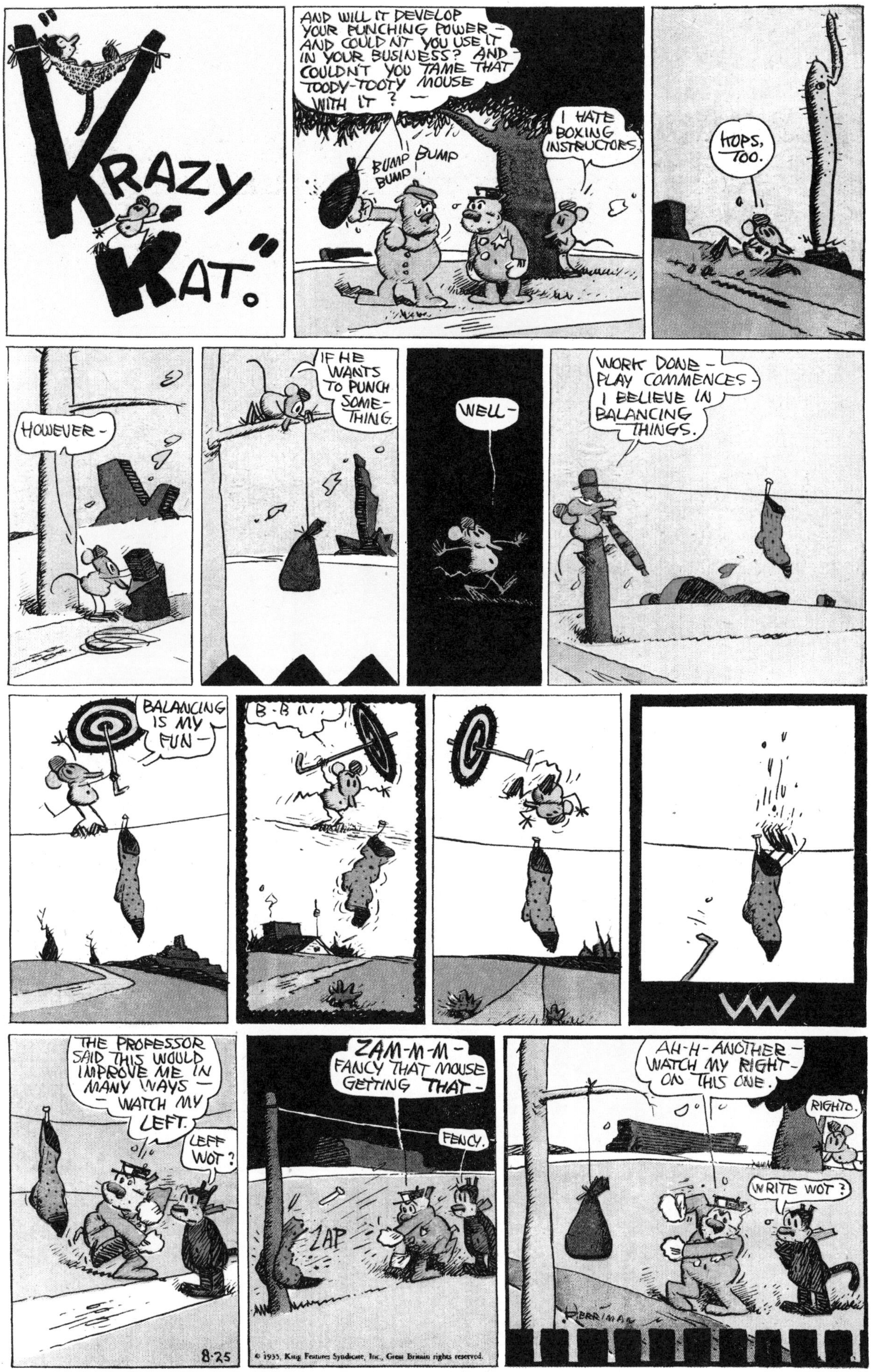
"Krazy Kat."
AND WILL IT DEVELOP YOUR PUNCHING POWER— AND COULD'NT YOU USE IT IN YOUR BUSINESS? AND COULDN'T YOU TAME THAT TOODY-TOOTY MOUSE WITH IT? —
BUMP BUMP BUMP!
I HATE BOXING INSTRUCTORS.
HOPS, TOO.
HOWEVER—
IF HE WANTS TO PUNCH SOME-THING.
WELL—
WORK DONE— PLAY COMMENCES— I BELIEVE IN BALANCING THINGS.
BALANCING IS MY FUN—
B-B !!!
THE PROFESSOR SAID THIS WOULD IMPROVE ME IN MANY WAYS — WATCH MY LEFT.
LEFF WOT?
ZAM-M-M— FANCY THAT MOUSE GETTING THAT—
FENCY.
ZAP
AH-H-ANOTHER— WATCH MY RIGHT— ON THIS ONE.
RIGHTO.
WRITE WOT?
HERRIMAN
8·25
© 1935, King Features Syndicate, Inc., Great Britain rights reserved.

August 25th, 1935.

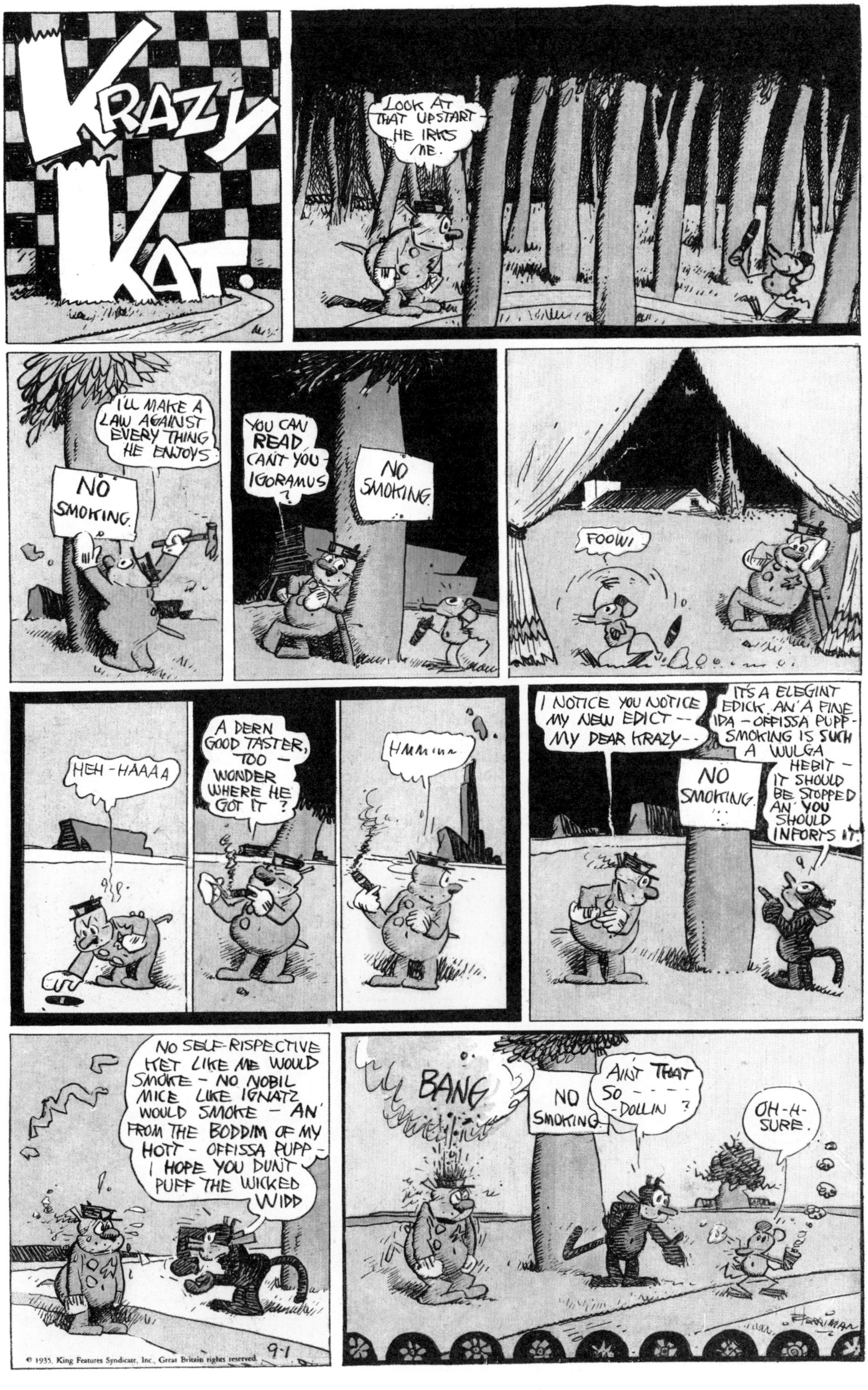
KRAZY KAT
LOOK AT THAT UPSTART HE IRKS ME.
I'LL MAKE A LAW AGAINST EVERY THING HE ENJOYS
NO SMOKING
YOU CAN READ CAN'T YOU IGORAMUS ?
NO SMOKING
FOOW!
HEH-HAAAA
A DERN GOOD TASTER, TOO – WONDER WHERE HE GOT IT ?
HMMMM
I NOTICE YOU NOTICE MY NEW EDICT -- MY DEAR KRAZY --
IT'S A ELEGINT EDICK AN' A FINE IDA – OFFISSA PUPP – SMOKING IS SUCH A WULGA HEBIT – IT SHOULD BE STOPPED AN' YOU SHOULD INFORM IT.
NO SMOKING
NO SELF-RISPECTIVE KET LIKE ME WOULD SMOKE – NO NOBIL MICE LIKE IGNATZ WOULD SMOKE – AN' FROM THE BODDIM OF MY HOTT – OFFISSA PUPP – I HOPE YOU DUNT PUFF THE WICKED WIDD
9-1
© 1935, King Features Syndicate, Inc., Great Britain rights reserved.
BANG
NO SMOKING
AIN'T THAT SO ---- DOLLIN ?
OH-H-SURE.
HERRIMAN

September 1st, 1935.

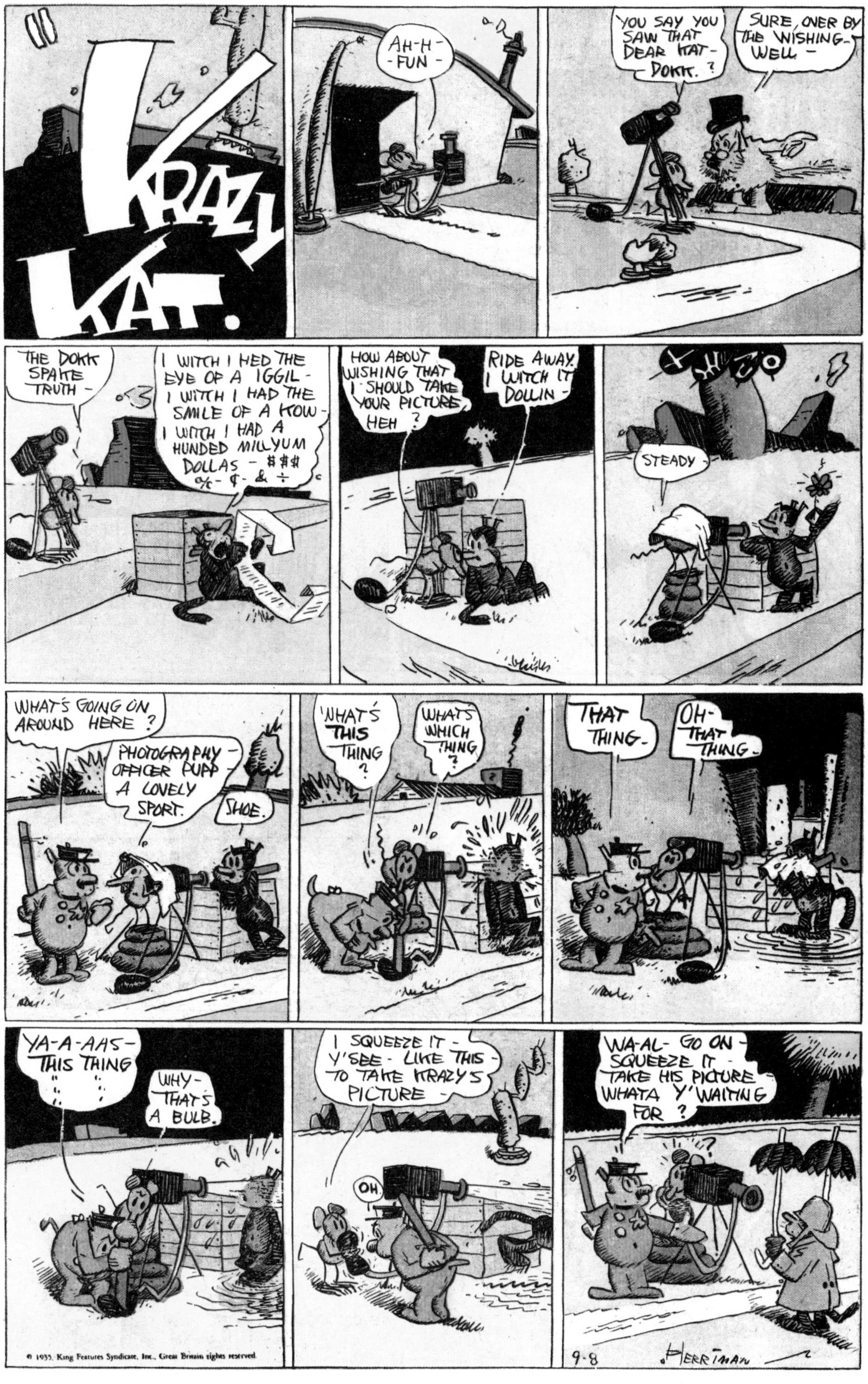
KRAZY KAT.
AH-H- -FUN-
YOU SAY YOU SAW THAT DEAR KAT-DOKK. ?
SURE, OVER BY THE WISHING-WELL-
THE DOKK SPAKE TRUTH-
I WITCH I HED THE EYE OF A IGGIL- I WITCH I HAD THE SMILE OF A KOW- I WITCH I HAD A HUNDED MILLYUM DOLLAS - $$$ %- ¢- & ÷
HOW ABOUT WISHING THAT I SHOULD TAKE YOUR PICTURE, HEH ?
RIDE AWAY. I WITCH IT DOLLIN-
STEADY
WHAT'S GOING ON AROUND HERE ?
PHOTOGRAPHY OFFICER PUPP A LOVELY SPORT.
SHOE.
WHAT'S THIS THING ?
WHAT'S WHICH THING ?
THAT THING.
OH- THAT THING.
YA-A-AAS- THIS THING
WHY- THAT'S A BULB.
I SQUEEZE IT - Y'SEE - LIKE THIS TO TAKE KRAZY'S PICTURE -
OH
WA-AL- GO ON- SQUEEZE IT - TAKE HIS PICTURE - WHATA Y' WAITING FOR ?
© 1935, King Features Syndicate, Inc., Great Britain rights reserved.
9-8
HERRIMAN

September 8th, 1935.

KRAZY KAT
KOUSIN KETFISH, YOU IS INWITED TO A KETNIP POTTY — AN' YOU MUSS COME — — R.S.V.P.
HOW CAN I — ?
HE MUSS COME.
PLUMBING
HE MUSS —
GIT IN, THIS POTTY WOULD N'T BE ONE HUNDED PITZENT SOCIAL UNLESS YOU WAS THERE IN PERTZIN —
IN THAT CASE, I'LL COME.
ENT TEBBY KET WILL BE THERE, ULSO UNKIL TOM KET — MR. ALEC. KET — KOUSIN KET BOID — ME — YOU — US — EVVA-BODDA —
AND WILL THAT AWFUL MOUSE — IGNATZ, BE THERE ?
WA-A-LL — NO — L'IL DOLLIN — HE'S GOT A BIG BITZNITZ DILL ON — HE'S TOO BITZI FOR OUR L'IL POTTIES — L'IL BITZI BEE.
THAT'S GOOD.
I'LL TRACK THIS TRAIL OF WATER BACK TO WHERE IT STARTS — I SUSPECT SOMETHING.
THOUGHT SO
IT RUNS OUT FASTER THAN I CAN POUR IT IN —
WAL, POUR IT IN FASTER — RASCAL —
HERRIMAN
9-15

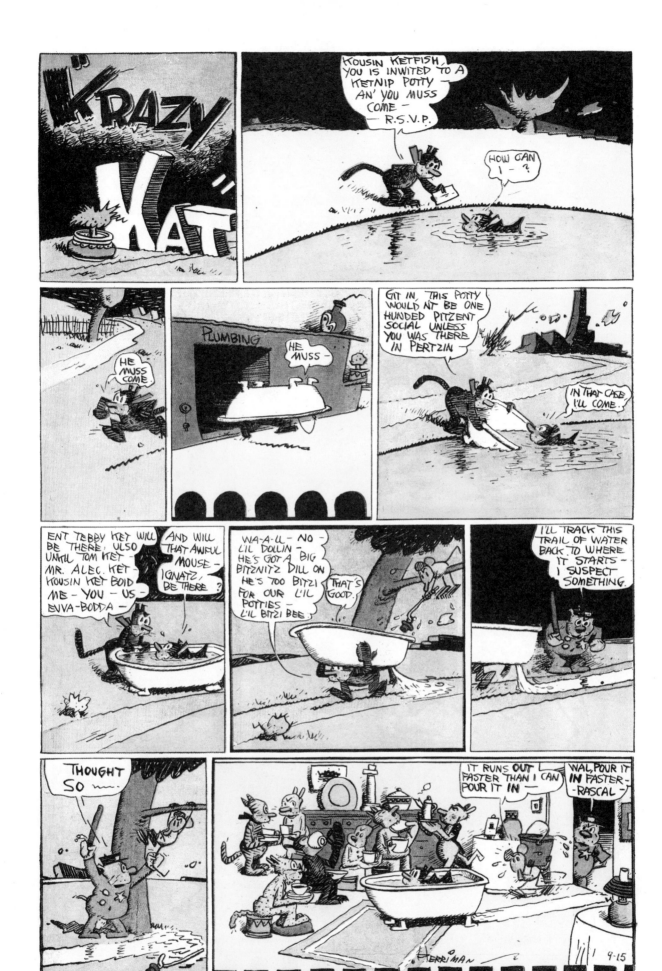

September 15th, 1935.

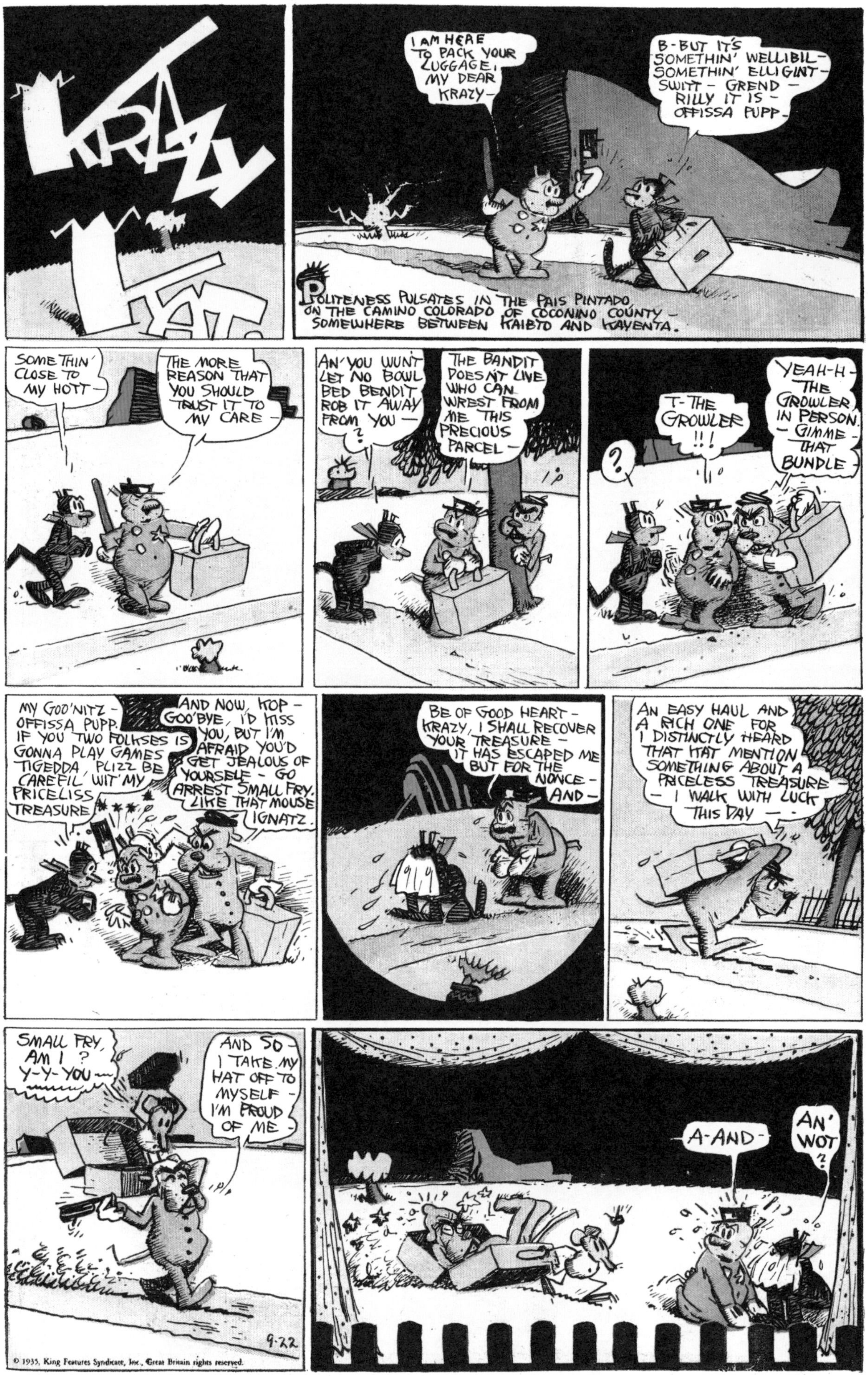
KRAZY KAT
I AM HERE TO PACK YOUR LUGGAGE, MY DEAR KRAZY -
B-BUT IT'S SOMETHIN' WELLIBIL - SOMETHIN' ELLIGINT - SWITT - GREND - RILLY IT IS - OFFISSA PUPP -
POLITENESS PULSATES IN THE PAIS PINTADO, ON THE CAMINO COLORADO OF COCONINO COUNTY - SOMEWHERE BETWEEN KAIBTO AND KAYENTA.
SOME THIN' CLOSE TO MY HOTT -
THE MORE REASON THAT YOU SHOULD TRUST IT TO MY CARE -
AN' YOU WUNT LET NO BOWL BED BENDIT ROB IT AWAY FROM YOU - ?
THE BANDIT DOESN'T LIVE WHO CAN WREST FROM ME THIS PRECIOUS PARCEL -
T-THE GROWLER !!!
YEAH-H - THE GROWLER IN PERSON. - GIMME THAT BUNDLE -
MY GOO'NITZ - OFFISSA PUPP. IF YOU TWO FOLKSES IS GONNA PLAY GAMES TIGEDDA, PLIZZ BE CAREFIL WIT MY PRICELISS TREASURE
AND NOW, KOP - GOO'BYE, I'D KISS YOU, BUT I'M AFRAID YOU'D GET JEALOUS OF YOURSELF - GO ARREST SMALL FRY, LIKE THAT MOUSE IGNATZ.
BE OF GOOD HEART - KRAZY, I SHALL RECOVER YOUR TREASURE - IT HAS ESCAPED ME BUT FOR THE NONCE - AND -
AN EASY HAUL AND A RICH ONE FOR I DISTINCTLY HEARD THAT KAT MENTION SOMETHING ABOUT A PRICELESS TREASURE - I WALK WITH LUCK THIS DAY -
SMALL FRY, AM I ? Y-Y-YOU -
AND SO - I TAKE MY HAT OFF TO MYSELF - I'M PROUD OF ME -
A-AND -
AN' WOT ?
9-22
© 1935, King Features Syndicate, Inc., Great Britain rights reserved.

September 22nd, 1935.

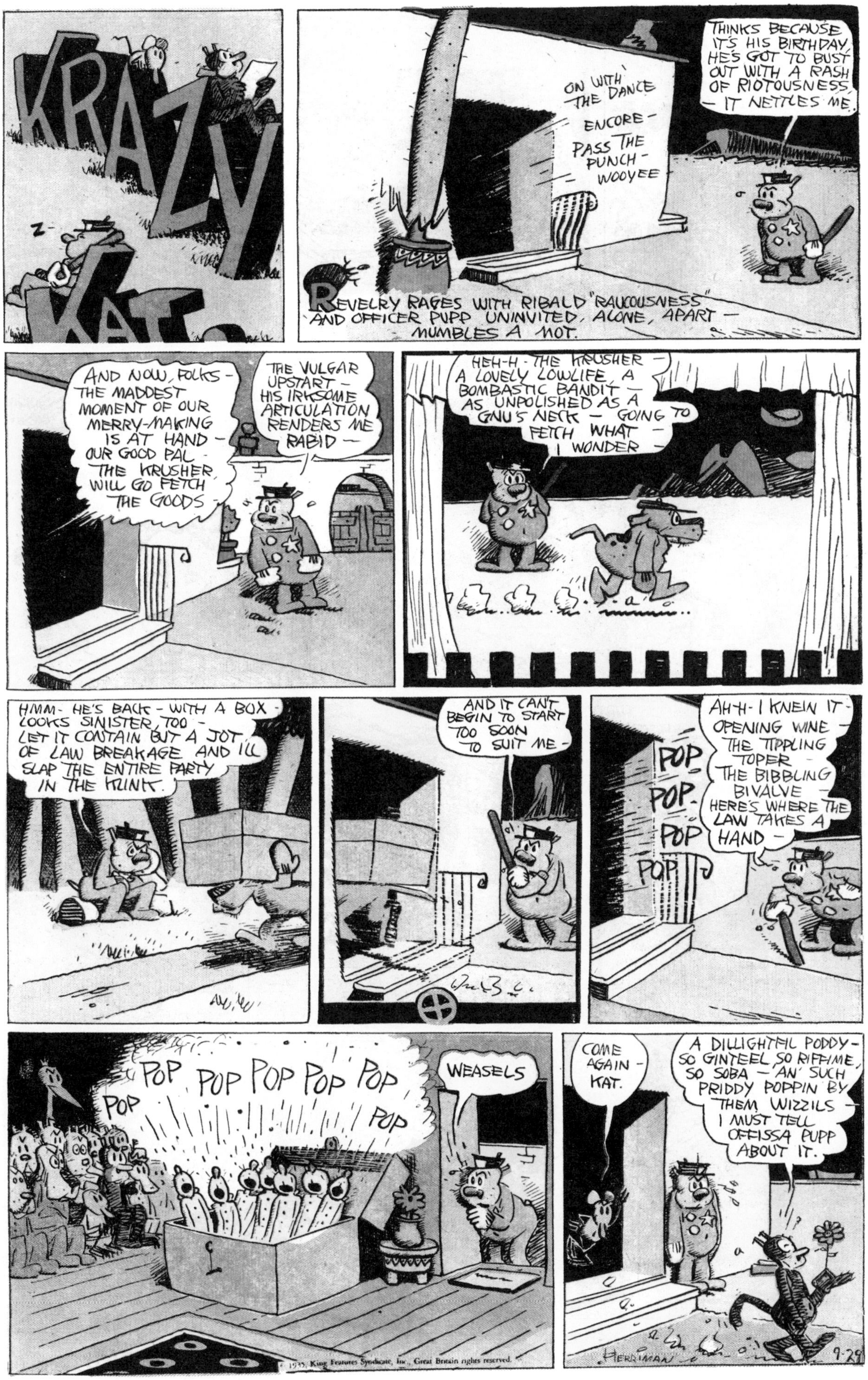
KRAZY KAT
Z-
ON WITH THE DANCE
ENCORE -
PASS THE PUNCH -
WOOYEE
THINKS BECAUSE IT'S HIS BIRTHDAY, HE'S GOT TO BUST OUT WITH A RASH OF RIOTOUSNESS. — IT NETTLES ME.
REVELRY RAGES WITH RIBALD "RAUCOUSNESS" AND OFFICER PUPP UNINVITED, ALONE, APART — MUMBLES A MOT.
AND NOW, FOLKS - THE MADDEST MOMENT OF OUR MERRY-MAKING IS AT HAND - OUR GOOD PAL THE KRUSHER WILL GO FETCH THE GOODS
THE VULGAR UPSTART - HIS IRKSOME ARTICULATION RENDERS ME RABID -
HEH-H - THE KRUSHER - A LOVELY LOWLIFE, A BOMBASTIC BANDIT - AS UNPOLISHED AS A GNU'S NECK - GOING TO FETCH WHAT - I WONDER -
HMM - HE'S BACK - WITH A BOX - LOOKS SINISTER, TOO - LET IT CONTAIN BUT A JOT OF LAW BREAKAGE AND I'LL SLAP THE ENTIRE PARTY IN THE KLINK.
AND IT CAN'T BEGIN TO START TOO SOON TO SUIT ME -
POP POP POP POP
AH-H - I KNEW IT - OPENING WINE - THE TIPPLING TOPER - THE BIBBLING BIVALVE - HERE'S WHERE THE LAW TAKES A HAND -
POP POP POP POP POP POP POP
WEASELS
COME AGAIN KAT.
A DILLIGHTFIL PODDY - SO GINTEEL SO RIFFIME, SO SOBA - AN' SUCH PRIDDY POPPIN BY THEM WIZZILS - I MUST TELL OFFISSA PUPP ABOUT IT.
© 1935, King Features Syndicate, Inc., Great Britain rights reserved.
HERRIMAN 9-29

September 29th, 1935.

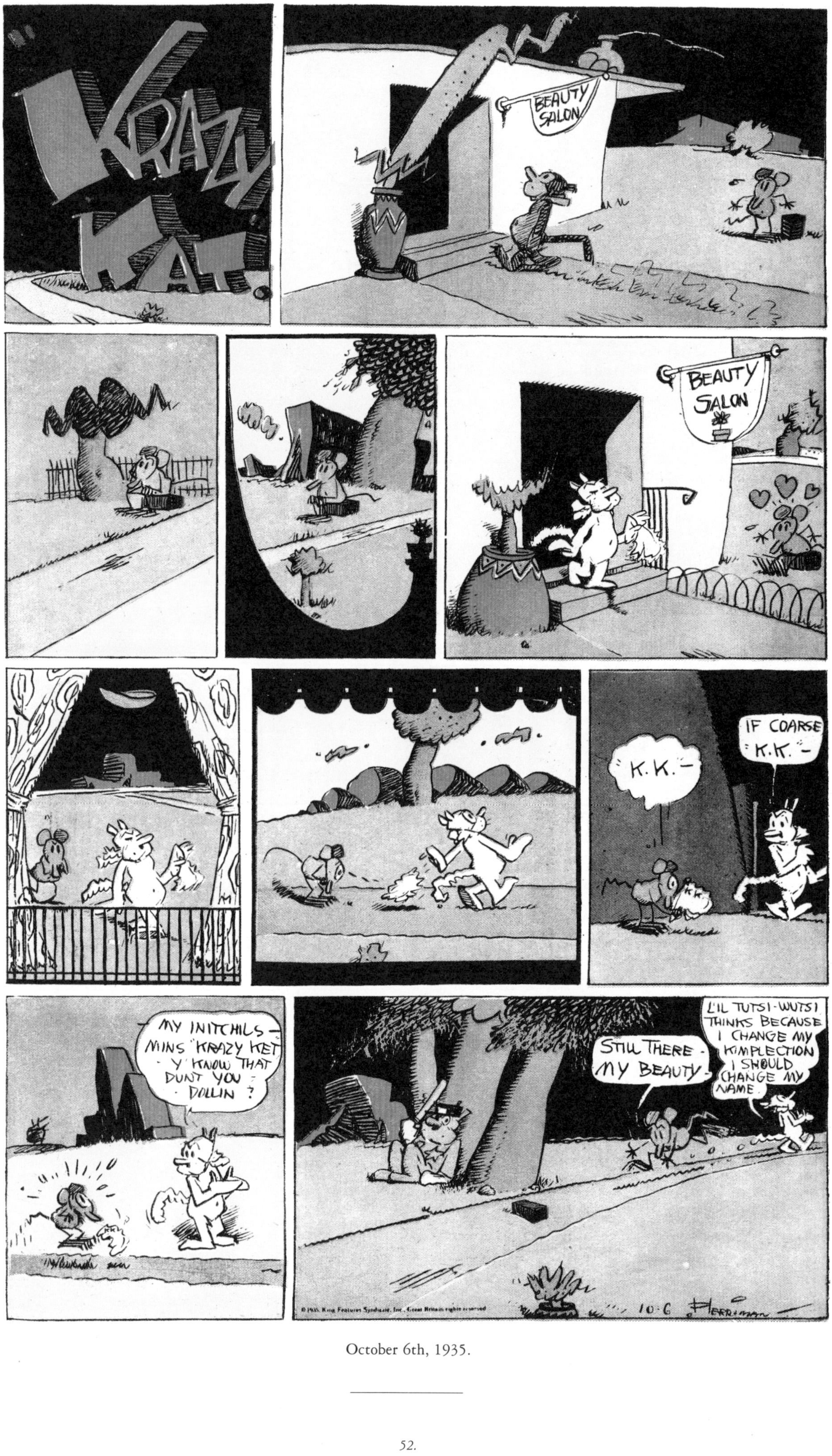
KRAZY KAT
BEAUTY SALON
BEAUTY SALON
K.K. —
IF COARSE K.K. —
MY INITCHILS — MINS "KRAZY KET" — Y' KNOW THAT DUNT YOU — DOLLIN ?
STILL THERE — MY BEAUTY —
L'IL TUTSI-WUTSI THINKS BECAUSE I CHANGE MY KIMPLECTION I SHOULD CHANGE MY NAME.
© 1935, King Features Syndicate, Inc., Great Britain rights reserved
10-6
Herriman

October 6th, 1935.

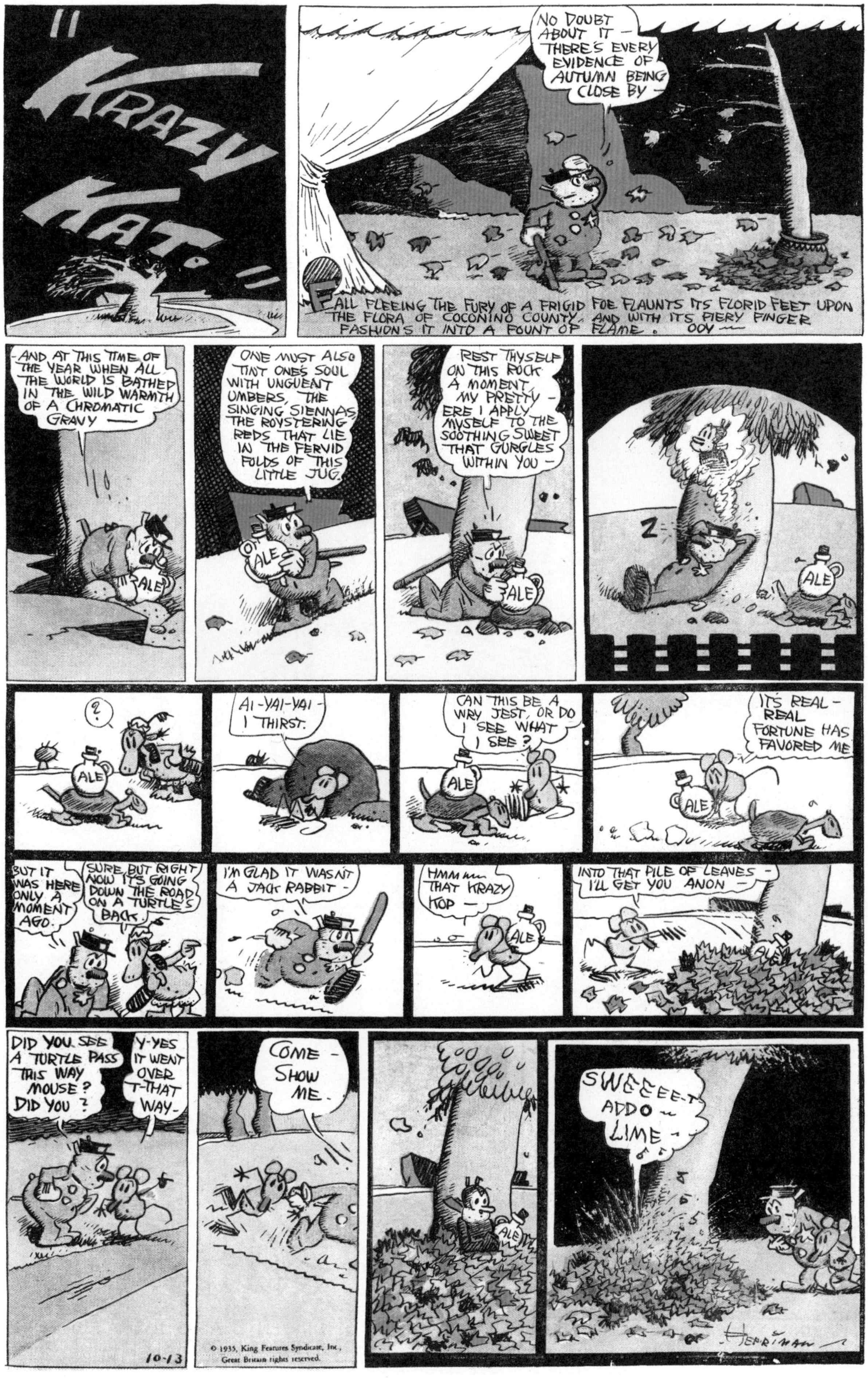
Krazy Kat
No doubt about it — there's every evidence of autumn being close by —
Fall fleeing the fury of a frigid foe flaunts its florid feet upon the flora of Coconino County, and with its fiery finger fashions it into a fount of flame. ooy —
—And at this time of the year when all the world is bathed in the wild warmth of a chromatic gravy —
One must also tint one's soul with unguent umbers, the singing siennas, the roystering reds that lie in the fervid folds of this little jug.
ALE
Rest thyself on this rock a moment, my pretty — ere I apply myself to the soothing sweet that gurgles within you —
Z
ALE
?
Ai-yai-yai — I thirst.
Can this be a wry jest, or do I see what I see?
It's real — real fortune has favored me
But it was here only a moment ago.
Sure, but right now it's going down the road on a turtle's back.
I'm glad it wasn't a jack rabbit —
Hmm — that Krazy Kop —
Into that pile of leaves — I'll get you anon —
Did you see a turtle pass this way mouse? Did you?
Y-yes it went over t-that way —
Come — show me.
Sweeeee-t addo — lime —
10-13
© 1935, King Features Syndicate, Inc., Great Britain rights reserved.
Herriman

October 13th, 1935.

KRAZY KAT.
IT IS NO FOOL'S FANCY - OFFICER PUPP - IT IS A BOOMERANG BRICK - AND WITH MY OWN FAIR FINGERS HAVE I FASHIONED IT - AND CONCEIVED IT WITH MY OWN MASTER MIND - HOW DO YOU LIKE IT ?
I HATE IT - GO.
PFFF
- KNOW WHAT THIS IS, MY DEAR KRAZY ?
IT'S A HOTZ-SHOE AINT IT ?
NO -
PRETZIL - ?
A HOOK AN' EYES ?
NO -
DUNT TELL ME - DUNT TELL ME I'LL GETZ IT - MY MINE IS FUNCTIONING.
WAIT TILL I GET RID OF IT - AND I'LL TELL YOU -
NOW YOU TELL ME - AN' SEE IF YOU THINK IT'S THE SAME THING I THINK IT IS -
OF COURSE, IT IS - OF COURSE, IT IS -
TELL ME -
IT'S ...
PSSST-T-T THE TIME HAS COME FOR YOU TO GO WITH ME
KLONK
IF COARSE, IT'S SHAPED LIKE THE LETTA "U" - BUT IT AINT A "U," IS IT ?
NO.
© 1935, King Features Syndicate, Inc., Great Britain rights reserved.
10-20
HERRIMAN

October 20th, 1935.

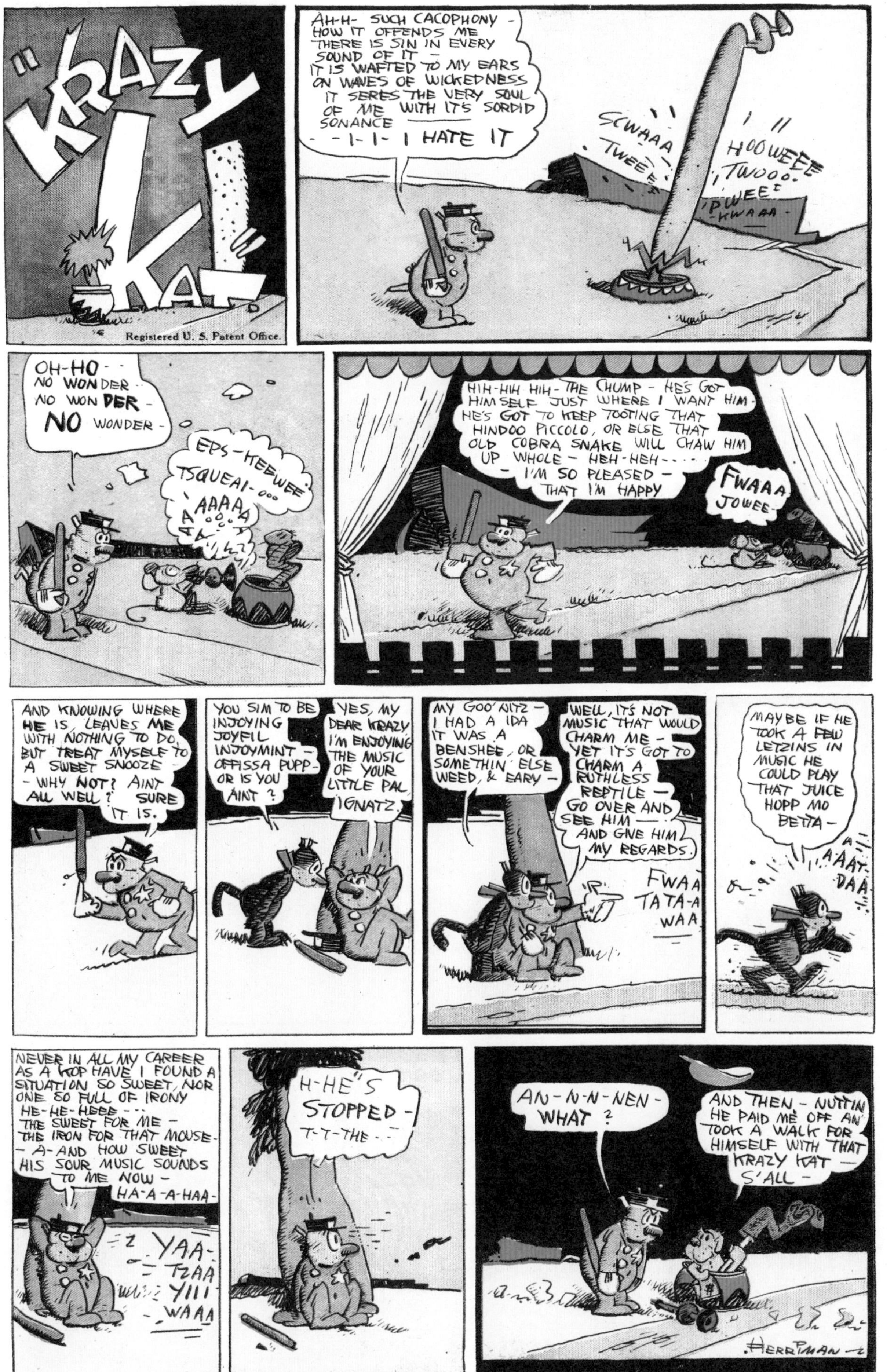
"KRAZY KAT"
Registered U. S. Patent Office.
AH-H- SUCH CACOPHONY - HOW IT OFFENDS ME THERE IS SIN IN EVERY SOUND OF IT - IT IS WAFTED TO MY EARS ON WAVES OF WICKEDNESS IT SERES THE VERY SOUL OF ME WITH IT'S SORDID SONANCE - - - I-I- I HATE IT
SCWAAA TWEEE
HOOWEEE TWOOO PWEEE KWAAA
OH-HO- NO WONDER NO WONDER NO WONDER -
EPS-HEEWEE TSQUEAI-ooo AAAA
HIH-HIH HIH - THE CHUMP - HE'S GOT HIMSELF JUST WHERE I WANT HIM - HE'S GOT TO KEEP TOOTING THAT HINDOO PICCOLO, OR ELSE THAT OLD COBRA SNAKE WILL CHAW HIM UP WHOLE - HEH-HEH - - - - I'M SO PLEASED - THAT I'M HAPPY
FWAAA JOWEE
AND KNOWING WHERE HE IS, LEAVES ME WITH NOTHING TO DO, BUT TREAT MYSELF TO A SWEET SNOOZE - WHY NOT? AINT ALL WELL? SURE IT IS.
YOU SIM TO BE INJOYING JOYFIL INJOYMINT - OFFISSA PUPP - OR IS YOU AINT ?
YES, MY DEAR KRAZY I'M ENJOYING THE MUSIC OF YOUR LITTLE PAL IGNATZ.
MY GOO'NITZ - I HAD A IDA IT WAS A BENSHEE, OR SOMETHIN' ELSE WEED, & EARY -
WELL, IT'S NOT MUSIC THAT WOULD CHARM ME - YET IT'S GOT TO CHARM A RUTHLESS REPTILE - GO OVER AND SEE HIM - AND GIVE HIM MY REGARDS.
FWAA TATA-A WAA
MAYBE IF HE TOOK A FEW LETZINS IN MUSIC HE COULD PLAY THAT JUICE HOPP MO BETTA -
A-AAAT-DAA
NEVER IN ALL MY CAREER AS A KOP HAVE I FOUND A SITUATION SO SWEET, NOR ONE SO FULL OF IRONY HE-HE-HEEE - - - THE SWEET FOR ME - THE IRON FOR THAT MOUSE - A- AND HOW SWEET HIS SOUR MUSIC SOUNDS TO ME NOW - HA-A-A-HAA -
YAA- TZAA YIII WAAA
10-27
H-HE'S STOPPED - T-T-THE - -
© 1935, King Features Syndicate, Inc., Great Britain rights reserved.
AN-N-N-NEN - WHAT ?
AND THEN - NUTTIN HE PAID ME OFF AN' TOOK A WALK FOR HIMSELF WITH THAT KRAZY KAT - S'ALL -
HERRIMAN

October 27th, 1935.

"KRAZY KAT."
SWEET LITTLE FOLKS, EVEN IF THEY ARE BUT MICE - AND EVEN IF THEIR FATHER IS THAT SINFUL, SINISTER, SCORPION, IGNATZ - THEY CAN'T HELP IT - AND THERE IS THAT IN MY HEART THAT GOES OUT TO THEM — - POBRECITOS -
AND THIS FAIR FEMMY - HIS SPOUSE - WHAT BLINDING STORM STEERED HER COURSE ON LIFE'S SEA AS THAT VANDAL'S MATE - - IT SADDENS ME AI-AI-AI -
AND HERE AM I - WIELDING THE WAND OF LAW UPON HIM - BACKED BY A TIN BUZZER - AND A BRASS BUTTON - MAKING A CHRONIC JAIL WREN OUT OF HIM - HE THEIR PROVIDER - PROTECTOR
I COULD HAVE AS WELL USED KINDNESS - SANS CLUB, SANS BADGE, SANS BUTTONS, SANS JAIL — SANS - - -
MY CONSCIENCE HAS AT LAST FOUND ME OUT - AND FOUND ME AT FAULT -
OFFICER PUPP — OFFICER-R-R PUPP —
OH-H- CONSCIENCE HAVE M-MERCY I-I-I'LL -
YOU'LL WHAT ?
I'LL DO BETTER - I'LL BE KIND, SWEET - PATIENT - TOLERANT -
WILL YOU PUT THAT DOWN IN WRITING ?
and, hereafter, instead of the law's bitter fervor, I will try the milk of kindness, the unction of gentleness — SIGNED Officer B. Pupp.
?
THIS WILL ALSO PLEASE THAT DEAR KAT.
IT MUST BE A L'IL GAME, HIM, AN' OFFISSA PUPP IS PLAYING — SO, I WUNT INTA-FEE - - -
ZIP
HERRIMAN 11-3
© 1935, King Features Syndicate, Inc., Great Britain rights reserved.

November 3rd, 1935.

"KRAZY KAT."
Registered U. S. Patent Office
I HAVE LONG DESIRED TO DELVE INTO THE DEPTHS OF HIS MORALS, KRAZY LEND ME YOUR PURSE FOR THE NONCE - AND I SHALL ATTEMPT MY WHIM -
IF HE TAKES IT I WILL ARREST HIM FOR THE DISHONEST WRETCH THAT HE IS - IF HE DOESN'T, I'LL FIND SOME OTHER REASON TO JAIL HIM.
RIGHT ABOUT HERE - IS WHERE HE'LL PASS -
THE TRAP IS SET - AND I WILL THIS DAY PENETRATE THAT WHICH I HAVE LONG SUSPECTED BEING SINS FAVORITE ABODE - THAT MOUSE'S SOUL.
AH-H-H - THE POLTROON - HE COMES - TO HIS DOOM -
$
THE GROWLER !!!
RIGHT - AND LAY OFFA THAT POKE -
OOH-H - PRETTY - PRETTY -
AH-H, BUT, MY DEAR MR. GROWLER --- Y'SEE, T'WAS BUT A JEST, A QUIP - S-SURELY, YOU'RE NOT GOING TO KEEP IT ---
AIN'T YOU THE FUNNY KOP?!!!
11-10
BUT, OFFISSA PUPP YOU AIN'T TOLD ME YET - DID HE TOOK IT - OR DID HE NOT TOOK IT? ENSA ME.
DRINK UP, PAL - DRINK UP - HAVE ANOTHER -
HERRIMAN

November 10th, 1935.

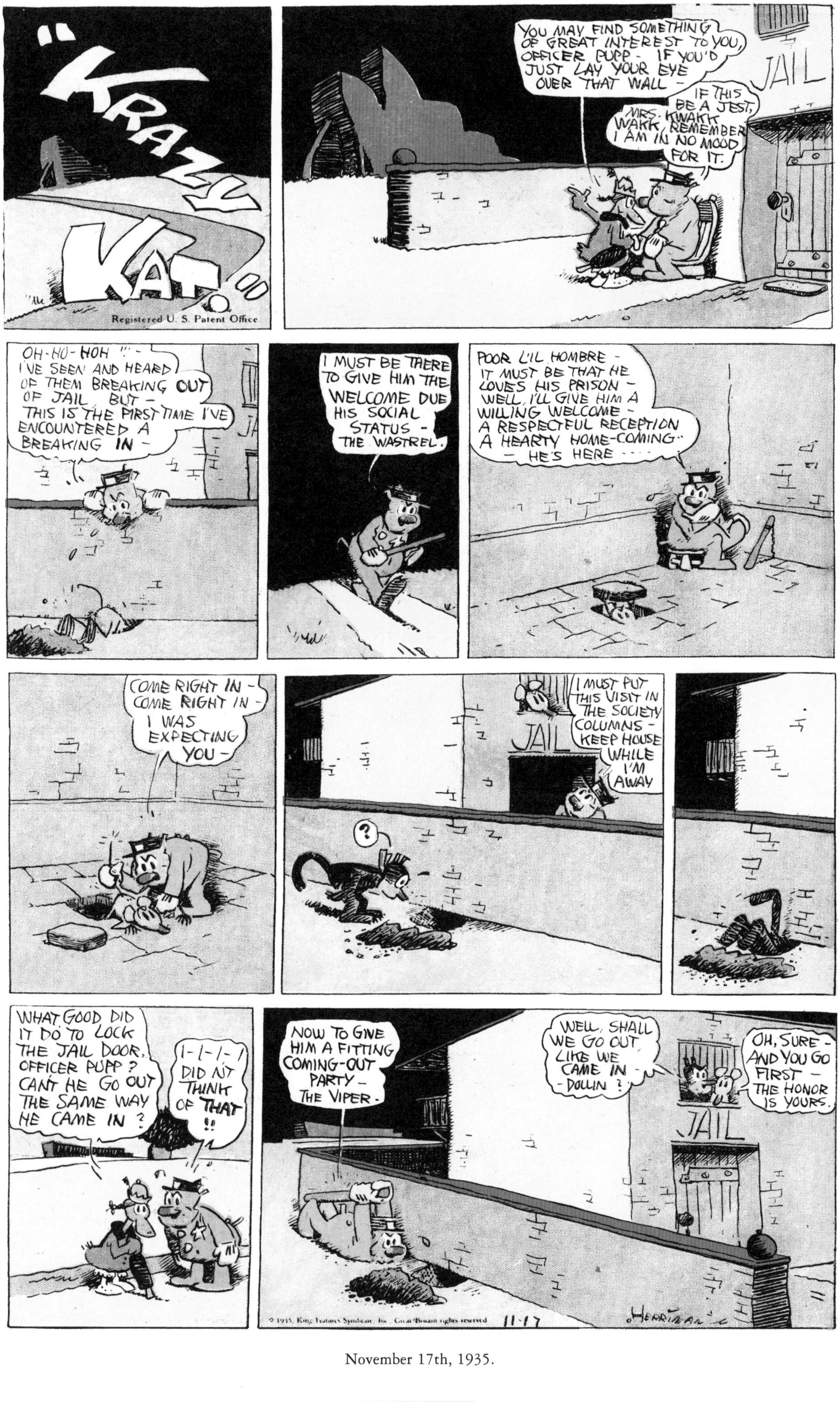
"KRAZY KAT"
Registered U. S. Patent Office
YOU MAY FIND SOMETHING OF GREAT INTEREST TO YOU, OFFICER PUPP - IF YOU'D JUST LAY YOUR EYE OVER THAT WALL -
IF THIS BE A JEST, MRS. KWAKK WAKK, REMEMBER I AM IN NO MOOD FOR IT.
JAIL
OH-HO-HOH !! - I'VE SEEN AND HEARD OF THEM BREAKING OUT OF JAIL BUT - THIS IS THE FIRST TIME I'VE ENCOUNTERED A BREAKING IN -
I MUST BE THERE TO GIVE HIM THE WELCOME DUE HIS SOCIAL STATUS - THE WASTREL.
POOR L'IL HOMBRE - IT MUST BE THAT HE LOVES HIS PRISON - WELL, I'LL GIVE HIM A WILLING WELCOME - A RESPECTFUL RECEPTION A HEARTY HOME-COMING - - HE'S HERE - - -
COME RIGHT IN - COME RIGHT IN - I WAS EXPECTING YOU -
I MUST PUT THIS VISIT IN THE SOCIETY COLUMNS - KEEP HOUSE WHILE I'M AWAY
JAIL
?
WHAT GOOD DID IT DO TO LOCK THE JAIL DOOR, OFFICER PUPP? CAN'T HE GO OUT THE SAME WAY HE CAME IN?
I-I-I-I DID N'T THINK OF THAT !!
NOW TO GIVE HIM A FITTING COMING-OUT PARTY - THE VIPER -
WELL, SHALL WE GO OUT LIKE WE CAME IN - DOLLIN?
OH, SURE - AND YOU GO FIRST - THE HONOR IS YOURS.
JAIL
© 1935, King Features Syndicate, Inc. Great Britain rights reserved
11-17
HERRIMAN

November 17th, 1935.

"KRAZY KAT."
Registered U. S. Patent Office
IN THE DIAMOND DAZZLE OF WHITE MESA'S BEAUTÉ BLANCHE, A WEEPING WILLOW DROOPS ADRIP WITH TEARS - KEEPING AT FLOOD A LACHRYMAL LAGOON - UPON WHOSE AQUEOUS BOUNTY A WATER-MELON HAS THRIVEN INTO A MAGNITUDINOUS MATURITY.
T'IS SO INDEED IN KAIBITO.
IF I KNOW MY MELLINS I'D SAY THIS ONE IS RIPE AN' FIDDIL TO EAT --- SO -
UMMM YMMM
S'FUNNA I FILL A GOOD KRY OF TEARS COMIN' ON A-AA-AAA---
AYAAAA WAAAAAA
AA-AAA-AAA AA-AA AAAAAA -
?
I-I-NEVER SAW SUCH TEARS - NOR EVER SUCH WOFUL WEEPING - I-II---
SHAAA - I CAN'T SMACK A KRYING KAT - I HAVE NO HEART FOR SUCH LOW-DOWNESS - - AWAY, BRICK I CAN'T DO IT.
AAAAA
HAH - THAT MOUSE'S WICKED WORK - AND HOW SORELY HE MUST HAVE HURT THAT DEAR KAT - TO BRING ON SUCH WEEPING, SUCH TEARS
BUT ERE I SET ABOUT TO BRING THE BRIGAND TO JUSTICE, I'LL TREAT MYSELF TO A NIBBLE OF THIS LUSCIOUS LEGUME - IT WILL GIVE ME COURAGE - AND -
I-I-I WEEP - I SEEM TO CRY - I AM IN TEARS - I-I-I GUSH WITH THEM - AA WAAA -
A-WAAA -
Y'YOU - YOU AND YOUR KROCODILE TEARS -
JAIL
AH, BUT WE KNOW, EH? WE WHO HAVE SEEN THE TRICKLE OF A WEEPING WILLOW'S TEARS - THE FOUNT FROM WHICH A MELON QUAFFED.
© 1935, King Features Syndicate, Inc. Great Britain rights reserved.
11-24 HERRIMAN

November 24th, 1935.

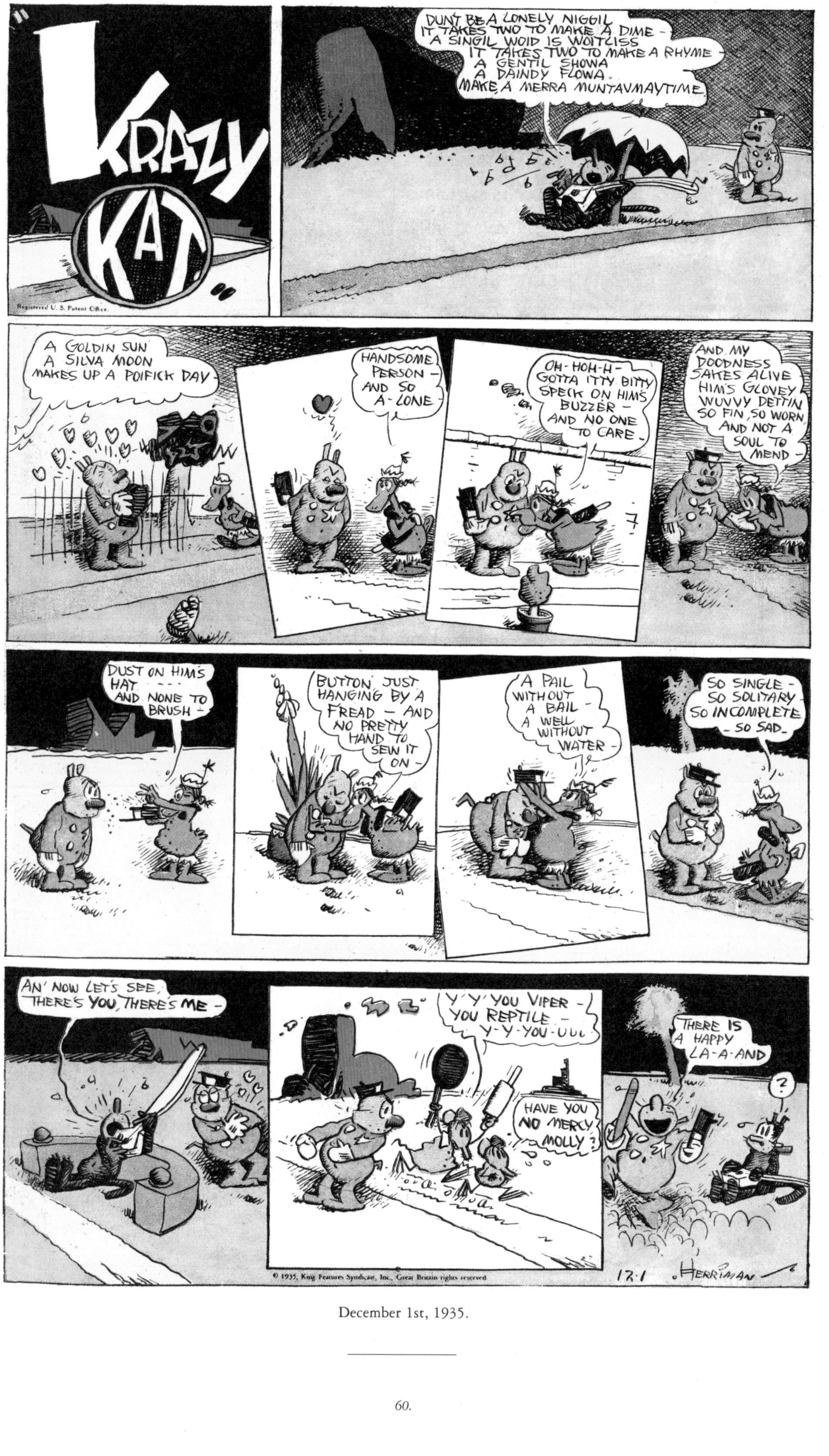

KRAZY KAT
Registered U. S. Patent Office.
DUN'T BE A LONELY NIGGIL
IT TAKES TWO TO MAKE A DIME -
A SINGIL WOID IS WOITLISS
IT TAKES TWO TO MAKE A RHYME -
A GENTIL SHOWA
A DAINDY FLOWA.
MAKE A MERRA MUNTAVMAYTIME.
A GOLDIN SUN A SILVA MOON MAKES UP A POIFICK DAY -
HANDSOME PERSON - AND SO A-LONE -
OH-HOH-H - GOTTA ITTY BITTY SPECK ON HIM'S BUZZER - AND NO ONE TO CARE -
AND MY DOODNESS SAKES ALIVE HIM'S GLOVEY WUVVY DETTIN SO FIN, SO WORN, AND NOT A SOUL TO MEND -
DUST ON HIM'S HAT --- AND NONE TO BRUSH -
BUTTON JUST HANGING BY A FREAD - AND NO PRETTY HAND TO SEW IT ON -
A PAIL WITHOUT A BAIL - A WELL WITHOUT WATER -
SO SINGLE - SO SOLITARY - SO INCOMPLETE - SO SAD -
AN' NOW LET'S SEE, THERE'S YOU, THERE'S ME -
Y-Y-YOU VIPER - YOU REPTILE - Y-Y-YOU-UUU
HAVE YOU NO MERCY, MOLLY?
THERE IS A HAPPY LA-A-AND
?
© 1935, King Features Syndicate, Inc., Great Britain rights reserved.
12-1
HERRIMAN

December 1st, 1935.

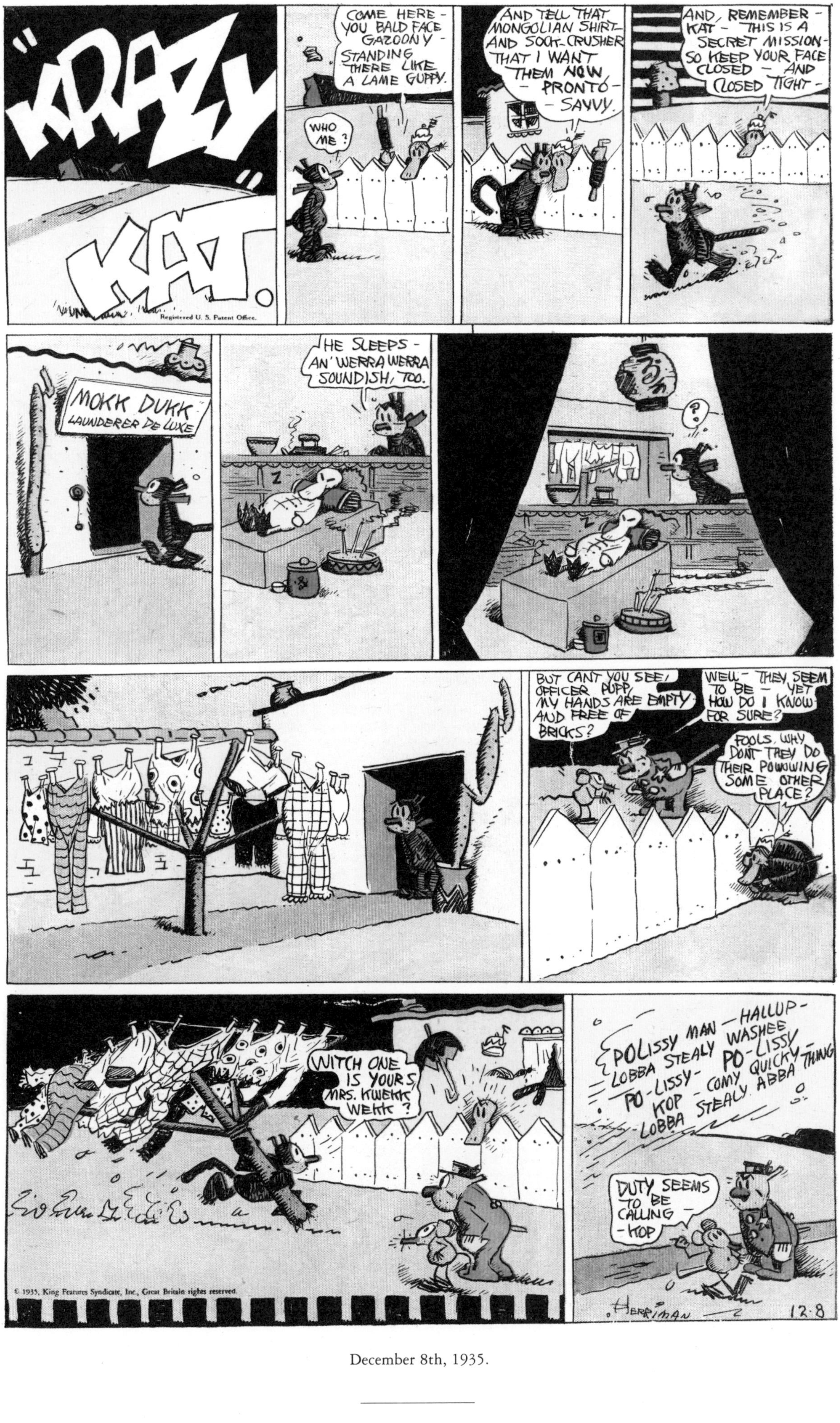
"KRAZY KAT."
Registered U. S. Patent Office.
COME HERE - YOU BALD FACE GAZOONY - STANDING THERE LIKE A LAME GUPPY.
WHO ME ?
AND TELL THAT MONGOLIAN SHIRT AND SOCK CRUSHER THAT I WANT THEM NOW, - PRONTO - - SAVVY.
AND, REMEMBER KAT - THIS IS A SECRET MISSION - SO KEEP YOUR FACE CLOSED - AND CLOSED TIGHT -
MOKK DUKK LAUNDERER DE LUXE
HE SLEEPS - AN' WERRA WERRA SOUNDISH, TOO.
?
BUT CANT YOU SEE, OFFICER PUPP, MY HANDS ARE EMPTY AND FREE OF BRICKS?
WELL - THEY SEEM TO BE - YET HOW DO I KNOW FOR SURE?
FOOLS, WHY DONT THEY DO THEIR POWWOWING SOME OTHER PLACE?
WITCH ONE IS YOURS, MRS. KWEKK WEKK ?
POLISSY MAN - HALLUP - LOBBA STEALY WASHEE PO-LISSY - PO-LISSY KOP - COMY QUICKY - LOBBA STEALY ABBA THING
DUTY SEEMS TO BE CALLING - KOP
© 1935, King Features Syndicate, Inc., Great Britain rights reserved.
HERRIMAN 12·8

December 8th, 1935.

KRAZY KAT
Registered U. S. Patent Office.
KRAZY KAT, HAVING FASHIONED A PASTY, FILLED WITH AN OLEAGINOUS AMPLITUDE OF APPLE – SEEKS A SPOT WHERE IN TO COOL THE CONFECTION.
HUH-HUH-HUH NO BRIZZ OUTSIDE.
SO I'LL KIMMENTZ A BRIZZ OF WIN' FROM THE INSIDE, A OTTAFITCHIL ZEPPA, AS IT WAS.
PIE – APPLE PIE – MY SIN – mmmm.
FUFF
ITS TEMPITURE HAS WENT DOWN – ONE MORE PUFF OF BRIZZ AN' IT WILL BE KOOL LIKE A KUKUMBA.
WHAT KIND OF BALLY BALDERDASH IS THIS, TRYING TO BUILD A NEST IN THAT CACTUS BUSH? – THINK YOU'RE A WREN?
FUFF
© 1935, King Features Syndicate, Inc., Great Britain rights reserved
WUNT L'IL PITZ EPPIL PIE, DOLLIN?
NAH
JAIL
12-15
HERRIMAN

December 15th, 1935.

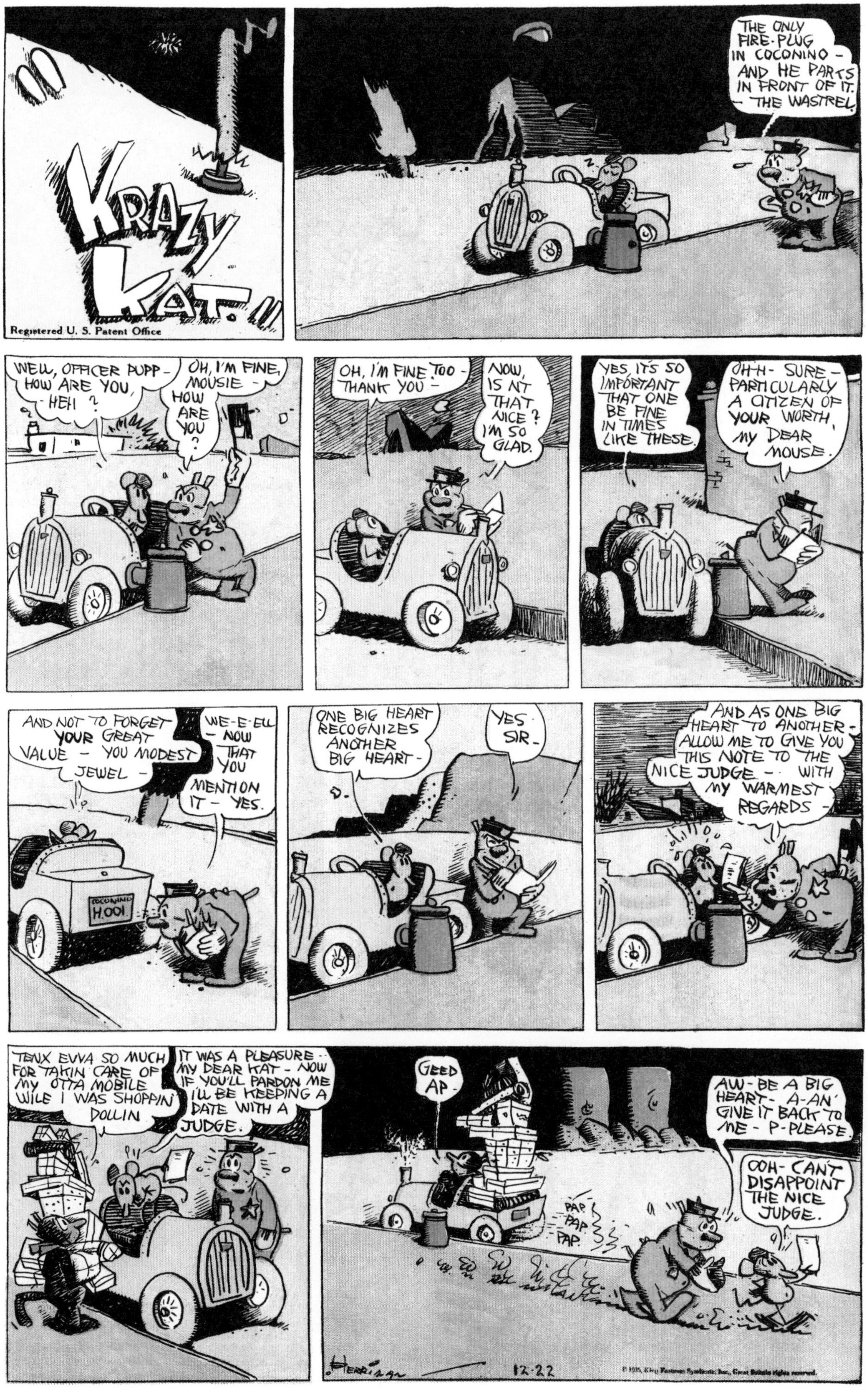
Krazy Kat
Registered U. S. Patent Office
THE ONLY FIRE-PLUG IN COCONINO - AND HE PARKS IN FRONT OF IT. - THE WASTREL.
WELL, OFFICER PUPP - HOW ARE YOU, - HEH ?
OH, I'M FINE, MOUSIE - HOW ARE YOU ?
OH, I'M FINE TOO - THANK YOU -
NOW, IS N'T THAT NICE ? I'M SO GLAD.
YES, IT'S SO IMPORTANT THAT ONE BE FINE IN TIMES LIKE THESE.
OH-H - SURE - PARTICULARLY A CITIZEN OF YOUR WORTH, MY DEAR MOUSE.
AND NOT TO FORGET YOUR GREAT VALUE - YOU MODEST JEWEL -
WE-E-ELL - NOW THAT YOU MENTION IT - YES.
COCONINO H.001
ONE BIG HEART RECOGNIZES ANOTHER BIG HEART -
YES SIR -
AND AS ONE BIG HEART TO ANOTHER - ALLOW ME TO GIVE YOU THIS NOTE TO THE NICE JUDGE - WITH MY WARMEST REGARDS -
TENX EVVA SO MUCH FOR TAKIN CARE OF MY OTTA MOBILE WILE I WAS SHOPPIN' DOLLIN
IT WAS A PLEASURE - MY DEAR KAT - NOW IF YOU'LL PARDON ME I'LL BE KEEPING A DATE WITH A JUDGE.
GEED AP -
PAP PAP PAP
AW - BE A BIG HEART - A-AN' GIVE IT BACK TO ME - P-PLEASE
OOH - CAN'T DISAPPOINT THE NICE JUDGE.
HERRIMAN
12-22

December 22nd, 1935.

KRAZY KAT
Registered U. S. Patent Office.
IT'S A PRIVATE TELEFOAM, OFFISSA PUPP - BITWIN IGNATZ MICE & ME ----- I'M LITZNIN' TO HIS SWITT WOICE RIDE NOW.
MMM-
HERE, YOU LITZIN -
AND IF THAT KRAZY KOP IS AROUND LET HIM HEAR THE VOICE OF HIS MOST ARDENT DISLIKER - ME - IGNATZ MOUSE
!
NOT ONLY HAS HE TRIFLED WITH THE PRIDE IN ME, BUT HE HAS TRODDEN UPON THE HIGH DIGNITY OF THE LAW -- WORM.
HAH-H -- DOES THIS DAUNT ME?
NO - A THOUSAND NOES IT BUT SPURS ME ON --
YA-A-A TRICKERY
YES-SIR - IGNATZ MOUSE, THE OLD TRICKSTER.
AND HIGH CLASS TRICKERY, TOO - EH, KOPPIE ?
GOO'-BYE, FOLKS!
12-29
© 1935, King Features Syndicate, Inc., Great Britain rights reserved.
Herriman

December 29th, 1935.

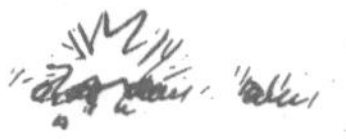

1936.

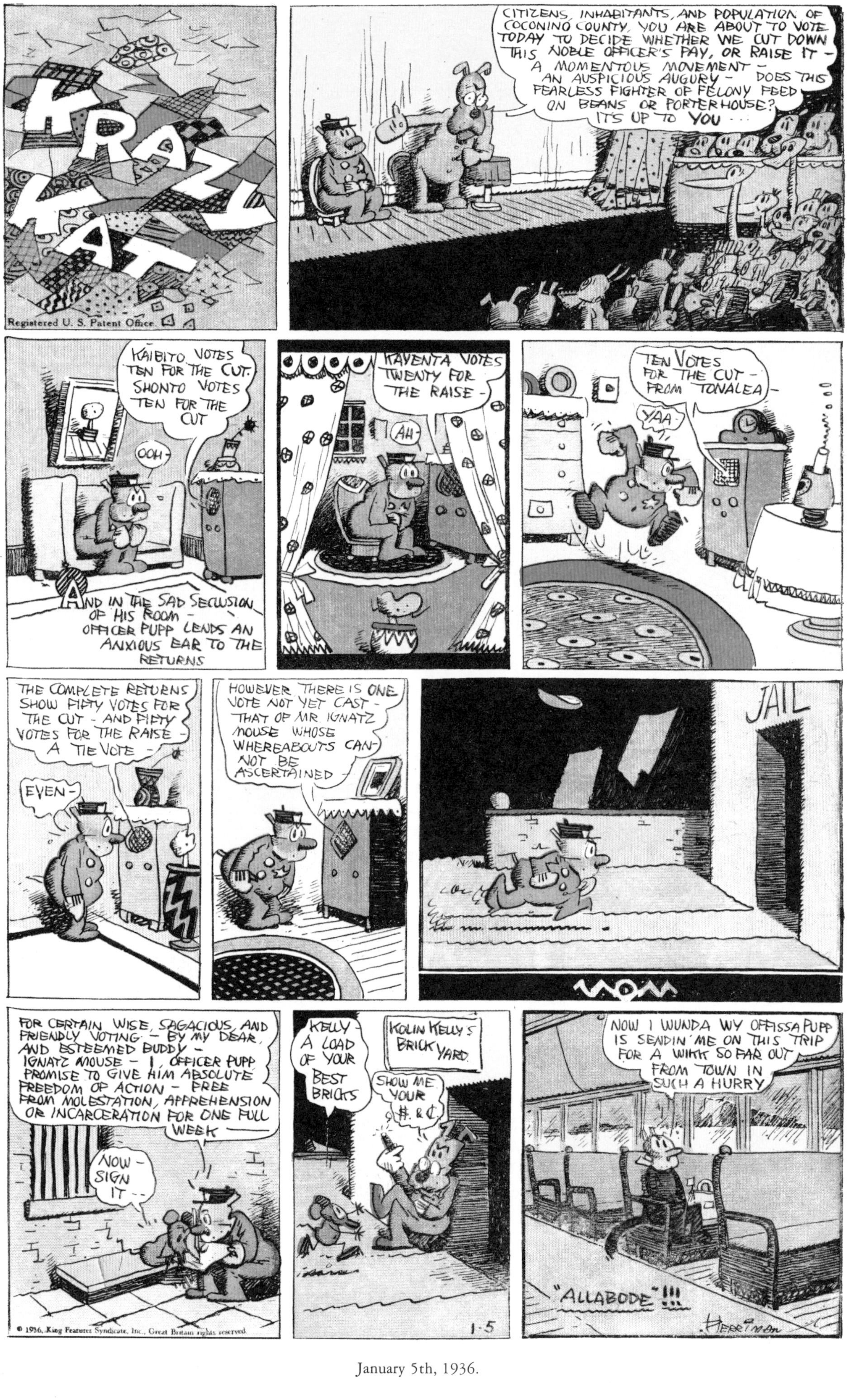
KRAZY KAT
Registered U. S. Patent Office.
CITIZENS, INHABITANTS, AND POPULATION OF COCONINO COUNTY, YOU ARE ABOUT TO VOTE TODAY TO DECIDE WHETHER WE CUT DOWN THIS NOBLE OFFICER'S PAY, OR RAISE IT - A MOMENTOUS MOVEMENT - AN AUSPICIOUS AUGURY - DOES THIS FEARLESS FIGHTER OF FELONY FEED ON BEANS OR PORTERHOUSE? IT'S UP TO YOU ...
AND IN THE SAD SECLUSION OF HIS ROOM - OFFICER PUPP LENDS AN ANXIOUS EAR TO THE RETURNS
KAIBITO VOTES TEN FOR THE CUT. SHONTO VOTES TEN FOR THE CUT
OOH -
KAYENTA VOTES TWENTY FOR THE RAISE -
AH -
TEN VOTES FOR THE CUT - FROM TONALEA -
YAA
THE COMPLETE RETURNS SHOW FIFTY VOTES FOR THE CUT - AND FIFTY VOTES FOR THE RAISE - A TIE VOTE -
EVEN -
HOWEVER THERE IS ONE VOTE NOT YET CAST - THAT OF MR IGNATZ MOUSE WHOSE WHEREABOUTS CAN-NOT BE ASCERTAINED -
JAIL
FOR CERTAIN WISE, SAGACIOUS, AND FRIENDLY VOTING - BY MY DEAR, AND ESTEEMED BUDDY - IGNATZ MOUSE - I, OFFICER PUPP PROMISE TO GIVE HIM ABSOLUTE FREEDOM OF ACTION - FREE FROM MOLESTATION, APPREHENSION OR INCARCERATION FOR ONE FULL WEEK
NOW - SIGN IT --
KOLIN KELLY'S BRICK YARD
KELLY - A LOAD OF YOUR BEST BRICKS
SHOW ME YOUR $. & ¢.
NOW I WUNDA WY OFFISSA PUPP IS SENDIN' ME ON THIS TRIP FOR A WIKK SO FAR OUT FROM TOWN IN SUCH A HURRY
"ALLABODE" !!!
© 1936, King Features Syndicate, Inc., Great Britain rights reserved.
1-5
HERRIMAN

January 5th, 1936.

KRAZY KAT
Registered U. S. Patent Office.
HIS FACE FULL OF A FANCY INNOCENCE, - HIS POSTURE, HIS EYE, HIS MIEN - EXUDE THE AURA OF SILLY SANCTITUDE - - BUT - - - -
THOSE ARMS - BEHIND HIS BACK - BODES NO GOOD -
SIN LURKS THERE - HE CONCEALS AN EVIL - A BRICK.
THE POLTROON - I'LL DRAG HIS SECRET INTO THE LIGHT - THE WORLD MUST SEE THE VILLAINY HE HIDES.
THE GROWLER -
IN PERSON -
OKE
STICK 'EM UP !!!
STIGG WOT OP ?
I NEED A DIME - GUESS I'LL GO HELP MYSELF TO A COUPLE OF BANKS.
?
PARDON.
HEH ?
STIGG WOT OP ?
WELL - ALL IS WELL.
HERRIMAN
1-12
© 1936, King Features Syndicate, Inc., Great Britain rights reserved.

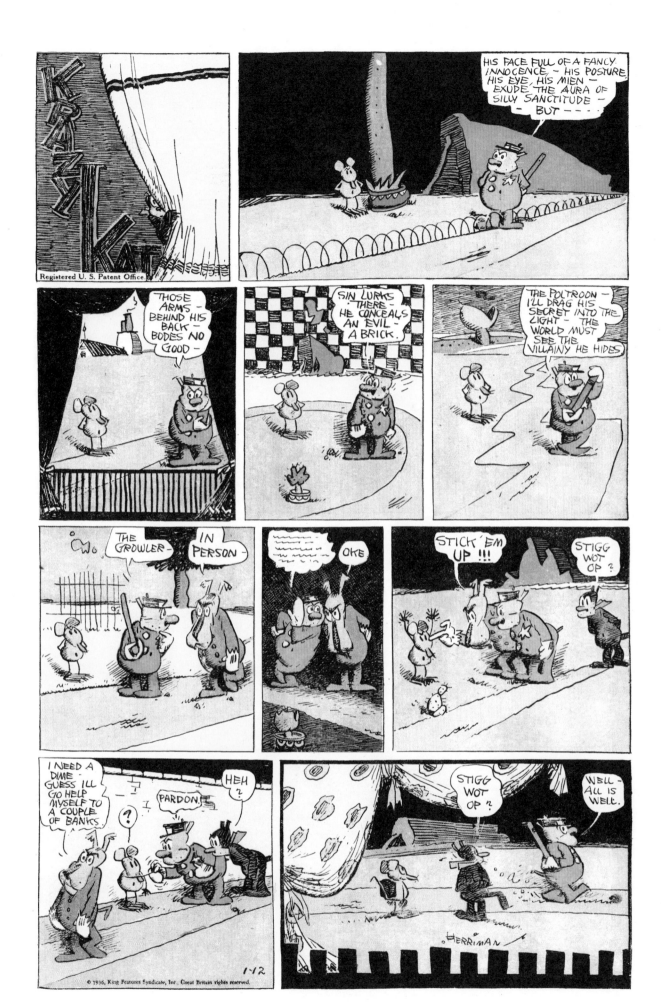

January 12th, 1936.

"KRAZY KAT"
Registered U. S. Patent Office.
RASCAL !!!
GOT YOU, HAVE NT I, MOUSE ?
YOU HAVE, INDEED KOP.
WHAT'S THAT Y'GOT THERE ?
A DOLLAR, KOP - CASH
HMMMM SUPPOSE I FINE YOU A DOLLAR - MOUSE ?
A GOOD IDEA - KOP -
YOU'RE FINED - GO !!!
FINE - I'M GOING.
A FEW MORE CASH FINES LIKE THIS AND COCONINO COUNTY WILL MORE THAN BALANCE ITS BUDGET.
L'IL JOE - L'IL BRIGHT-EYED FOURS - LOOKIN' AT ME SO SWEET.
OH-HO MORE CRIME - MORE FINE
I'M JUST LOOKING FOR A STOUT-HEARTED - IRON-NERVED TWO-FISTED SPORT TO FADE ME - - WHO SAYS I CAN'T MAKE THESE LITTLE FOURS? - L'IL JOE WHO SAYS I CAN'T ?
HOT DOLLAR IN HAT.
FADE HIM - FOURS ARE HARD TO ROLL - FADE HIM - - - HE CAN'T MAKE A L'IL JOE - - - - FADE HIM - -
TEMPTATION
THERE THEY ARE - LITTLE BRIGHT-EYED FOURS - L'IL JOE - LOOKING AT ME SO SWE-E-E-ET -
HE DONE IT !!!
MUST DICES HAVE NUTTIN' BUT FOUR DOTS ON THEM - OFFISSA PUPP ?
N-NO
THERE Y'ARE, MOUSIE, DON'T SAY I NEVER PAYS UP MY OWINGS -
OLE HONEST JODY - - SQUARE AS A BILLIARD BALL.
© 1936, King Features Syndicate, Inc., Great Britain rights reserved.
1-19
HERRIMAN

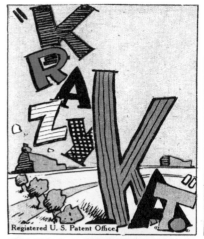

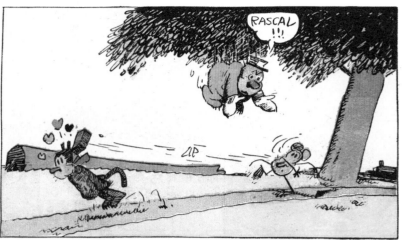

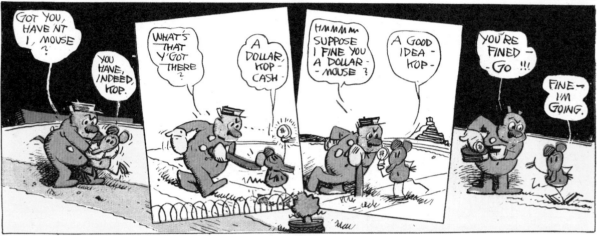

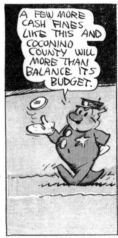

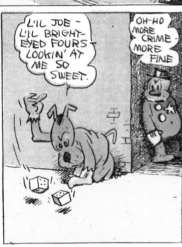

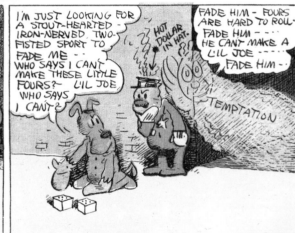

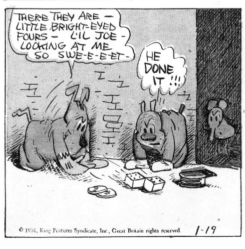

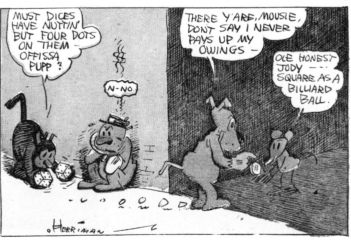

January 19th, 1936.

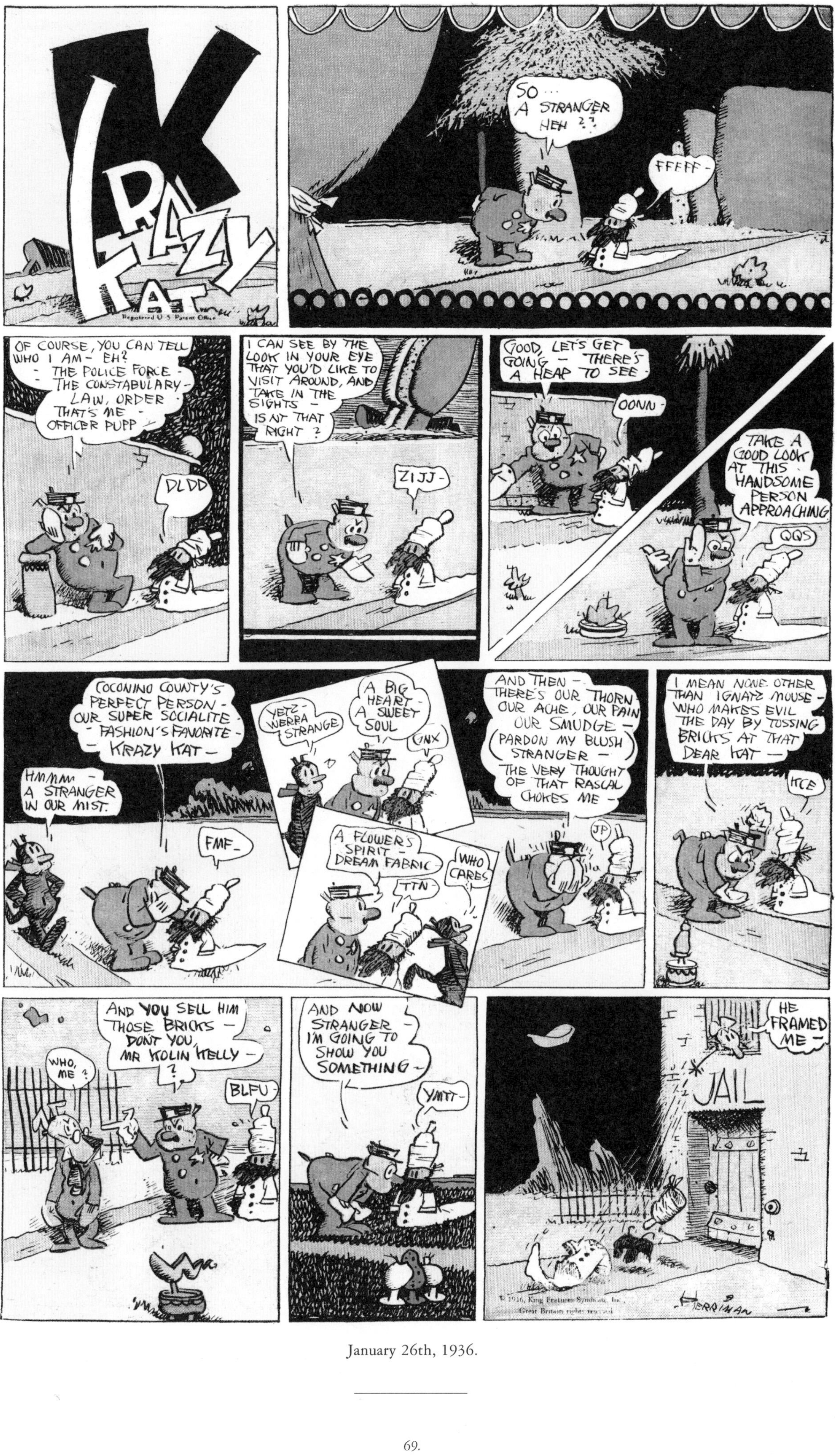
Krazy Kat
Registered U.S. Patent Office
SO ... A STRANGER HEH ??
FFFFF -
OF COURSE, YOU CAN TELL WHO I AM - EH? - THE POLICE FORCE - THE CONSTABULARY - LAW, ORDER - THAT'S ME - OFFICER PUPP -
DLDD
I CAN SEE BY THE LOOK IN YOUR EYE THAT YOU'D LIKE TO VISIT AROUND, AND TAKE IN THE SIGHTS - IS N'T THAT RIGHT ?
ZIJJ -
GOOD, LET'S GET GOING - THERE'S A HEAP TO SEE -
OONN -
TAKE A GOOD LOOK AT THIS HANDSOME PERSON APPROACHING
QQS
COCONINO COUNTY'S PERFECT PERSON - OUR SUPER SOCIALITE - FASHION'S FAVORITE - KRAZY KAT -
HM/MM - A STRANGER IN OUR MIST.
FMF -
YETZ - WERRA STRANGE
A BIG HEART - A SWEET SOUL
GNX
A FLOWER'S SPIRIT - DREAM FABRIC -
WHO CARES
TTN -
AND THEN - THERE'S OUR THORN OUR ACHE, OUR PAIN OUR SMUDGE - (PARDON MY BLUSH STRANGER -) THE VERY THOUGHT OF THAT RASCAL CHOKES ME -
JP
I MEAN NONE OTHER THAN IGNATZ MOUSE - WHO MAKES EVIL THE DAY BY TOSSING BRICKS AT THAT DEAR KAT -
KCE
AND YOU SELL HIM THOSE BRICKS - DON'T YOU, MR KOLIN KELLY - ?
WHO, ME ?
BLFU -
AND NOW STRANGER I'M GOING TO SHOW YOU SOMETHING -
YMTT -
HE FRAMED ME -
JAIL
© 1936, King Features Syndicate, Inc. Great Britain rights reserved.
HERRIMAN

January 26th, 1936.

KRAZY KAT.
Registered U. S. Patent Office
ZIP
OF COURSE, IT IS TOO SLIPPERY TO CLIMB, MY DEAR KOP - THERE'S A BUCKET OF LARD ON THIS POLE.
Y-Y-YOU SCOUNDREL
NOT ONLY DOES LARD KEEP ONE FROM ASCENDING A POLE - IT ALSO SPOILS ONE'S BEST SUIT - AND ONES DIGNITY.
I REPEAT - SCOUNDREL
HEY - YOU - Y' WANT TO EARN A REWARD ?
YES - $$$$ $
$
PICK HIM OFF OF THAT POLE AND HAND HIM TO ME.
$
GOOD -
WHEN DO I GET MY REWARD - $$$
SINCE WHEN, MOUSE, DID YOU THINK YOU WERE SMARTER THAN ME - HEH ?
JAIL.
I WILL SPEAK TO THE POLICE COMMISSION, WHO WILL SPEAK TO THE MAYOR, WHO WILL SPEAK TO THE POPULATION, WHO WILL NO DOUBT VOTE TO AWARD YOU THE REWARD OF A MEDAL.
2-2
© 1936, King Features Syndicate, Inc. Great Britain rights reserved
JAIL
HERRIMAN

February 2nd, 1936.

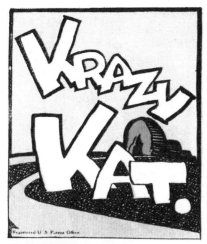

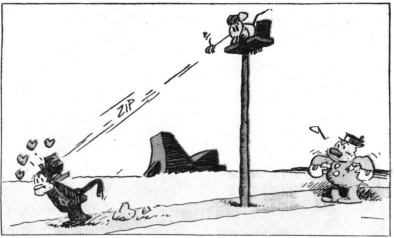

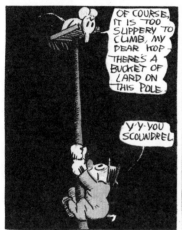

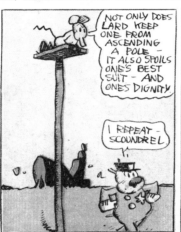

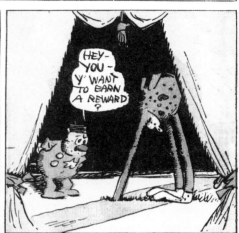

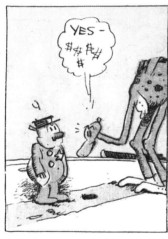

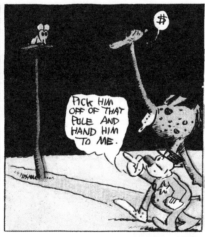

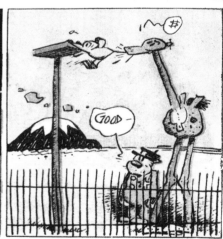

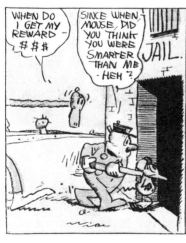

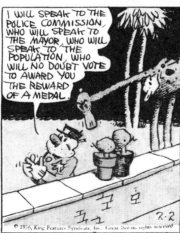

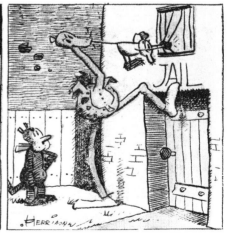

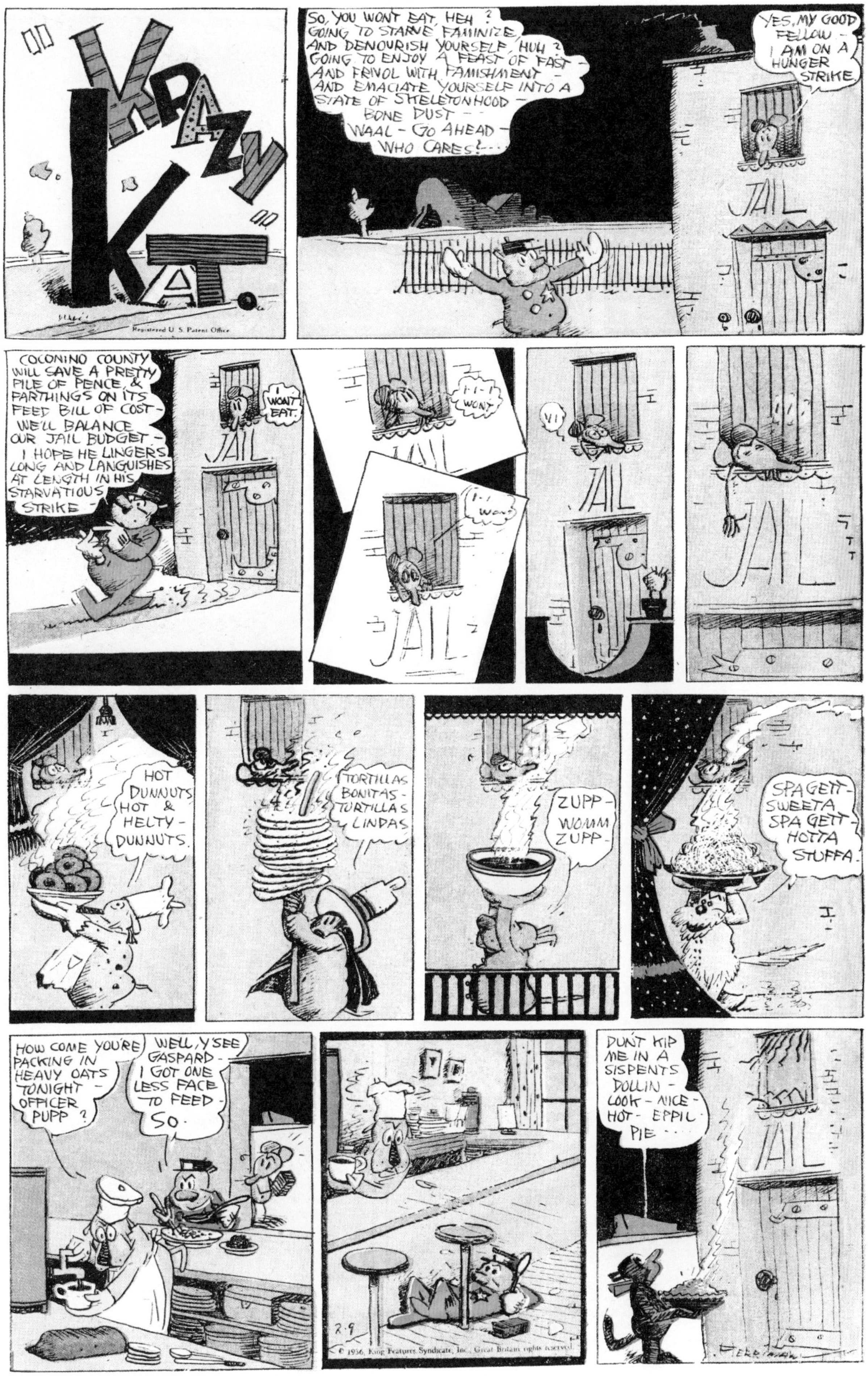
KRAZY KAT
Registered U. S. Patent Office
SO, YOU WONT EAT, HEH ? GOING TO STARVE FAMINIZE, AND DENOURISH YOURSELF, HUH ? GOING TO ENJOY A FEAST OF FAST - AND FRIVOL WITH FAMISHMENT - AND EMACIATE YOURSELF INTO A STATE OF SKELETONHOOD - BONE DUST - - WAAL - GO AHEAD - WHO CARES? - - -
YES, MY GOOD FELLOW - I AM ON A HUNGER STRIKE.
JAIL
COCONINO COUNTY WILL SAVE A PRETTY PILE OF PENCE, & FARTHINGS ON ITS FEED BILL OF COST - WE'LL BALANCE OUR JAIL BUDGET - I HOPE HE LINGERS LONG AND LANGUISHES AT LENGTH IN HIS STARVATIOUS STRIKE -
I WONT EAT.
JAIL
I-I-I WONT
I-I WONT
JAIL
JAIL
JAIL
HOT DUNNUTS HOT & HELTY DUNNUTS.
TORTILLAS BONITAS - TORTILLAS LINDAS
ZUPP - WOMM ZUPP -
SPAGETT - SWEETA SPA GETT - HOTTA STUFFA.
HOW COME YOU'RE PACKING IN HEAVY OATS TONIGHT - OFFICER PUPP ?
WELL, Y'SEE GASPARD - I GOT ONE LESS FACE TO FEED - SO.
© 1936, King Features Syndicate, Inc., Great Britain rights reserved.
DUN'T KIP ME IN A SISPENTS DOLLIN - LOOK - NICE - HOT - EPPIL - PIE - - -
JAIL

February 9th, 1936.

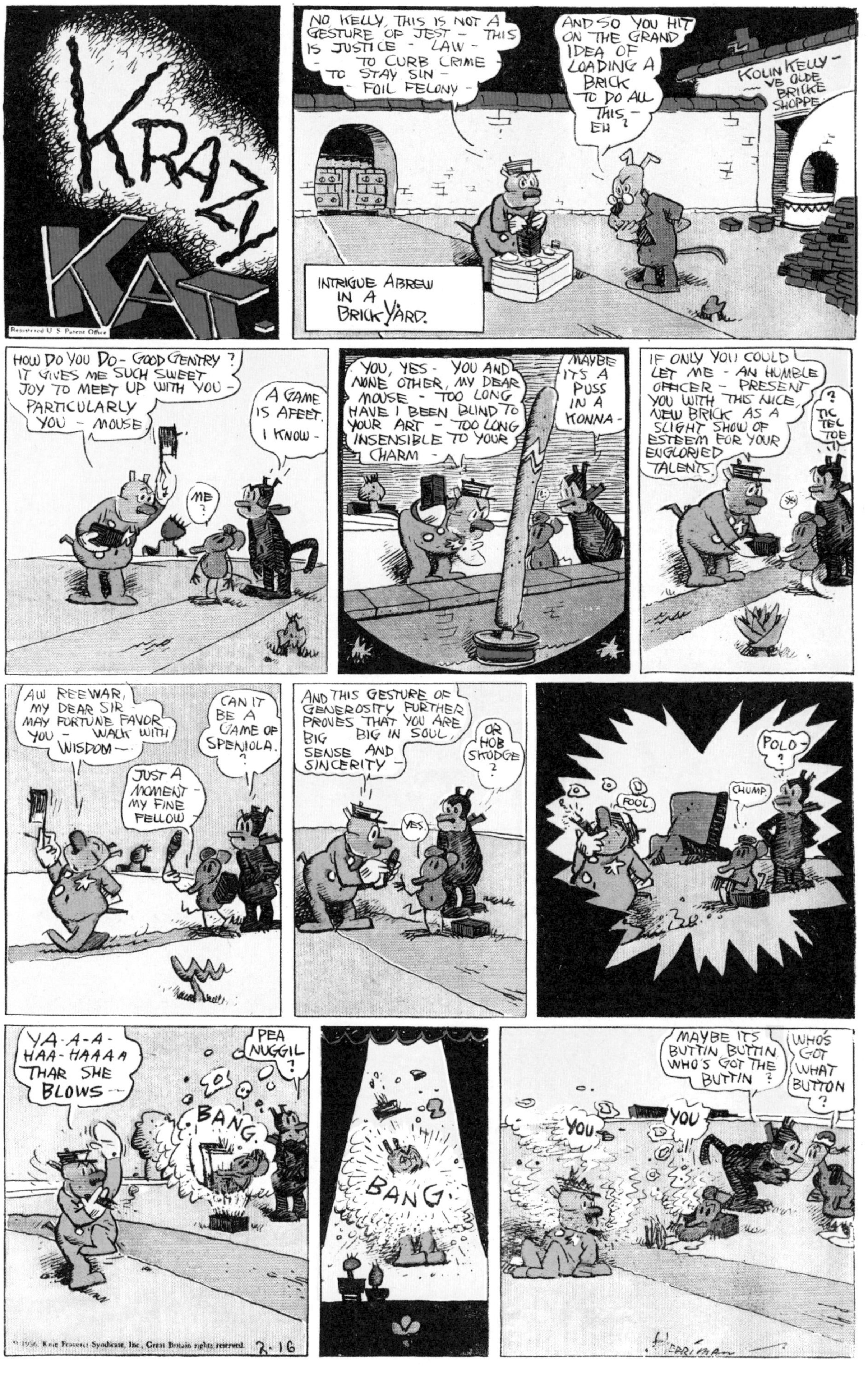
KRAZY KAT
Registered U.S. Patent Office
NO KELLY, THIS IS NOT A GESTURE OF JEST - THIS IS JUSTICE - LAW - - TO CURB CRIME - TO STAY SIN - - FOIL FELONY -
AND SO YOU HIT ON THE GRAND IDEA OF LOADING A BRICK TO DO ALL THIS, - EH ?
KOLIN KELLY - YE OLDE BRICKE SHOPPE
INTRIGUE ABREW IN A BRICK YARD.
HOW DO YOU DO - GOOD GENTRY ? IT GIVES ME SUCH SWEET JOY TO MEET UP WITH YOU - PARTICULARLY YOU - MOUSE.
A GAME IS AFEET. I KNOW -
ME ?
YOU, YES - YOU AND NONE OTHER, MY DEAR MOUSE - TOO LONG HAVE I BEEN BLIND TO YOUR ART - TOO LONG INSENSIBLE TO YOUR CHARM -
MAYBE IT'S A PUSS IN A KONNA -
IF ONLY YOU COULD LET ME - AN HUMBLE OFFICER - PRESENT YOU WITH THIS NICE NEW BRICK AS A SLIGHT SHOW OF ESTEEM FOR YOUR ENGLORIED TALENTS.
? TIC TEC TOE
AW REEWAR, MY DEAR SIR - MAY FORTUNE FAVOR YOU - WALK WITH WISDOM -
CAN IT BE A GAME OF SPENIOLA. ?
JUST A MOMENT MY FINE FELLOW
AND THIS GESTURE OF GENEROSITY FURTHER PROVES THAT YOU ARE BIG BIG IN SOUL, SENSE AND SINCERITY -
OR HOB SKODGE ?
YES.
POLO - ?
FOOL
CHUMP
YA-A-A- HAA-HAAAA THAR SHE BLOWS -
PEA NUGGIL ?
BANG
© 1936, King Features Syndicate, Inc., Great Britain rights reserved.
2-16
BANG
MAYBE ITS BUTTIN BUTTIN WHO'S GOT THE BUTTIN ?
WHO'S GOT WHAT BUTTON ?
YOU
YOU
HERRIMAN

February 16th, 1936.

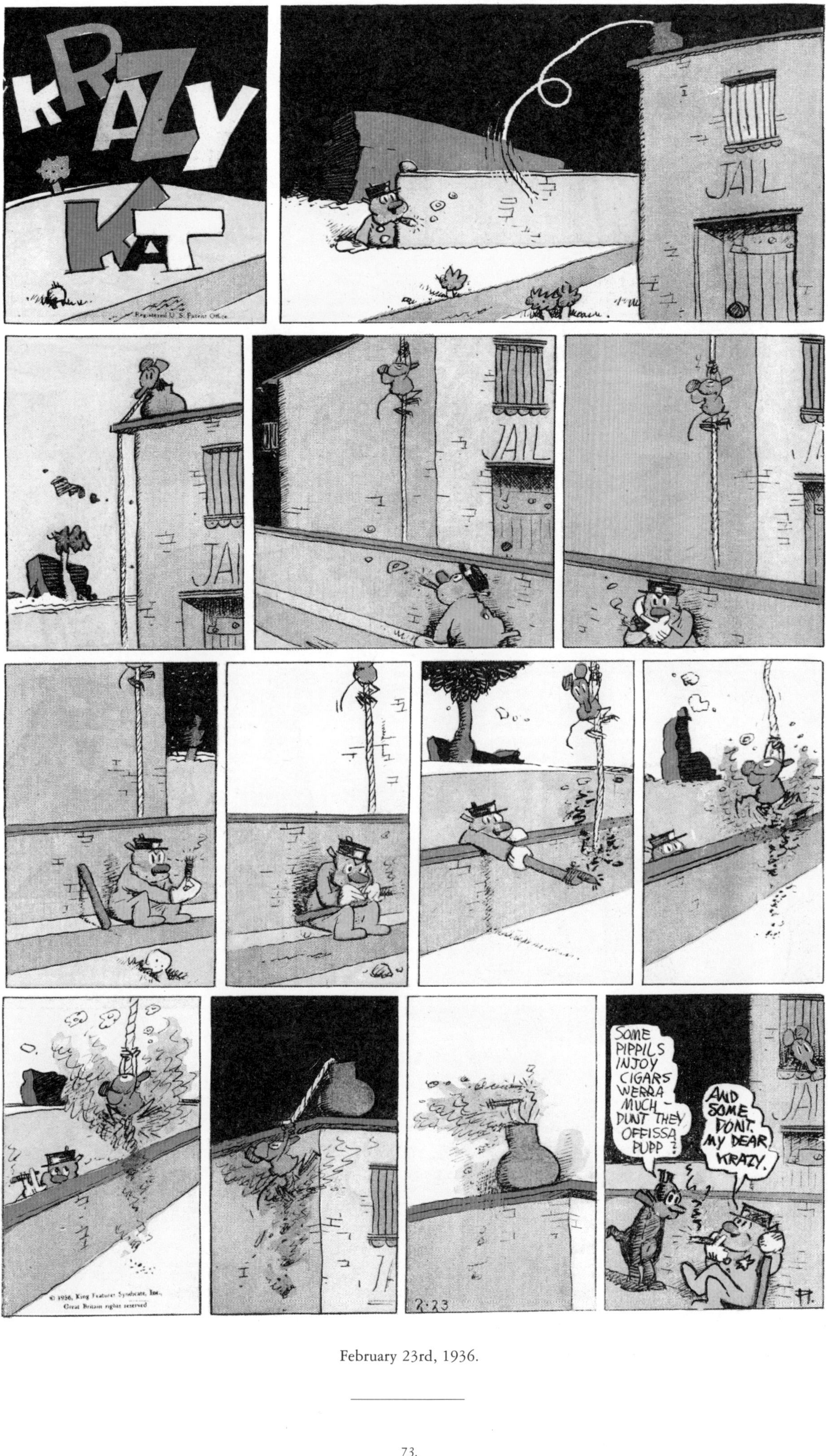
KRAZY KAT
Registered U.S. Patent Office
JAIL
JAIL
JAIL
SOME PIPPILS INJOY CIGARS WERRA MUCH - DUNT THEY OFFISSA PUPP ?
AND SOME DONT. MY DEAR KRAZY.
JAIL
© 1936, King Features Syndicate, Inc., Great Britain rights reserved
2-23

February 23rd, 1936.

KRAZY KAT.
Registered U.S. Patent Office
OH, A SUN IS SHINING BRIDE ON MY OLD KENTOKKIL HOMES ·· ···
YOU'RE SURE THE SUN IS SHINING THERE - HEH ?
WA-AL-L- NO
AND HOW DO YOU KNOW THAT HOME IS OLD - HOW DO YOU KNOW THAT ?
UH-H-H A-AHH-
AND HOW COME YOU CALL IT YOUR HOME - DO YOU OWN IT ?
- W- W-
WERE YOU EVER IN KENTUCKY- ?
ALMOST.
Y' DON'T EVEN KNOW WHERE KENTUCKY IS —
DO. YOU ?
WHAT DO YOU SUPPOSE THE FOLKS IN KENTUCKY WOULD THINK OF ALL THIS -
I WUNDA -
I'VE ALMOST A MIND TO START A FEUD WITH HIM -
!
IMPOSTOR -
SING ME A SONG - KRAZY - A SONG OF THE SUNNY SOUTH - "MY OLD KENTUCKY HOME" —
JAIL.
3·1
© 1936, King Features Syndicate, Inc., Great Britain rights reserved
HERRIMAN

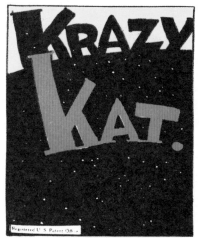

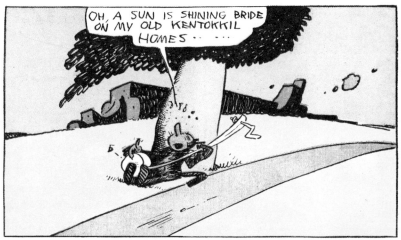

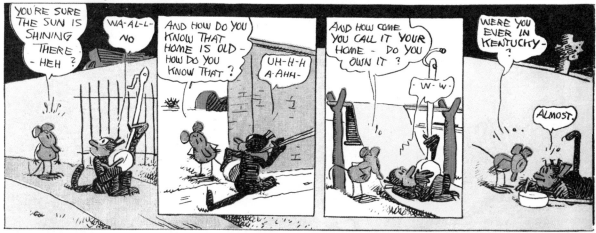

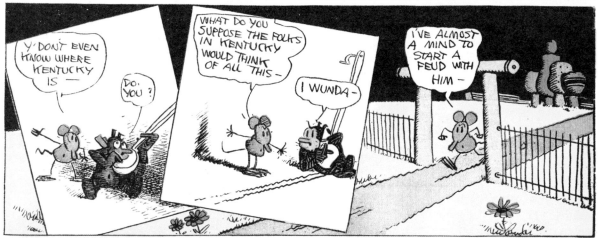

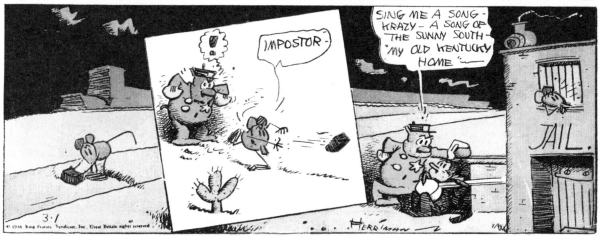

March 1st, 1936.

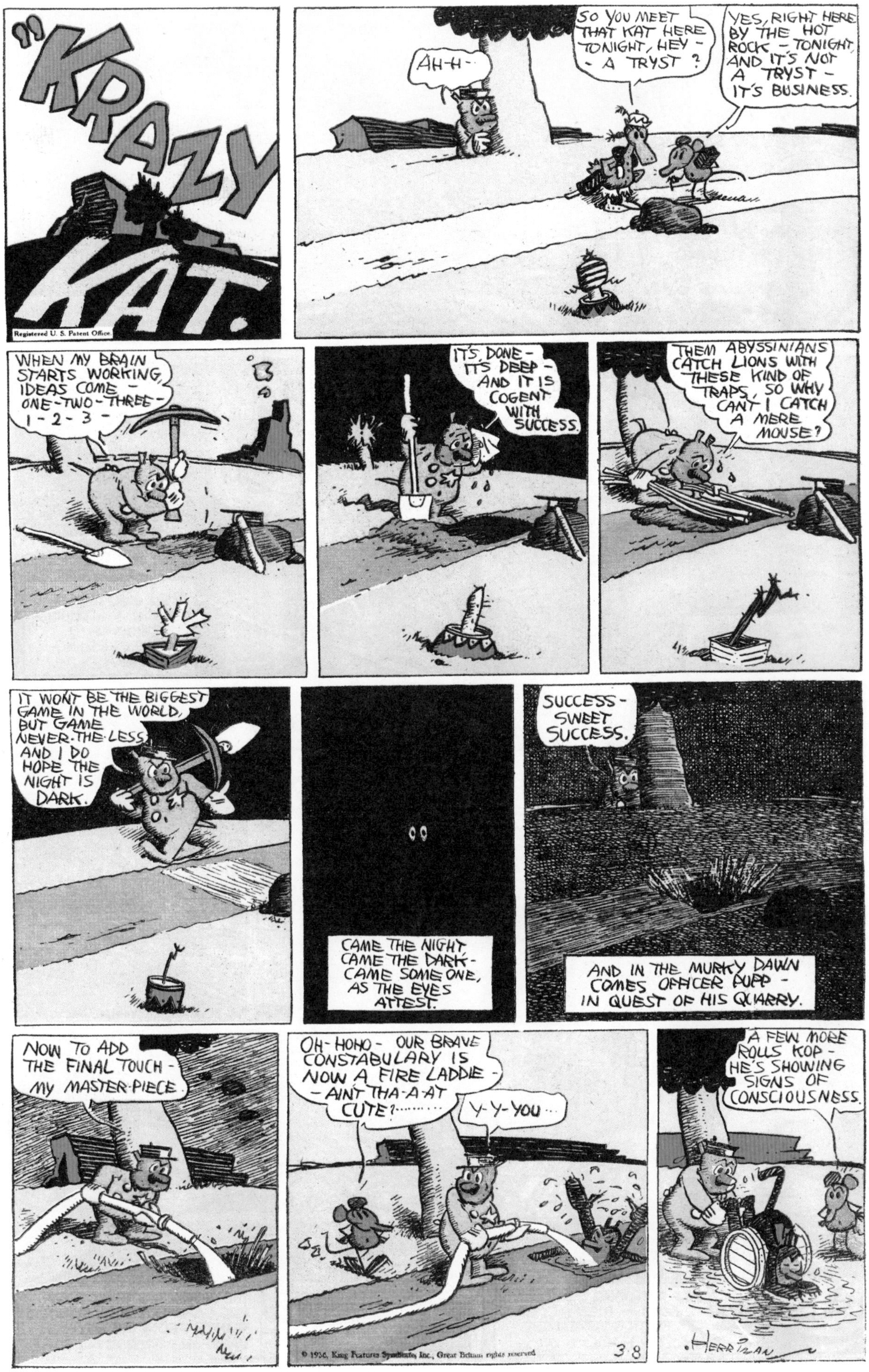
"KRAZY KAT."
Registered U. S. Patent Office
AH-H-
SO YOU MEET THAT KAT HERE TONIGHT, HEY - - A TRYST ?
YES, RIGHT HERE BY THE HOT ROCK - TONIGHT, AND IT'S NOT A TRYST - IT'S BUSINESS.
WHEN MY BRAIN STARTS WORKING, IDEAS COME - ONE-TWO-THREE - 1 - 2 - 3 -
IT'S DONE - IT'S DEEP - AND IT IS COGENT WITH SUCCESS.
THEM ABYSSINIANS CATCH LIONS WITH THESE KIND OF TRAPS, SO WHY CAN'T I CATCH A MERE MOUSE?
IT WON'T BE THE BIGGEST GAME IN THE WORLD, BUT GAME NEVER-THE-LESS. AND I DO HOPE THE NIGHT IS DARK.
CAME THE NIGHT, CAME THE DARK - CAME SOME ONE, AS THE EYES ATTEST.
SUCCESS - SWEET SUCCESS.
AND IN THE MURKY DAWN COMES OFFICER PUPP - IN QUEST OF HIS QUARRY.
NOW TO ADD THE FINAL TOUCH - MY MASTER-PIECE
OH-HOHO - OUR BRAVE CONSTABULARY IS NOW A FIRE LADDIE - - AIN'T THA-A-AT CUTE?.........
Y-Y-YOU...
A FEW MORE ROLLS KOP - HE'S SHOWING SIGNS OF CONSCIOUSNESS.
© 1936, King Features Syndicate, Inc., Great Britain rights reserved
3 8
HERRIMAN

March 8th, 1936.

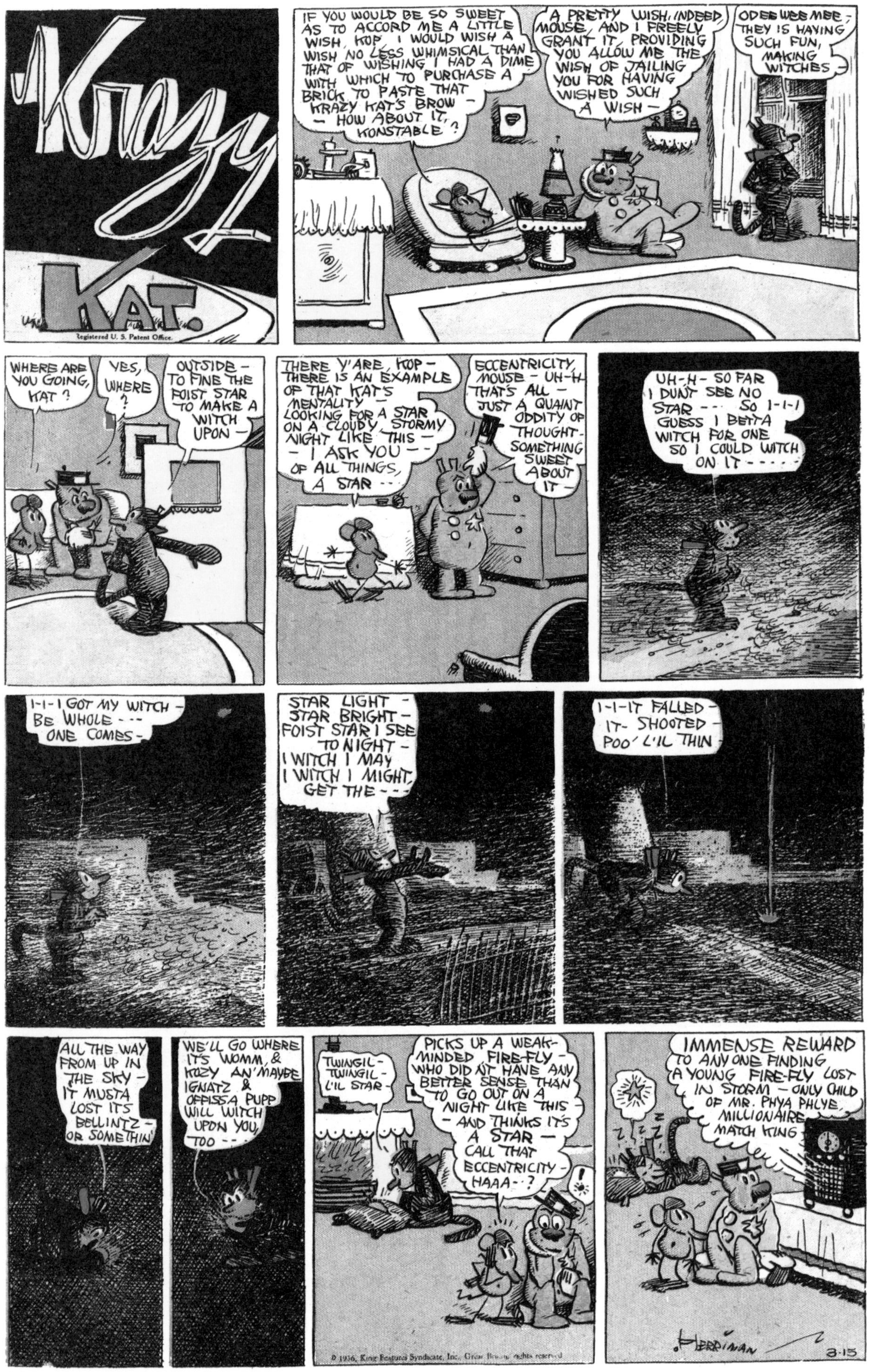
Krazy Kat.
Registered U. S. Patent Office.
IF YOU WOULD BE SO SWEET AS TO ACCORD ME A LITTLE WISH, KOP, I WOULD WISH A WISH NO LESS WHIMSICAL THAN THAT OF WISHING I HAD A DIME WITH WHICH TO PURCHASE A BRICK TO PASTE THAT KRAZY KAT'S BROW — HOW ABOUT IT, KONSTABLE?
A PRETTY WISH, INDEED MOUSE, AND I FREELY GRANT IT, PROVIDING YOU ALLOW ME THE WISH OF JAILING YOU FOR HAVING WISHED SUCH A WISH —
ODEE WEE MEE — THEY IS HAVING SUCH FUN, MAKING WITCHES —
WHERE ARE YOU GOING, KAT?
YES, WHERE?
OUTSIDE — TO FINE THE FOIST STAR TO MAKE A WITCH UPON —
THERE Y'ARE, KOP — THERE IS AN EXAMPLE OF THAT KAT'S MENTALITY — LOOKING FOR A STAR ON A CLOUDY, STORMY NIGHT LIKE THIS — I ASK YOU — OF ALL THINGS, A STAR —
ECCENTRICITY, MOUSE — UH-H THAT'S ALL — JUST A QUAINT ODDITY OF THOUGHT — SOMETHING SWEET ABOUT IT —
UH-H — SO FAR I DUN'T SEE NO STAR — SO I-I-I GUESS I BETTA WITCH FOR ONE SO I COULD WITCH ON IT ----
I-I-I GOT MY WITCH — BE WHOLE — ONE COMES —
STAR LIGHT — STAR BRIGHT — FOIST STAR I SEE TO NIGHT — I WITCH I MAY I WITCH I MIGHT, GET THE ---
I-I-IT FALLED — IT SHOOTED — POO' L'IL THIN
ALL THE WAY FROM UP IN THE SKY — IT MUSTA LOST ITS BELLINTZ — OR SOMETHIN'
WE'LL GO WHERE IT'S WOMM, & KRAZY AN' MAYBE IGNATZ & OFFISSA PUPP WILL WITCH UPON YOU, TOO --
TWINGIL — TWINGIL — L'IL STAR —
PICKS UP A WEAK-MINDED FIRE-FLY WHO DID NOT HAVE ANY BETTER SENSE THAN TO GO OUT ON A NIGHT LIKE THIS — AND THINKS IT'S A STAR — CALL THAT ECCENTRICITY — HAAA --?
IMMENSE REWARD TO ANY ONE FINDING A YOUNG FIRE-FLY LOST IN STORM — ONLY CHILD OF MR. PHYA PHLYE, MILLIONAIRE MATCH KING
© 1936, King Features Syndicate, Inc., Great Britain rights reserved
Herriman 3-15

March 15th, 1936.

"KRAZY
Kat.
Registered U. S. Patent Office.
HELLO!, MITZIS LADY BUGG -
HELLO, KAT.
BETTA FLY IWWAY TO YOUR HOME - - YETZ ?
NO.
LADY BUGG - LA-A-ADY BUGG - PLIZ FLY IWWAY - HOME.
WHY ?
BECAUSE YOUR HOUSE IS ON FIRE -
NA-AH-H -
BUT YOUR L'IL CHILDRINS IS ALL ILLONE.
DON'T BE SILLY.
WHAT'S UP DOWN HERE ?
I'M ESKIN' THIS L'IL LADY BUGG TO GO HOME IT'S ON FIRE, AN' HER CHILDRINS IS ILLONE -
WELL - WHAT OF IT ?
WOODEN YOU GO, IF YOUR HOME WAS ON FIRE, AN' YOUR CHILDRINS WAS ILLONE ?
OF COURSE I WOULD.
WELL, WHY DUN'T THIS SILLY L'IL LADY BUGG GO HOME ?
BECAUSE THAT LADY BUG HAS NO HOME, SO IT'S NOT ON FIRE -
AND BESIDES, HE'S A BACHELOR, AND HAS NO CHILDREN -
GOOD NIGHT FOLKS.
WHATS UP - DOWN HERE ?
3-22.
HERRIMAN

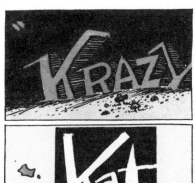

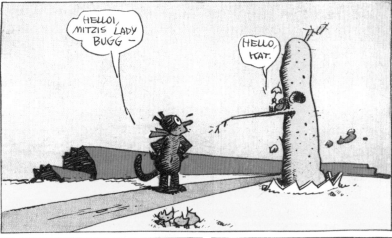

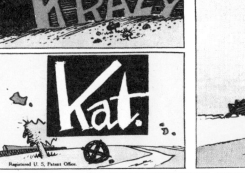

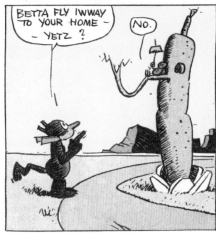

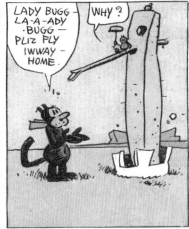

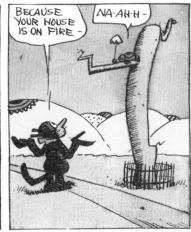

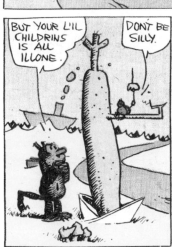

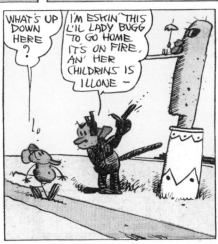

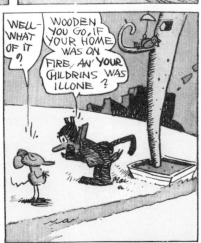

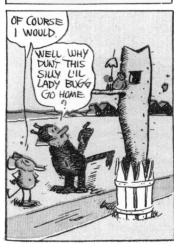

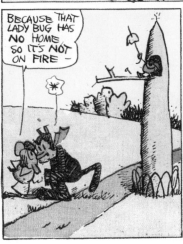

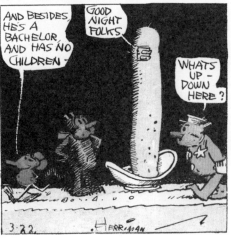

March 22nd, 1936.

KRAZY KAT
Registered U S Patent Office
KLIKK, AND IT LIGHTS - NEVER FAILS NOR FALTERS - NO MESS, NO MUSS - FLUSH WITH FLASH, FLARE AND FIRE, STOKES A STOGIE, SEEGAR, OR SIGGAREET WITH EQUAL IMPUNITY - AND IT'S A BONNIE GIFTIE TO COCONINO COUNTY'S BEST KOP - "OFFICER BULL PUPP" - WITH MY COMPLIMENTS
ZIP
© 1936, King Features Syndicate, Inc., Great Britain rights reserved.
AND COCONINO COUNTY'S BEST KOP RETURNS THE COMPLIMENT
JAIL
3.29

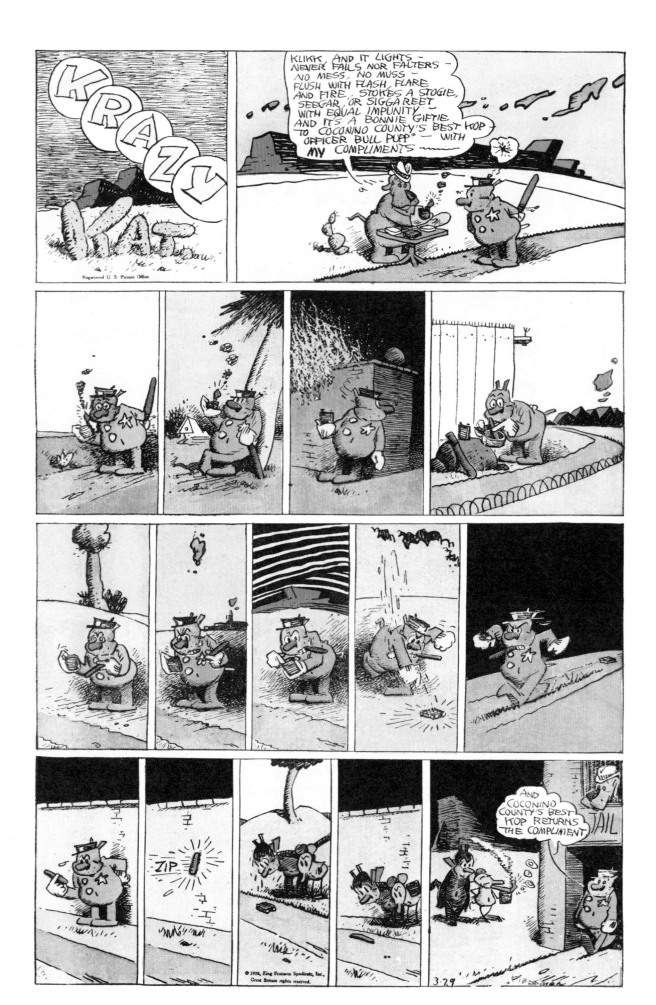

March 29th, 1936.

KRAZY KAT.
Registered U. S. Patent Office
AH-H, ME - KRAZY - LEAP YEAR - WHAT A BOON TO US WIDOWS -
IT IS - HEH?
I AM YET COMELY -
SVELTE -
CHIC -
COY -
I WUNDA WOT MRS KWEKK WEKK MEANT WEN SHE SAID LIP YEAR WAS A BOOM TO A WIDDA - I'LL ESK MR. GOOSEBERRY SPRIG, HE SHOULD KNOW.
GOOSEBERRY SPRIG DUCK DUKE.
AN' SHE SAID LIP YEAR IS A BOOM TO A WIDDA - A-A-AN -
M-MY WORD -
WY?
I'LL TELL YOU NEXT YEAR - WHEN I COME BACK -
AN' SHE SAID - LIP YEAR IS A BOOM TO A WIDDA - N-N ---
MOKK DUKK LAUNDERER DE LUXE.
WY?
I COME BACK BIME-BYE - ONE YEE - I TELL YOU - NOW I GO HIP QUICK - GOO'BYE -
OH, WELL - FATE, I GUESS, JUST FATE
4-4
HERRIMAN

April 4th, 1936.

KRAZY KAT.
ME, THE BEST OF THE BETTER BARTERERS OF TRADE RAT CLANS - AND NOT A BEAN WITH WHICH TO BAIT A BARGAIN - I AM NON-PLUSSED.
HM-MMM. CONSIDERABLE IMPEDIMENTA - A MESS OF NEEDLESSNESSES, OF NO USEFUL HELP TO HIM -
SILLY HAT - HOLELESS BUTTONS, A STAR WITHOUT GLITTER, A HICKORY MACE - BUT ME, THE FAIR EXCHANGER WILL FIX IT.
HUH-H-- ANOTHER ONE CLUTTERED UP WITH UNUSABLES, AND FUTILES, AND NOT GOODS - I'LL FIX THAT, TOO -
I DON'T KNOW WHAT GOOD THAT HAT, THAT CLUB, THAT STAR, OR THOSE BUTTONS WILL DO HIM ?
AND I DON'T KNOW WHAT GOOD THIS BRICK WILL DO HIM - SO IT'S AN EVEN TRADE -
MY SPECIALTY - GOO'BYE - FOLKS.
NOW, WOT GOOD IS A OUT FIDDIL LIKE THIS TO A MICE ?
RIDDIKKILLIS
AN' WOT GOOD IS A BRICK TO A KOP ?
EVVA THIN'S TURSY-TOPVY -
SO UNRISSINIBIL -
FAIR SWAP MINT -
4-11
HERRIMAN

April 11th, 1936.

KRAZY KAT
Registered U. S. Patent Office.
URGENT BUSINESS WAITS FOR NO SLUMBERER --
Z
SOMETHING WITH A SINISTER SEMBLANCE OF STEALING HAPPENS IN KOLIN KELLY'S BRICK-YARD.
OH-HOH
AND WHEN YOU AWOKE UP - A NICE NEW, FRESH-BAKED BRICK HAD BEEN STOLEN FROM YOUR KILN - IS THAT IT, KELLY?
Y'DANG YIPPIN' IT IS, KOP - AND IT'S UP TO YOU, AS GUARDEEN OF LAW AND ORDER TO GET IT BACK - SAVVY?
AH-H-H-
UNSQUAT YOURSELF OFFA THAT BOX, MOUSE - LET'S SEE WHAT YOU'RE HIDING UNDER IT -
LIFT Y'SELF, RASCAL, LET'S LOOK -
REMEMBER I'M JUST A BYSTANDING SPECTATOR IN THIS -
4-18
© 1936, King Features Syndicate, Inc., Great Britain rights reserved.
HA-HAAA - IT WAS A MORAL VICTORY ANY-WAY HU-HU -
DONT MISS.
MY AIM IS UNERRING.

April 18th, 1936.

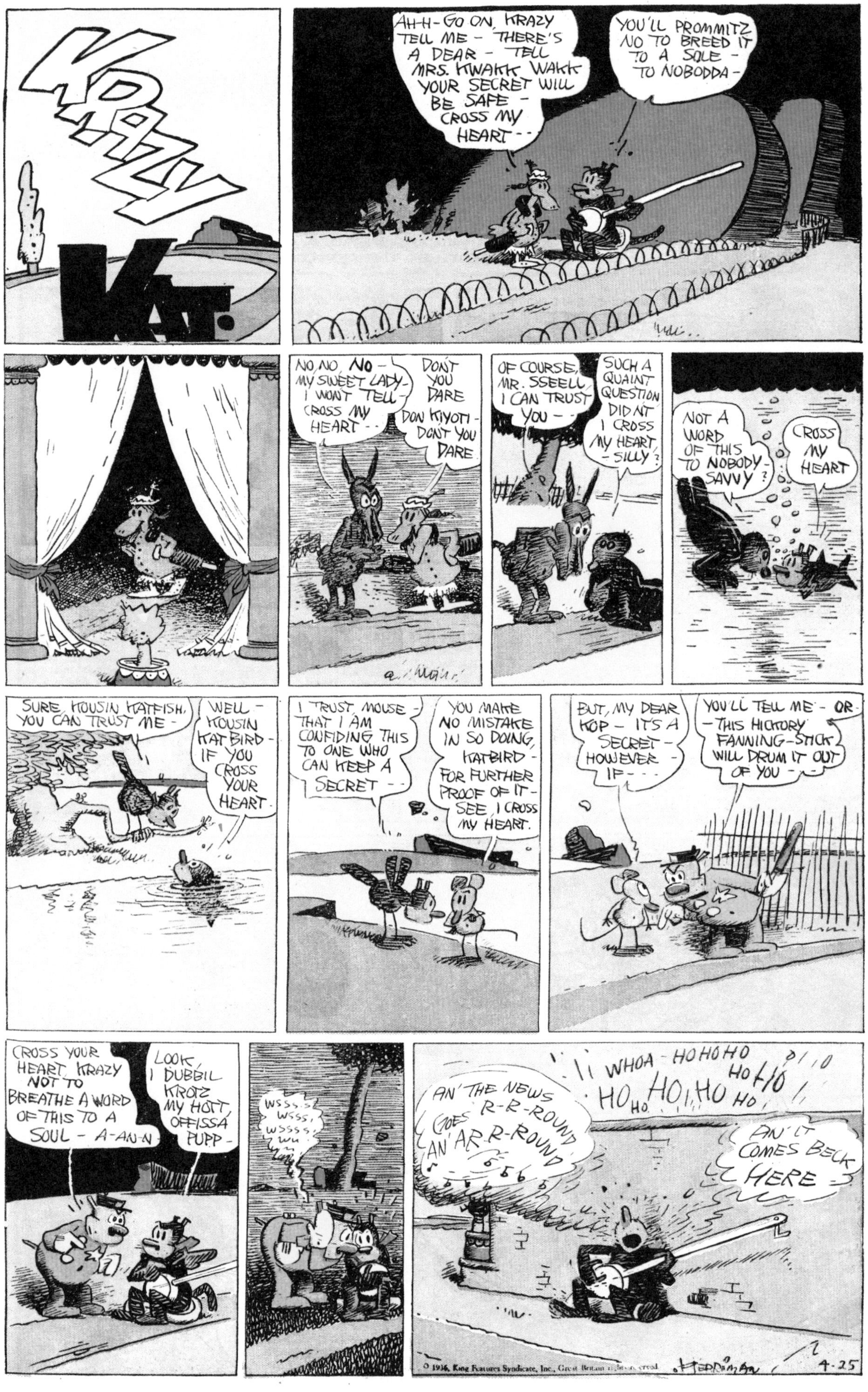
KRAZY KAT.
AH-H - GO ON, KRAZY TELL ME - THERE'S A DEAR - TELL MRS. KWAKK WAKK YOUR SECRET WILL BE SAFE - CROSS MY HEART - -
YOU'LL PROMMITZ NO TO BREED IT TO A SOLE - TO NOBODDA -
NO, NO, NO - MY SWEET LADY - I WONT TELL - CROSS MY HEART - -
DON'T YOU DARE DON KIYOTI - DONT YOU DARE
OF COURSE, MR. SSEELL, I CAN TRUST YOU - -
SUCH A QUAINT QUESTION DID NT I CROSS MY HEART, - SILLY ?
NOT A WORD OF THIS TO NOBODY - SAVVY ?
CROSS MY HEART
SURE, KOUSIN KATFISH, YOU CAN TRUST ME -
WELL - KOUSIN KATBIRD - IF YOU CROSS YOUR HEART.
I TRUST, MOUSE - THAT I AM CONFIDING THIS TO ONE WHO CAN KEEP A SECRET - -
YOU MAKE NO MISTAKE IN SO DOING, KATBIRD - FOR FURTHER PROOF OF IT - SEE, I CROSS MY HEART.
BUT, MY DEAR KOP - IT'S A SECRET - HOWEVER - IF - - -
YOU'LL TELL ME - OR - THIS HICKORY FANNING-STICK WILL DRUM IT OUT OF YOU - -
CROSS YOUR HEART, KRAZY NOT TO BREATHE A WORD OF THIS TO A SOUL - A-AN-N
LOOK, I DUBBIL KROTZ MY HOTT, OFFISSA PUPP -
WSSSS WSSS, WSSSS, WU
WHOA - HO HO HO HO HO HO, HO HO HO HO
AN' THE NEWS GOES R-R-ROUND AN' AR-R-ROUND
AN' IT COMES BECK HERE
© 1936, King Features Syndicate, Inc., Great Britain rights reserved.
HERRIMAN
4-25

April 25th, 1936.

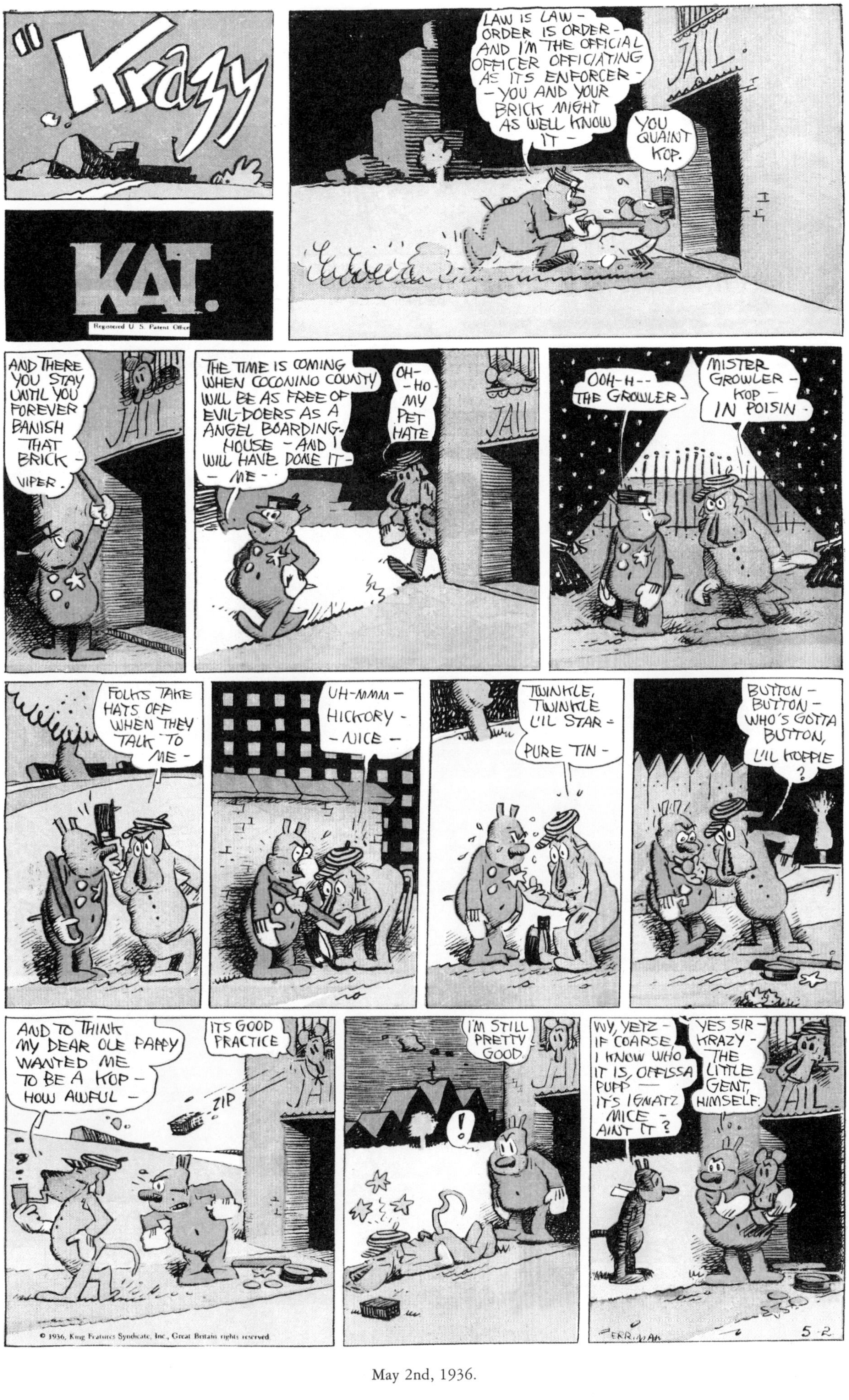
"Krazy
KAT.
Registered U.S. Patent Office
LAW IS LAW - ORDER IS ORDER - AND I'M THE OFFICIAL OFFICER OFFICIATING AS ITS ENFORCER - - YOU AND YOUR BRICK MIGHT AS WELL KNOW IT -
YOU QUAINT KOP.
JAIL
AND THERE YOU STAY UNTIL YOU FOREVER BANISH THAT BRICK - VIPER.
THE TIME IS COMING WHEN COCONINO COUNTY WILL BE AS FREE OF EVIL-DOERS AS A ANGEL BOARDING-HOUSE - AND I WILL HAVE DONE IT - ME -
OH - HO MY PET HATE
OOH-H -- THE GROWLER -
MISTER GROWLER - KOP - IN POISIN -
FOLKS TAKE HATS OFF WHEN THEY TALK TO ME -
UH-MMM - HICKORY - - NICE -
TWINKLE, TWINKLE L'IL STAR =
PURE TIN -
BUTTON - BUTTON - WHO'S GOTTA BUTTON, L'IL HOPPIE ?
AND TO THINK MY DEAR OLE PAPPY WANTED ME TO BE A KOP - HOW AWFUL -
ITS GOOD PRACTICE
ZIP
I'M STILL PRETTY GOOD.
!
WY, YETZ - IF COARSE, I KNOW WHO IT IS, OFFISSA PUPP — IT'S IGNATZ MICE - AINT IT ?
YES SIR - KRAZY - THE LITTLE GENT, HIMSELF.
© 1936, King Features Syndicate, Inc., Great Britain rights reserved.
5-2

May 2nd, 1936.

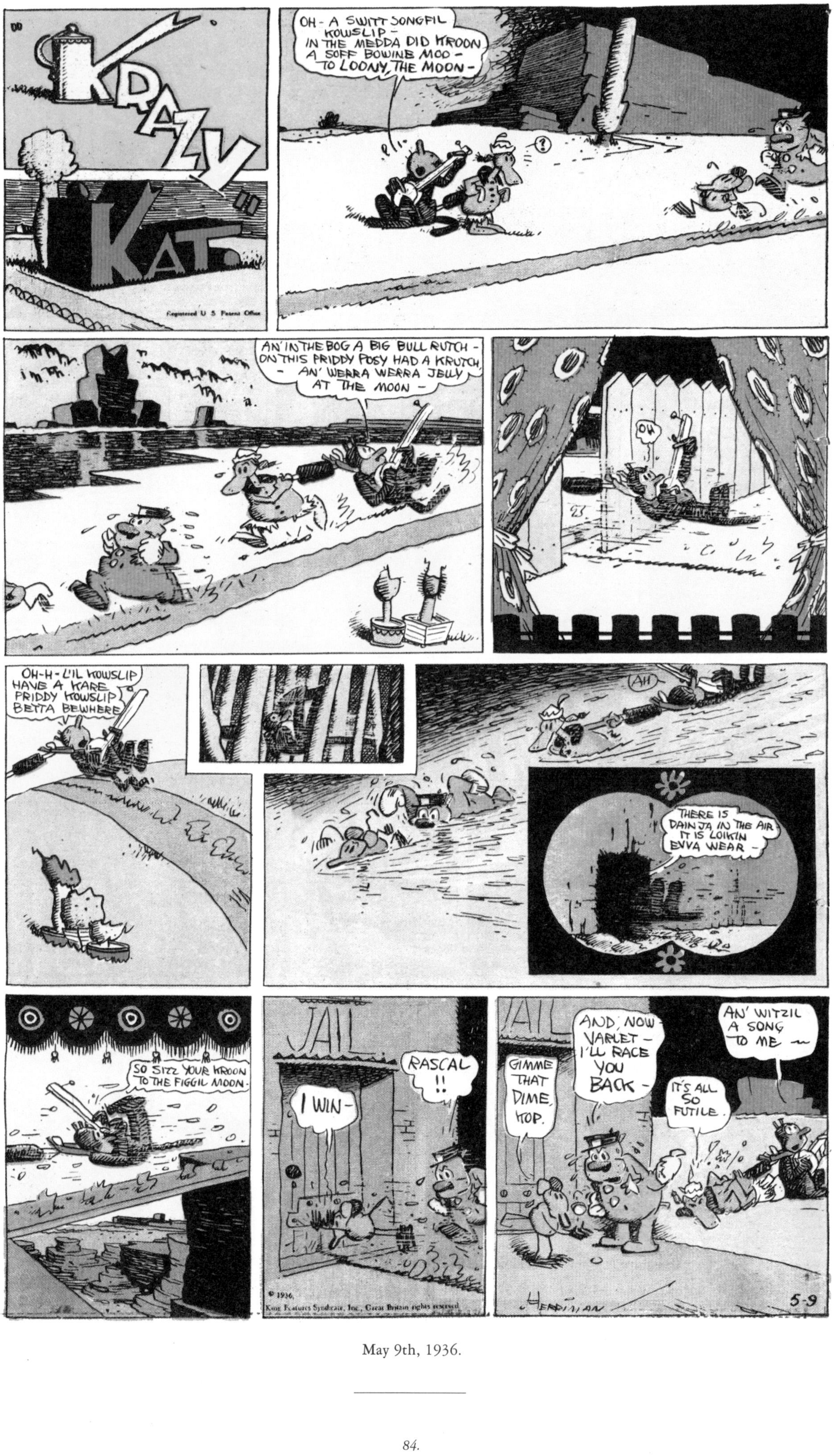
KRAZY KAT.
Registered U S Patent Office
OH - A SWITT SONGFIL KOWSLIP - IN THE MEDDA DID KROON A SOFF BOWINE MOO - TO LOONY, THE MOON -
?
AN' IN THE BOG A BIG BULL RUTCH - ON THIS PRIDDY POSY HAD A KRUTCH - AN' WERRA WERRA JELLY AT THE MOON -
OH
OH-H - L'IL KOWSLIP HAVE A KARE PRIDDY KOWSLIP BETTA BEWHERE
AH
THERE IS DAINJA IN THE AIR IT IS LOIKIN EVVA WEAR -
SO SIZZ YOUR KROON TO THE FIGGIL MOON -
JAIL
RASCAL !!
I WIN -
JAIL
GIMME THAT DIME, KOP.
AND, NOW - VARLET - I'LL RACE YOU BACK -
IT'S ALL SO FUTILE.
AN' WITZIL A SONG TO ME
© 1936, King Features Syndicate, Inc., Great Britain rights reserved.
HERRIMAN
5-9

May 9th, 1936.

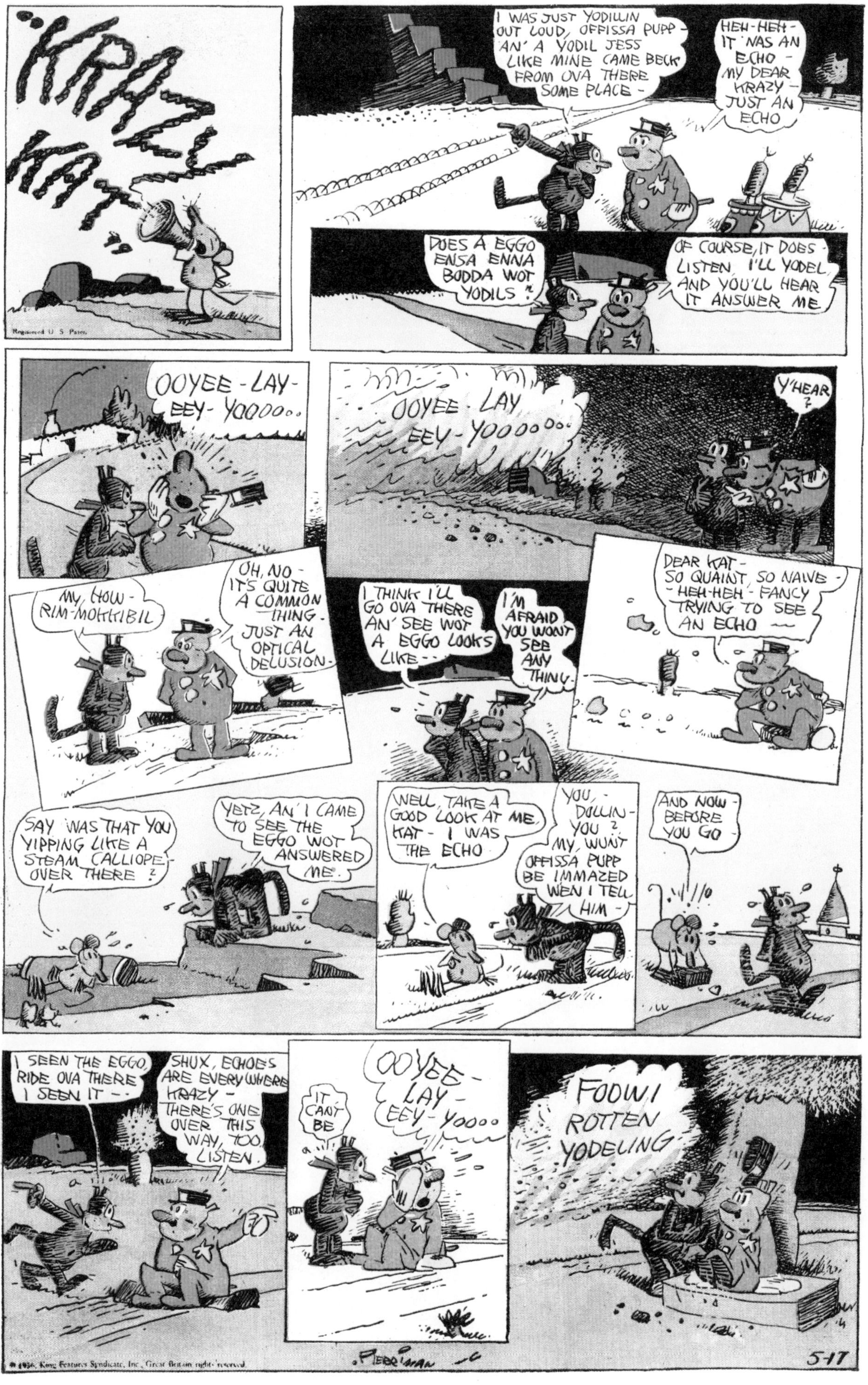

KRAZY KAT
Registered U. S. Patent
I WAS JUST YODILLIN OUT LOUD, OFFISSA PUPP - AN' A YODIL JESS LIKE MINE CAME BECK FROM OVA THERE SOME PLACE -
HEH-HEH - IT WAS AN ECHO - MY DEAR KRAZY - JUST AN ECHO
DOES A EGGO ENSA ENNA BODDA WOT YODILS ?
OF COURSE, IT DOES - LISTEN, I'LL YODEL, AND YOU'LL HEAR IT ANSWER ME
OOYEE - LAY - EEY - YOOOO...
OOYEE - LAY - EEY - YOOOOO...
Y'HEAR ?
MY, HOW - RIM - MOHHIBIL
OH, NO - IT'S QUITE A COMMON THING - JUST AN OPTICAL DELUSION -
I THINK I'LL GO OVA THERE AN' SEE WOT A EGGO LOOKS LIKE -
I'M AFRAID YOU WON'T SEE ANY THING -
DEAR KAT - SO QUAINT, SO NAIVE - HEH-HEH - FANCY TRYING TO SEE AN ECHO
SAY WAS THAT YOU YIPPING LIKE A STEAM CALLIOPE OVER THERE ?
YETZ, AN' I CAME TO SEE THE EGGO WOT ANSWERED ME.
WELL, TAKE A GOOD LOOK AT ME, KAT - I WAS THE ECHO
YOU, - DOLLIN - YOU ? MY, WUNT OFFISSA PUPP BE IMMAZED WEN I TELL HIM -
AND NOW - BEFORE YOU GO
I SEEN THE EGGO, RIDE OVA THERE I SEEN IT -
SHUX, ECHOES ARE EVERYWHERE KRAZY - THERE'S ONE OVER THIS WAY, TOO. LISTEN.
IT CAN'T BE
OOYEE - LAY - EEY - YOOOO
FOOW! ROTTEN YODELING
© 1936, King Features Syndicate, Inc., Great Britain rights reserved.
HERRIMAN
5-17

May 17th, 1936.

Registered U.S. Patent Office
KRAZY KAT
AH-H- ART HAS CALLED ME AND FOUND ME NOT WANTING - I HAVE LIMNED A MASTERPIECE
?
I MUST SEEK A SPOT PROPER AND FITTING FOR IT TO BE HUNG -
HUNG WHERE THE EYE OF THE WORLD MAY SEE -
DOLLIN
HE MUST NOT -
OFFISSA PUPP HAS A SINNISTA NOTION ABOUT THIS PITCHA -
WELL, MAYBE HE'S RIGHT - WHAT IS IT ?
HE WUNTS TO HENG IT
HM-M - ELECTROCUTION WOULD BE BETTER - STILL, IF HE WANTS HANGING - I KNOW JUST THE PLACE
RIGHT THERE
!
JAIL
FINE - IT'S A NATURAL.
JAIL
AND THERE, MY GOOD SIR IS THE ORIGINAL OF MY PICTURE.
MMM - IT SMACKS OF SIN AND FELONY - STILL ART KNOWS NO BARRIER - LET US ON TO YOUR MASTERPIECE
JAIL
THAT KOP WILL PROBABLY CALL THAT PICTURE - THE "JAIL-BIRD" - OR SOMETHING.
OR THE "MOANY LIZZIE."
HOW ABOUT "STORM AT SEA?"
ZIP
King Features Syndicate, Inc., Great Britain rights reserved.
5-24

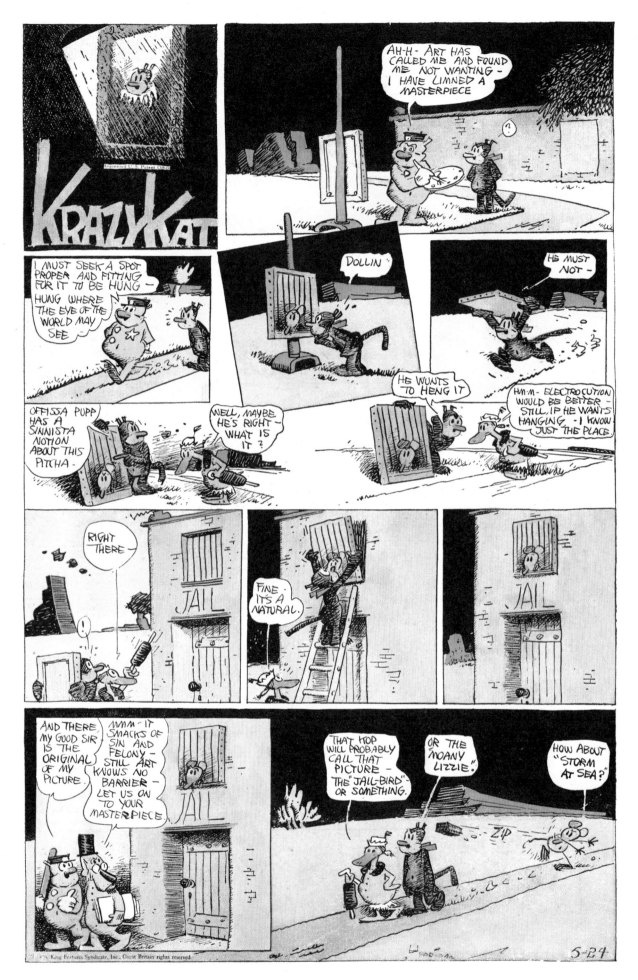

May 24th, 1936.

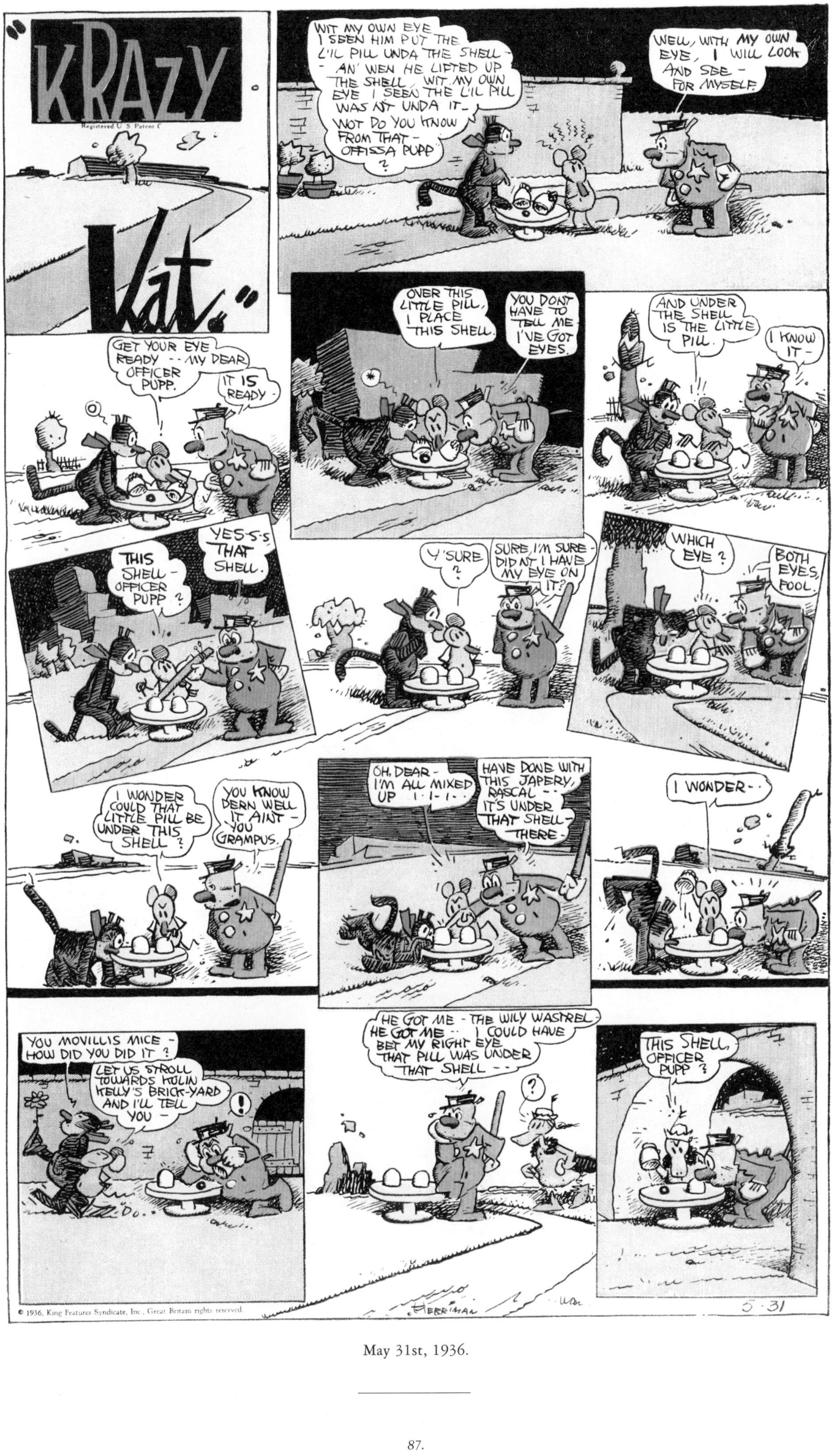
"KRAZY KAT"
Registered U.S. Patent O
WIT MY OWN EYE I SEEN HIM PUT THE L'IL PILL UNDA THE SHELL - AN' WEN HE LIFTED UP THE SHELL, WIT MY OWN EYE I SEEN THE L'IL PILL WAS N'T UNDA IT - WOT DO YOU KNOW FROM THAT - OFFISSA PUPP ?
WELL, WITH MY OWN EYE, I WILL LOOK AND SEE - FOR MYSELF.
GET YOUR EYE READY - - MY DEAR OFFICER PUPP.
IT IS READY -
OVER THIS LITTLE PILL, I PLACE THIS SHELL.
YOU DON'T HAVE TO TELL ME I'VE GOT EYES.
AND UNDER THE SHELL IS THE LITTLE PILL.
I KNOW IT -
THIS SHELL - OFFICER PUPP ?
YES-S-S THAT SHELL.
Y'SURE ?
SURE, I'M SURE DID N'T I HAVE MY EYE ON IT ?
WHICH EYE ?
BOTH EYES, FOOL.
I WONDER COULD THAT LITTLE PILL BE UNDER THIS SHELL ?
YOU KNOW DERN WELL IT AINT - YOU GRAMPUS.
OH, DEAR - I'M ALL MIXED UP I-I-I-
HAVE DONE WITH THIS JAPERY, RASCAL - IT'S UNDER THAT SHELL - THERE -
I WONDER - -
YOU MOVILLIS MICE - HOW DID YOU DID IT ?
LET US STROLL TOWARDS KOLIN KELLY'S BRICK-YARD AND I'LL TELL YOU -
!
HE GOT ME - THE WILY WASTREL HE GOT ME - - I COULD HAVE BET MY RIGHT EYE THAT PILL WAS UNDER THAT SHELL - -
?
THIS SHELL, OFFICER PUPP ?
© 1936, King Features Syndicate, Inc., Great Britain rights reserved.
HERRIMAN
5-31

May 31st, 1936.

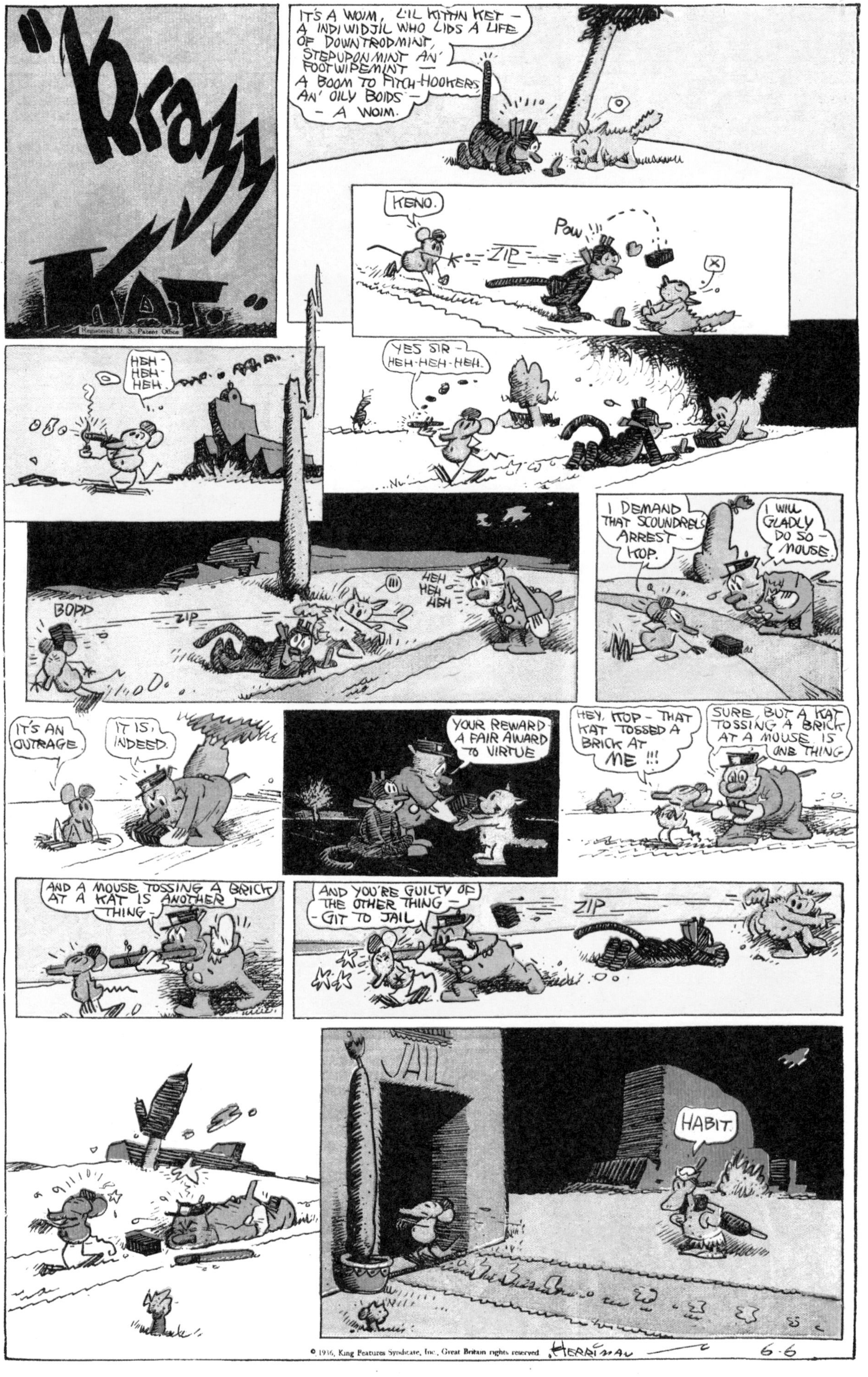
"Krazy Kat."
Registered U. S. Patent Office
IT'S A WOIM, L'IL KITTIN KET — A INDI WIDJIL WHO LIDS A LIFE OF DOWNTRODMINT, STEPUPONMINT AN' FOOTWIPEMINT — A BOOM TO FITCH-HOOKERS AN' OILY BOIDS — — A WOIM.
KENO.
POW !!
ZIP
HEH - HEH - HEH.
YES SIR - HEH-HEH-HEH.
BOPP
ZIP
HEH HEH HEH
I DEMAND THAT SCOUNDREL'S ARREST - KOP.
I WILL GLADLY DO SO - MOUSE.
IT'S AN OUTRAGE.
IT IS, INDEED.
YOUR REWARD A FAIR AWARD TO VIRTUE
HEY, KOP - THAT KAT TOSSED A BRICK AT ME !!!
SURE, BUT A KAT TOSSING A BRICK AT A MOUSE IS ONE THING
AND A MOUSE TOSSING A BRICK AT A KAT IS ANOTHER THING -
AND YOU'RE GUILTY OF THE OTHER THING - - GIT TO JAIL
ZIP
JAIL
HABIT.
HERRIMAN
6-6

June 6th, 1936.

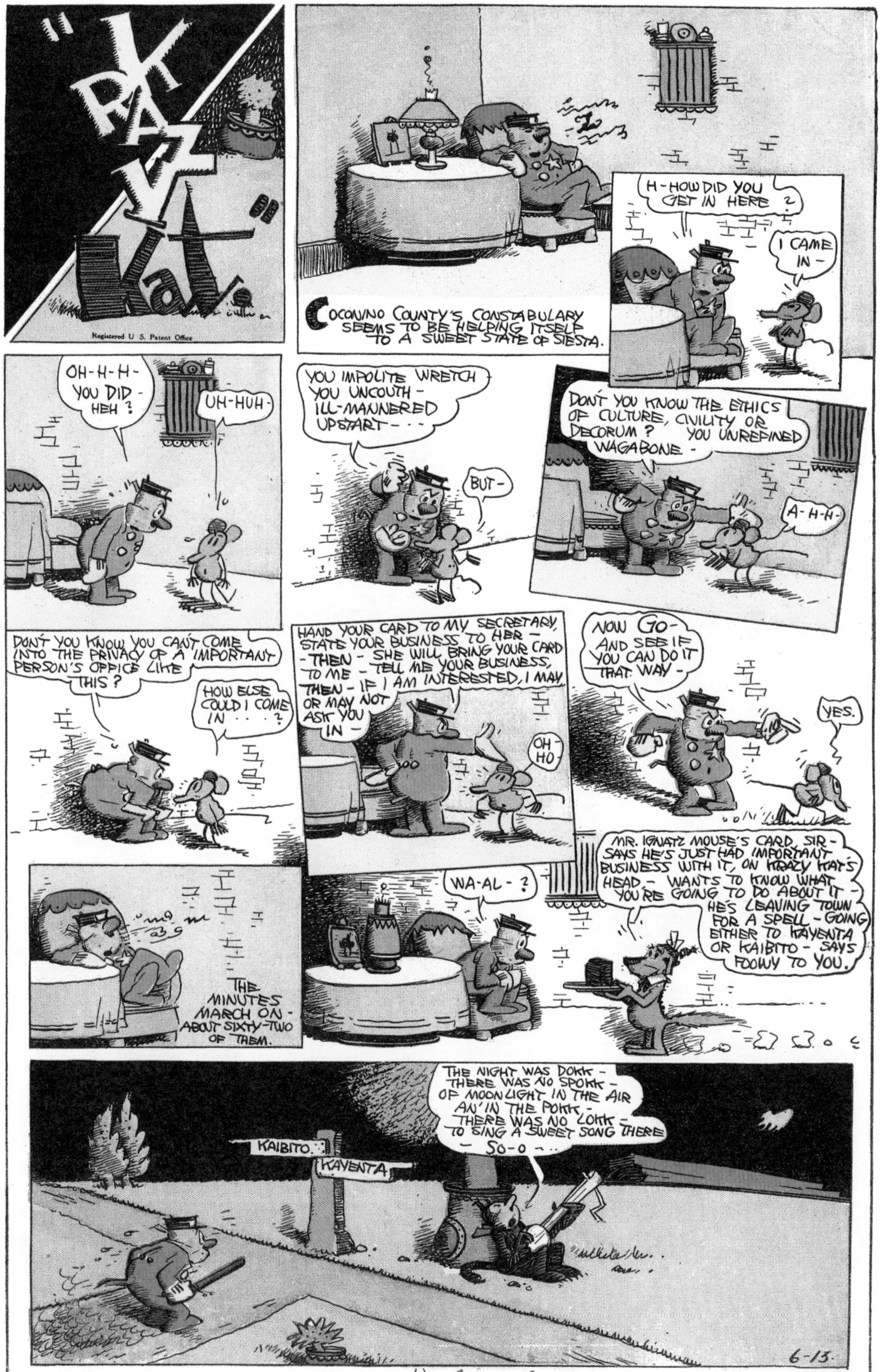
"Krazy Kat"
Registered U. S. Patent Office
Coconino County's constabulary seems to be helping itself to a sweet state of siesta.
H-how did you get in here?
I came in -
Oh-h-h - you did heh?
Uh-huh
You impolite wretch - you uncouth - ill-mannered upstart - - -
But -
Don't you know the ethics of culture, civility or decorum? You unrefined wagabone -
A-h-h-
Don't you know you can't come into the privacy of a important person's office like this?
How else could I come in . . . ?
Hand your card to my secretary, state your business to her - then - she will bring your card to me - tell me your business, then - if I am interested, I may or may not ask you in -
Oh-ho
Now go - and see if you can do it that way -
Yes.
The minutes march on - about sixty-two of them.
Wa-al - ?
Mr. Ignatz Mouse's card, sir - says he's just had important business with it, on Krazy Kat's head - wants to know what you're going to do about it - he's leaving town for a spell - going either to Kayenta or Kaibito - says fooey to you.
The night was dokk - there was no spokk - of moonlight in the air an' in the pokk - there was no lokk - to sing a sweet song there - so-o - -
Kaibito
Kayenta
6-13
Herriman
© 1936, King Features Syndicate, Inc., Great Britain rights reserved.

June 13th, 1936.

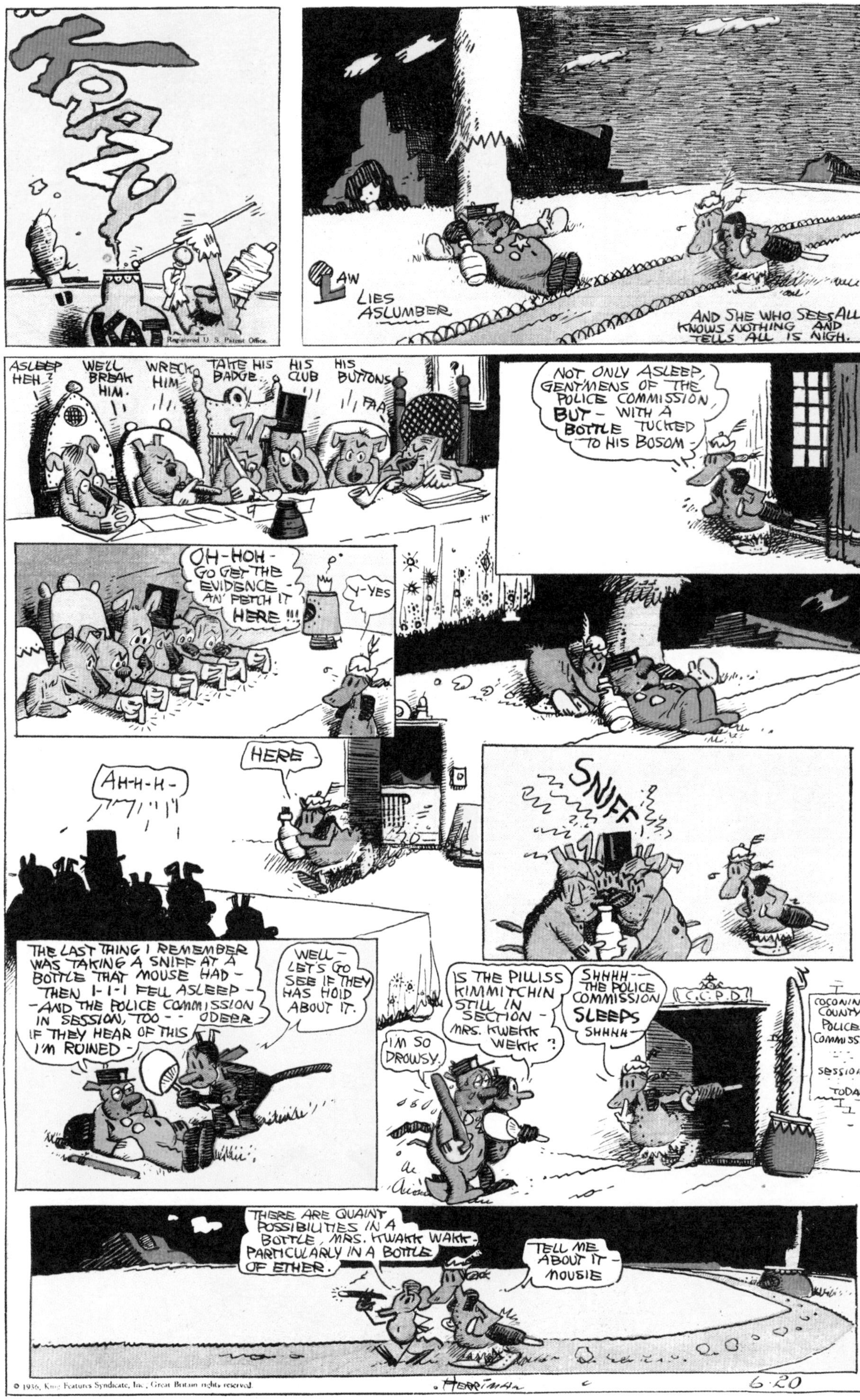

KRAZY "KAT"
Registered U. S. Patent Office.
LAW LIES ASLUMBER
AND SHE WHO SEES ALL KNOWS NOTHING AND TELLS ALL IS NIGH.
ASLEEP HEH?
WE'LL BREAK HIM.
WRECK HIM
TAKE HIS BADGE
HIS CLUB
HIS BUTTONS
NOT ONLY ASLEEP, GENT'MENS OF THE POLICE COMMISSION, BUT - WITH A BOTTLE TUCKED TO HIS BOSOM -
OH-HOH - GO GET THE EVIDENCE - AN' FETCH IT HERE!!!
Y-YES
HERE
AH-H-H-
SNIFF
THE LAST THING I REMEMBER WAS TAKING A SNIFF AT A BOTTLE THAT MOUSE HAD - THEN I-I-I FELL ASLEEP - AND THE POLICE COMMISSION IN SESSION, TOO - - IF THEY HEAR OF THIS I'M RUINED -
ODEER
WELL - LET'S GO SEE IF THEY HAS HOID ABOUT IT.
I'M SO DROWSY.
IS THE PILLISS KIMMITCHIN STILL IN SECTION - MRS. KWEKK WEKK?
SHHHH - THE POLICE COMMISSION SLEEPS SHHHH
C.C.P.D.
COCONINO COUNTY POLICE COMMISSION SESSION TODAY
THERE ARE QUAINT POSSIBILITIES IN A BOTTLE, MRS. KWAKK WAKK - PARTICULARLY IN A BOTTLE OF ETHER.
TELL ME ABOUT IT - MOUSIE
© 1936, King Features Syndicate, Inc., Great Britain rights reserved.
HERRIMAN
6-20

June 20th, 1936.

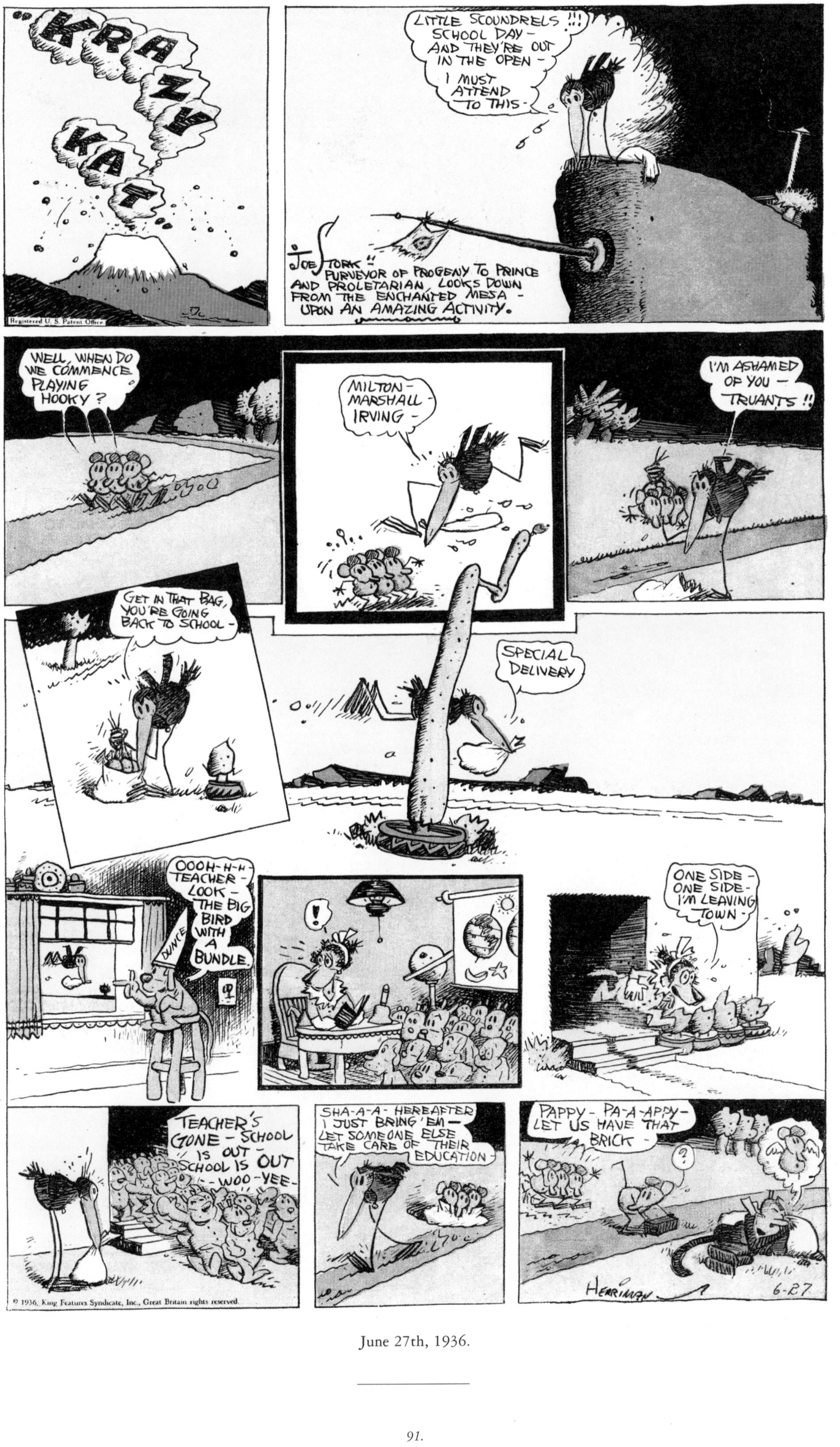
"KRAZY KAT"
Registered U. S. Patent Office
LITTLE SCOUNDRELS !!! SCHOOL DAY - AND THEY'RE OUT IN THE OPEN -
I MUST ATTEND TO THIS -
JOE STORK !! PURVEYOR OF PROGENY TO PRINCE AND PROLETARIAN, LOOKS DOWN FROM THE ENCHANTED MESA - UPON AN AMAZING ACTIVITY.
WELL, WHEN DO WE COMMENCE PLAYING HOOKY ?
MILTON - MARSHALL - IRVING -
I'M ASHAMED OF YOU - TRUANTS !!
GET IN THAT BAG, YOU'RE GOING BACK TO SCHOOL -
SPECIAL DELIVERY
OOOH-H-H TEACHER - LOOK - THE BIG BIRD WITH A BUNDLE.
DUNCE
ONE SIDE - ONE SIDE - I'M LEAVING TOWN -
TEACHER'S GONE - SCHOOL IS OUT - SCHOOL IS OUT - WOO-YEE -
SHA-A-A- HEREAFTER I JUST BRING 'EM - LET SOMEONE ELSE TAKE CARE OF THEIR EDUCATION -
PAPPY - PA-A-APPY - LET US HAVE THAT BRICK -
HERRIMAN
6-27
© 1936, King Features Syndicate, Inc., Great Britain rights reserved.

June 27th, 1936.

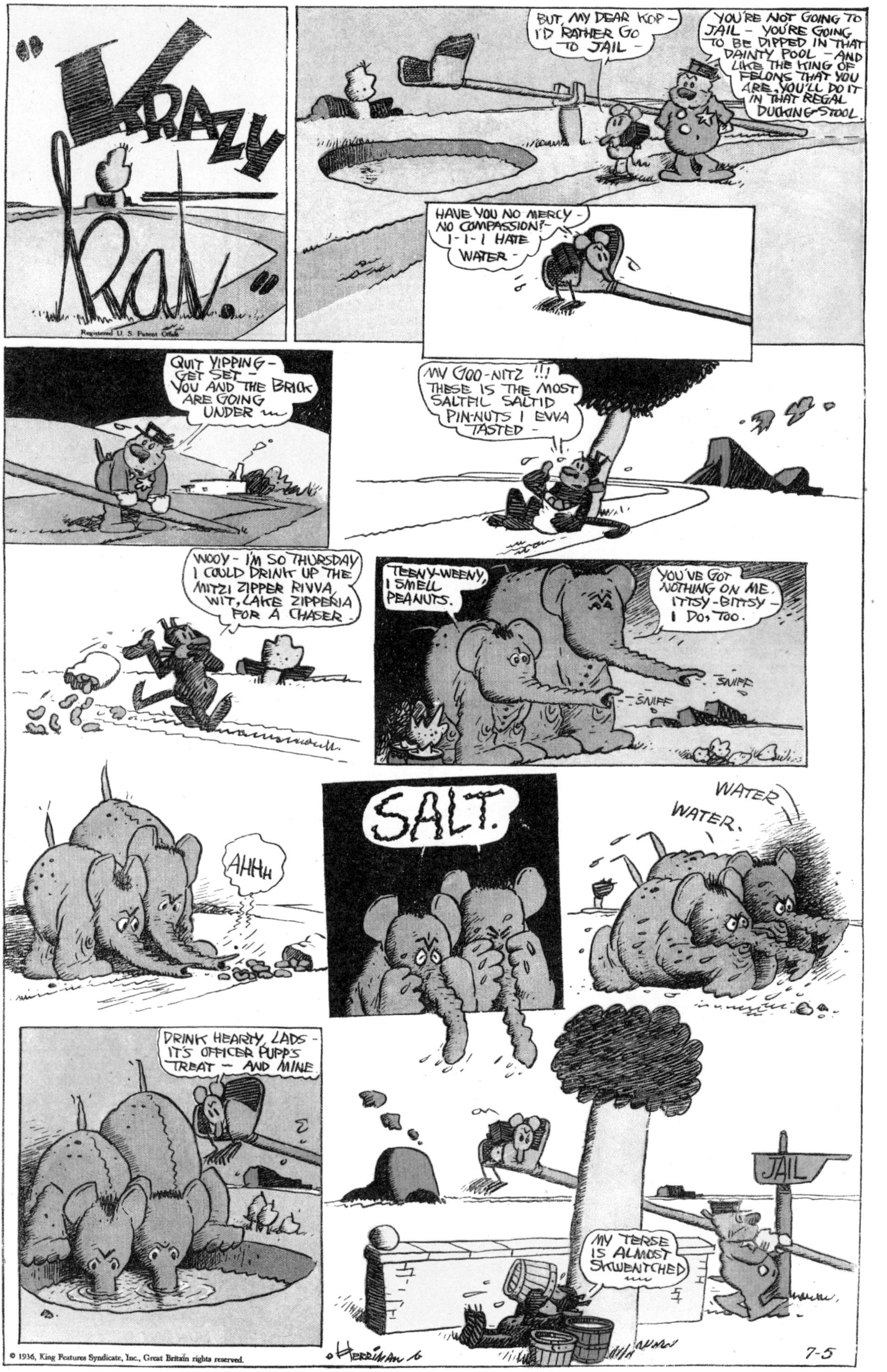
Krazy Kat.
Registered U. S. Patent Office
BUT, MY DEAR KOP - I'D RATHER GO TO JAIL -
YOU'RE NOT GOING TO JAIL - YOU'RE GOING TO BE DIPPED IN THAT DAINTY POOL - AND LIKE THE KING OF FELONS THAT YOU ARE, YOU'LL DO IT IN THAT REGAL DUCKING STOOL.
HAVE YOU NO MERCY - NO COMPASSION? - I-I-I HATE WATER -
QUIT YIPPING - GET SET - YOU AND THE BRICK ARE GOING UNDER
MY GOO-NITZ !!! THESE IS THE MOST SALTFIL SALTID PIN-NUTS I EVVA TASTED -
WOOY - I'M SO THURSDAY I COULD DRINK UP THE MITZI ZIPPER RIVVA, WIT, LAKE ZIPPERIA FOR A CHASER
TEENY-WEENY, I SMELL PEANUTS.
YOU'VE GOT NOTHING ON ME, ITTSY-BITTSY - I DO, TOO.
SNIFF
SNIFF
AHHH
SALT.
WATER
WATER.
DRINK HEARTY, LADS - IT'S OFFICER PUPP'S TREAT - AND MINE
JAIL
MY TERSE IS ALMOST SKWENTCHED
© 1936, King Features Syndicate, Inc., Great Britain rights reserved.
Herriman
7-5

July 5th, 1936.

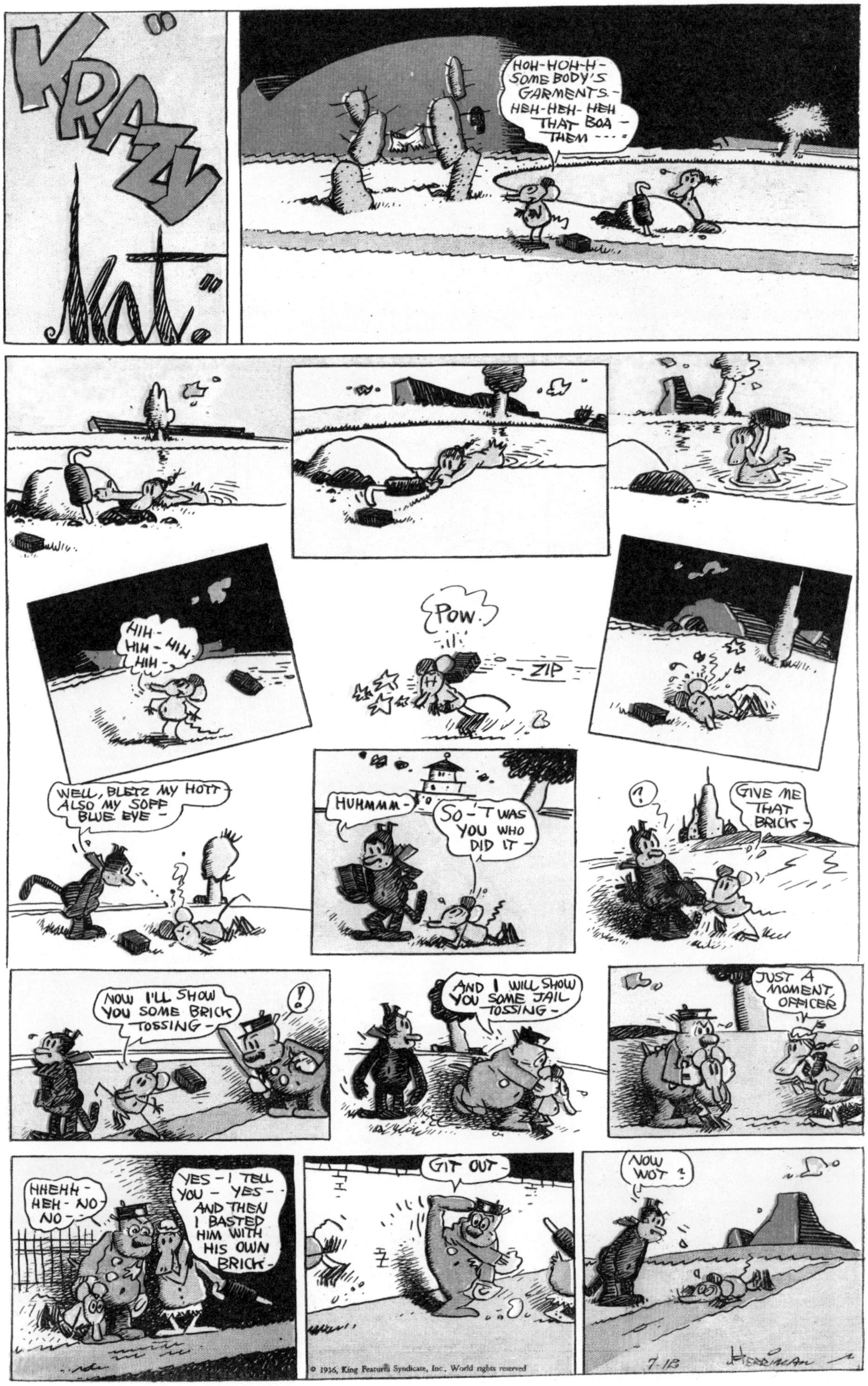

KRAZY KAT
HOH-HOH-H-
SOME BODY'S
GARMENTS-
HEH-HEH-HEH
THAT BOA
THEM---
HIH-HIH
HIH-
HIH-
POW
ZIP
WELL, BLETZ MY HOTT-
ALSO MY SOFF
BLUE EYE-
HUHMMM-
SO-'T WAS
YOU WHO
DID IT-
?
GIVE ME
THAT
BRICK-
NOW I'LL SHOW
YOU SOME BRICK
TOSSING-
!
AND I WILL SHOW
YOU SOME JAIL
TOSSING-
JUST A
MOMENT,
OFFICER
HHEHH-
HEH-NO
NO-
YES-I TELL
YOU-YES-
AND THEN
I BASTED
HIM WITH
HIS OWN
BRICK-
GIT OUT-
NOW
WOT ?
© 1936, King Features Syndicate, Inc., World rights reserved
7-12
HERRIMAN

July 12th, 1936.

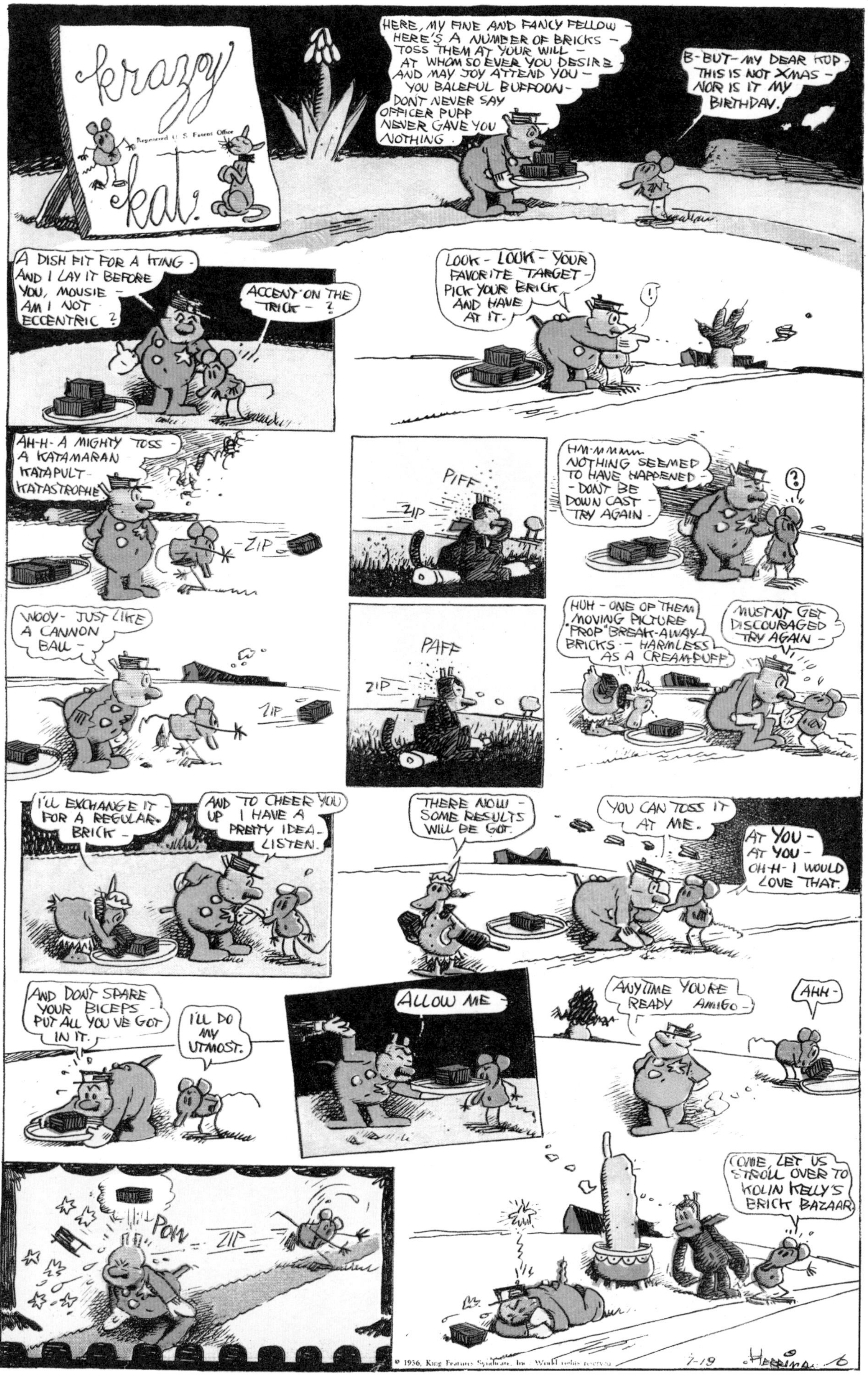

Krazy Kat
Registered U. S. Patent Office
HERE, MY FINE AND FANCY FELLOW - HERE'S A NUMBER OF BRICKS - TOSS THEM AT YOUR WILL - AT WHOM SO EVER YOU DESIRE AND MAY JOY ATTEND YOU - YOU BALEFUL BUFFOON - DONT NEVER SAY OFFICER PUPP NEVER GAVE YOU NOTHING.
B-BUT-MY DEAR KOP THIS IS NOT XMAS - NOR IS IT MY BIRTHDAY.
A DISH FIT FOR A KING - AND I LAY IT BEFORE YOU, MOUSIE - AM I NOT ECCENTRIC ?
ACCENT ON THE TRICK - ?
LOOK - LOOK - YOUR FAVORITE TARGET - PICK YOUR BRICK AND HAVE AT IT.
AH-H- A MIGHTY TOSS - A KATAMARAN KATAPULT KATASTROPHE
ZIP
PIFF
ZIP
HM-MMMM NOTHING SEEMED TO HAVE HAPPENED - DONT BE DOWN CAST - TRY AGAIN -
WOOY - JUST LIKE A CANNON BALL -
ZIP
PAFF
ZIP
HUH - ONE OF THEM MOVING PICTURE "PROP" BREAK-AWAY BRICKS - HARMLESS AS A CREAM-PUFF.
MUSTN'T GET DISCOURAGED TRY AGAIN -
I'LL EXCHANGE IT FOR A REGULAR BRICK -
AND TO CHEER YOU UP I HAVE A PRETTY IDEA - LISTEN.
THERE NOW - SOME RESULTS WILL BE GOT.
YOU CAN TOSS IT AT ME.
AT YOU - AT YOU - OH-H - I WOULD LOVE THAT.
AND DON'T SPARE YOUR BICEPS - PUT ALL YOU'VE GOT IN IT.
I'LL DO MY UTMOST.
ALLOW ME -
ANYTIME YOU'RE READY AMIGO -
AHH -
POW
ZIP
COME, LET US STROLL OVER TO KOLIN KELLY'S BRICK BAZAAR.
© 1936, King Features Syndicate, Inc. World rights reserved
7-19
Herriman

July 19th, 1936.

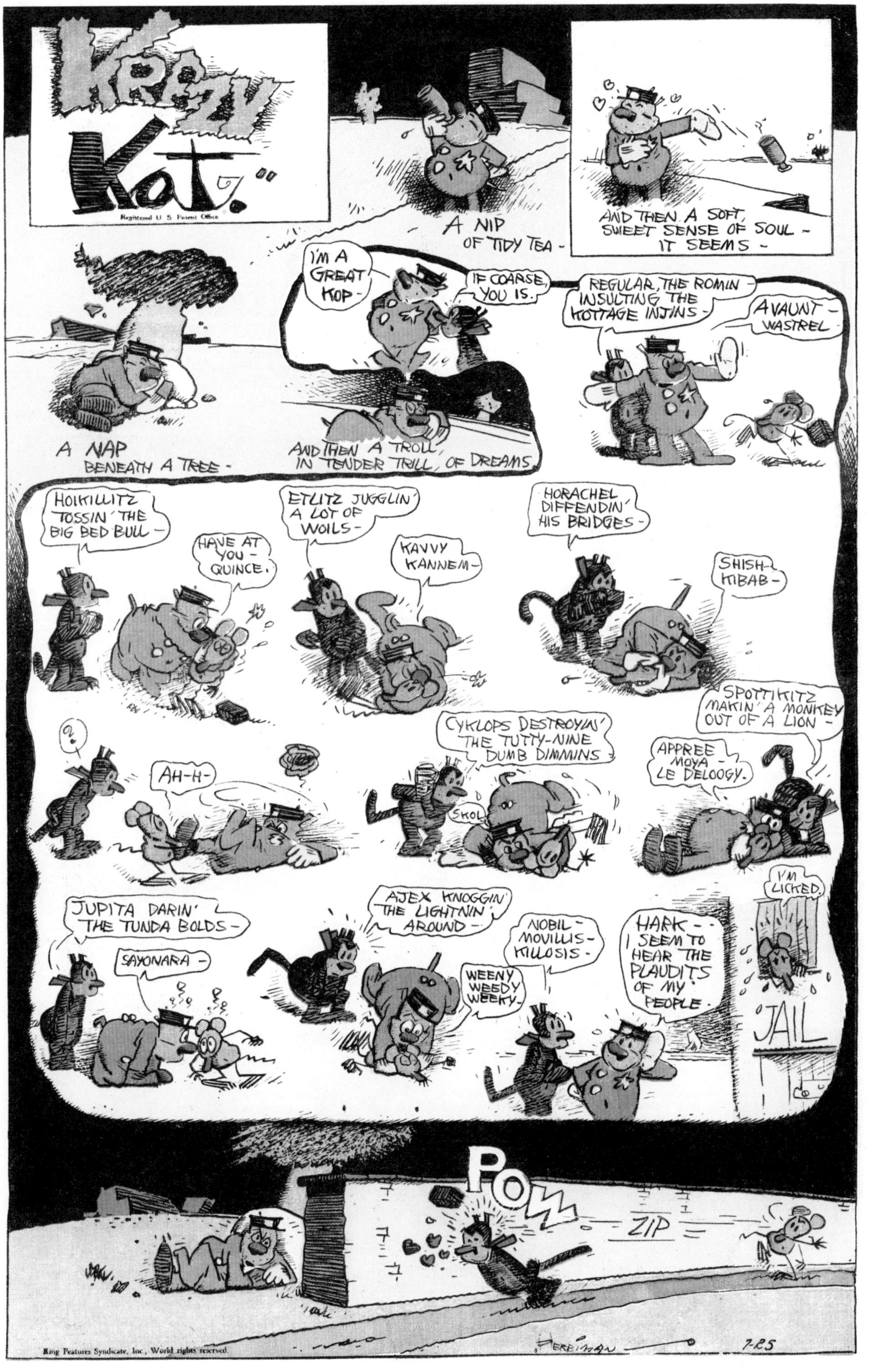
Krazy Kat
Registered U. S. Patent Office
A NIP OF TIDY TEA -
AND THEN A SOFT, SWEET SENSE OF SOUL - IT SEEMS -
A NAP BENEATH A TREE -
AND THEN A TROLL IN TENDER TRILL OF DREAMS
I'M A GREAT KOP -
IF COARSE, YOU IS.
REGULAR, THE ROMIN INSULTING THE KOTTAGE INJINS -
AVAUNT - WASTREL
HOIKILLITZ TOSSIN' THE BIG BED BULL -
HAVE AT YOU - QUINCE.
ETLITZ JUGGLIN' A LOT OF WOILS -
KAVVY KANNEM -
HORACHEL DIFFENDIN' HIS BRIDGES -
SHISH-KIBAB -
?
AH-H-
CYKLOPS DESTROYIN' THE TUTTY-NINE DUMB DIMMINS
SKOL
SPOTTIKITZ MAKIN' A MONKEY OUT OF A LION -
APPREE MOYA LE DELOOGY.
JUPITA DARIN' THE TUNDA BOLDS -
SAYONARA -
AJEX KNOGGIN' THE LIGHTNIN' AROUND -
WEENY WEEDY WEEKY.
NOBIL MOVILLIS KILLOSIS -
HARK - - I SEEM TO HEAR THE PLAUDITS OF MY PEOPLE.
I'M LICKED.
JAIL
POW
ZIP
King Features Syndicate, Inc., World rights reserved.
HERRIMAN
7-25

July 25th, 1936.

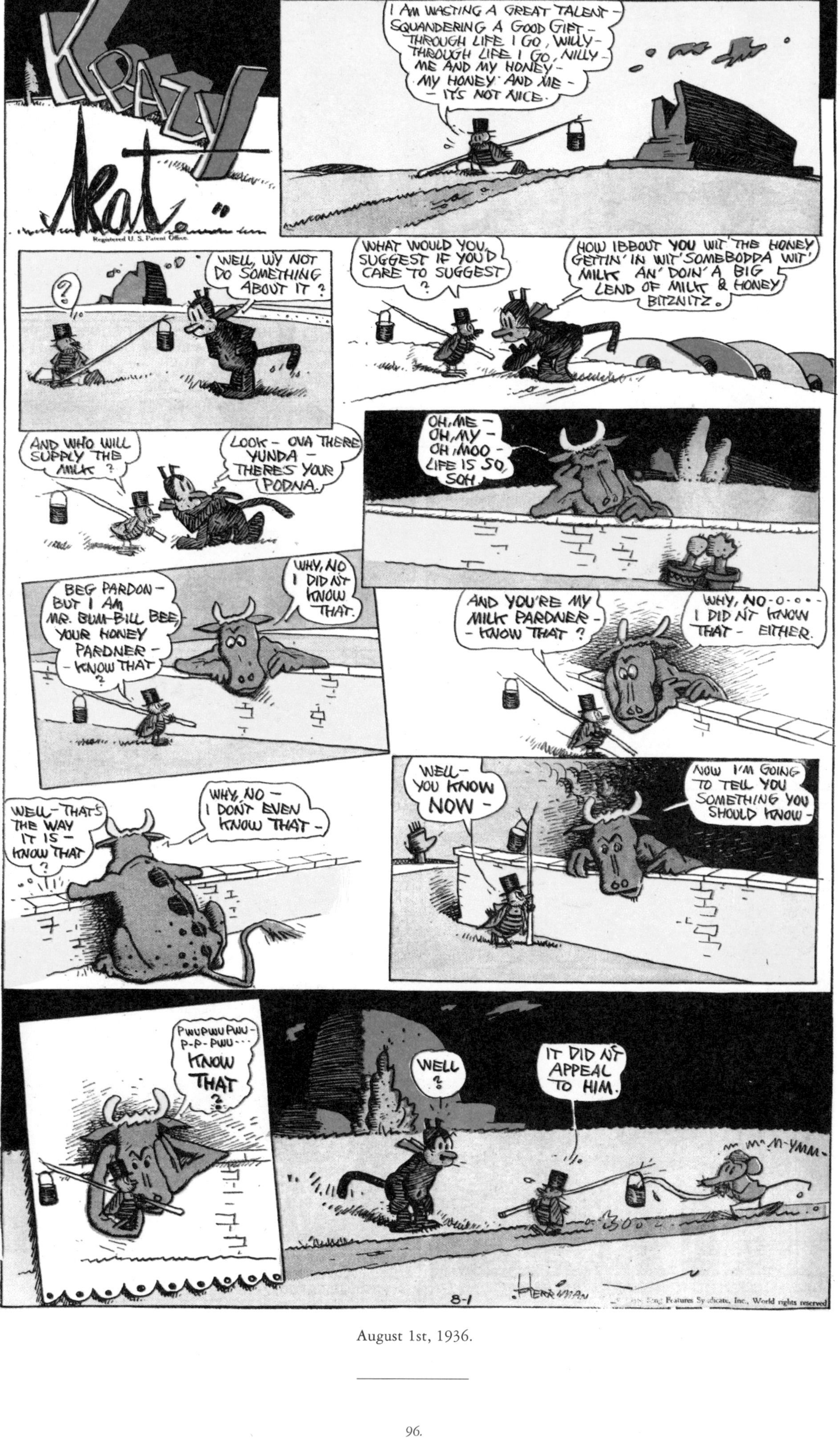
Krazy Kat
Registered U. S. Patent Office.
I AM WASTING A GREAT TALENT - SQUANDERING A GOOD GIFT - THROUGH LIFE I GO, WILLY - THROUGH LIFE I GO, NILLY - ME AND MY HONEY - MY HONEY AND ME - - IT'S NOT NICE.
?
WELL, WY NOT DO SOMETHING ABOUT IT ?
WHAT WOULD YOU, SUGGEST IF YOU'D CARE TO SUGGEST ?
HOW IBBOUT YOU WIT' THE HONEY GETTIN' IN WIT' SOMEBODDA WIT' MILK AN' DOIN' A BIG LEND OF MILK & HONEY BITZNITZ.
AND WHO WILL SUPPLY THE MILK ?
LOOK - OVA THERE YUNDA - THERE'S YOUR PODNA.
OH, ME - OH, MY - OH, MOO - LIFE IS SO, SOH.
BEG PARDON - BUT I AM MR. BUM-BILL BEE, YOUR HONEY PARDNER - - KNOW THAT ?
WHY, NO I DID N'T KNOW THAT.
AND YOU'RE MY MILK PARDNER - - KNOW THAT ?
WHY, NO - O - ○ - ○ - I DID N'T KNOW THAT - EITHER.
WELL - THAT'S THE WAY IT IS - KNOW THAT ?
WHY, NO - I DON'T EVEN KNOW THAT -
WELL - YOU KNOW NOW -
NOW I'M GOING TO TELL YOU SOMETHING YOU SHOULD KNOW -
PWUPWUPWU - P-P-PWU - - - KNOW THAT ?
WELL ?
IT DID N'T APPEAL TO HIM.
M'M-YMM-
8-1
HERRIMAN
Features Syndicate, Inc., World rights reserved

August 1st, 1936.

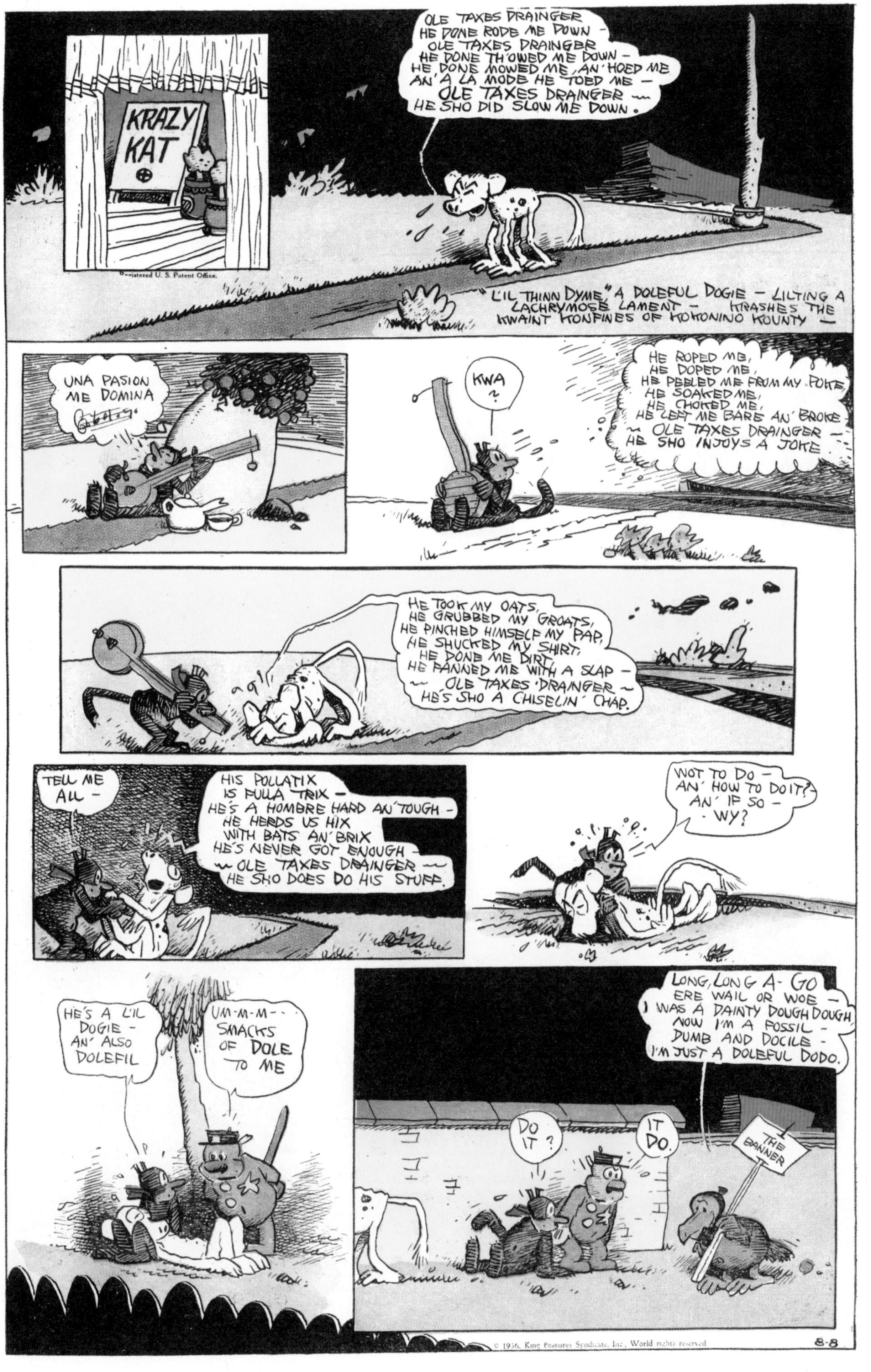
OLE TAXES DRAINGER HE DONE RODE ME DOWN — OLE TAXES DRAINGER HE DONE TH'OWED ME DOWN — HE DONE MOWED ME, AN' HOED ME AN' A LA MODE HE TOED ME — OLE TAXES DRAINGER — HE SHO DID SLOW ME DOWN.
KRAZY KAT
Registered U. S. Patent Office.
"LIL THINN DYME," A DOLEFUL DOGIE — LILTING A LACHRYMOSE LAMENT — KRASHES THE KWAINT KONFINES OF KOKONINO KOUNTY —
UNA PASION ME DOMINA
KWA ?
HE ROPED ME, HE DOPED ME, HE PEELED ME FROM MY POKE HE SOAKED ME, HE CHOKED ME, HE LEFT ME BARE AN' BROKE — OLE TAXES DRAINGER — HE SHO INJOYS A JOKE
HE TOOK MY OATS, HE GRUBBED MY GROATS, HE PINCHED HIMSELF MY PAP, HE SHUCKED MY SHIRT, HE DONE ME DIRT, HE FANNED ME WITH A SLAP — OLE TAXES DRAINGER — HE'S SHO A CHISELIN' CHAP.
TELL ME ALL —
HIS POLLATIX IS FULLA TRIX — HE'S A HOMBRE HARD AN' TOUGH — HE HERDS US HIX WITH BATS AN' BRIX HE'S NEVER GOT ENOUGH — OLE TAXES DRAINGER — HE SHO DOES DO HIS STUFF.
WOT TO DO — AN' HOW TO DO IT? — AN' IF SO — WY?
HE'S A LIL DOGIE — AN' ALSO DOLEFIL
UM-M-M — SMACKS OF DOLE TO ME
LONG, LONG A-GO ERE WAIL OR WOE — I WAS A DAINTY DOUGH DOUGH NOW I'M A FOSSIL — DUMB AND DOCILE — I'M JUST A DOLEFUL DODO.
DO IT ?
IT DO.
THE BANNER
© 1936, King Features Syndicate, Inc., World rights reserved.
8-8

August 8th, 1936.

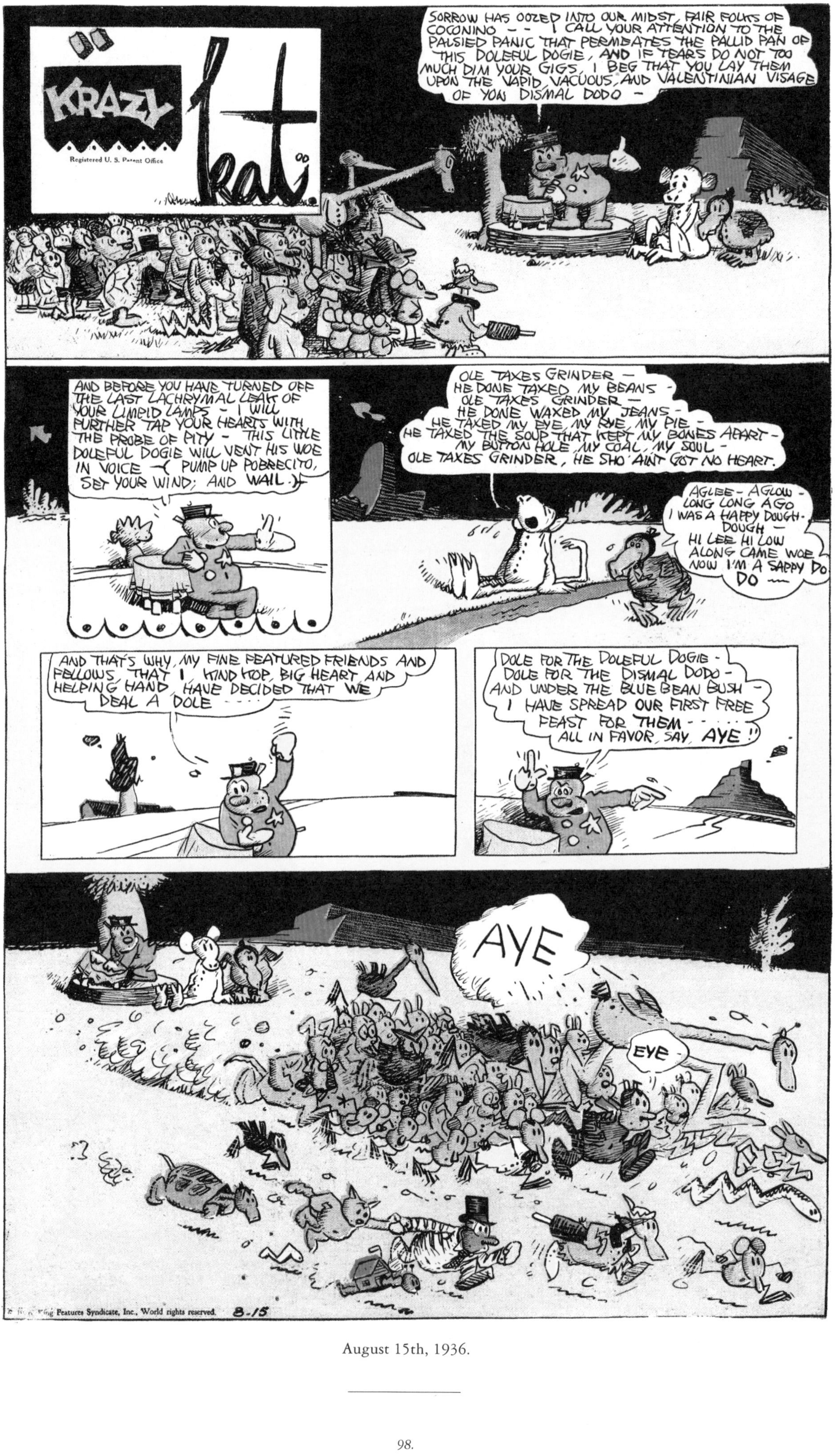
KRAZY Kat
Registered U. S. Patent Office
SORROW HAS OOZED INTO OUR MIDST, FAIR FOLKS OF COCONINO - - I CALL YOUR ATTENTION TO THE PALSIED PANIC THAT PERMEATES THE PALLID PAN OF THIS DOLEFUL DOGIE, AND IF TEARS DO NOT TOO MUCH DIM YOUR GIGS, I BEG THAT YOU LAY THEM UPON THE VAPID, VACUOUS, AND VALENTINIAN VISAGE OF YON DISMAL DODO -
AND BEFORE YOU HAVE TURNED OFF THE LAST LACHRYMAL LEAK OF YOUR LIMPID LAMPS - I WILL FURTHER TAP YOUR HEARTS WITH THE PROBE OF PITY - THIS LITTLE DOLEFUL DOGIE WILL VENT HIS WOE IN VOICE -(PUMP UP POBRECITO, SET YOUR WIND; AND WAIL.)-
OLE TAXES GRINDER - HE DONE TAXED MY BEANS - OLE TAXES GRINDER - HE DONE WAXED MY JEANS - HE TAXED MY EYE, MY RYE, MY PIE - HE TAXED THE SOUP THAT KEPT MY BONES APART - MY BUTTON HOLE, MY COAL, MY SOUL - OLE TAXES GRINDER, HE SHO' AIN'T GOT NO HEART.
AGLEE - AGLOW - LONG LONG AGO I WAS A HAPPY DOUGH-DOUGH - HI LEE HI LOW ALONG CAME WOE NOW I'M A SAPPY DO DO ~
AND THAT'S WHY, MY FINE FEATURED FRIENDS AND FELLOWS, THAT I, KIND HOP, BIG HEART AND HELPING HAND, HAVE DECIDED THAT WE DEAL A DOLE - - -
DOLE FOR THE DOLEFUL DOGIE - DOLE FOR THE DISMAL DODO - AND UNDER THE BLUE BEAN BUSH - I HAVE SPREAD OUR FIRST FREE FEAST FOR THEM - - - - ALL IN FAVOR, SAY, AYE !!
AYE
EYE
King Features Syndicate, Inc., World rights reserved.
8-15

August 15th, 1936.

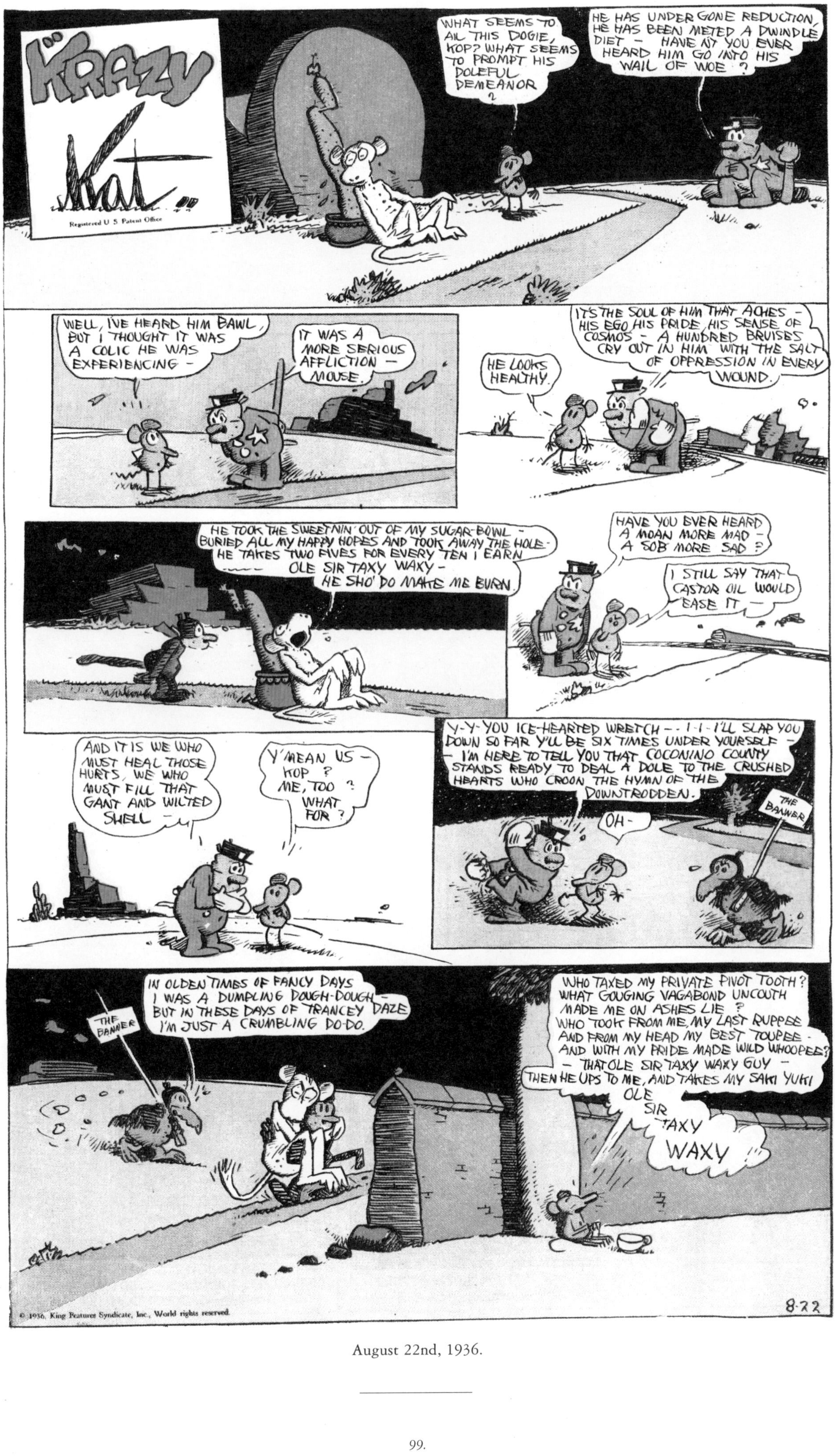
KRAZY KAT
Registered U.S. Patent Office
WHAT SEEMS TO AIL THIS DOGIE, KOP? WHAT SEEMS TO PROMPT HIS DOLEFUL DEMEANOR ?
HE HAS UNDER GONE REDUCTION, HE HAS BEEN METED A DWINDLE DIET - HAVE N'T YOU EVER HEARD HIM GO INTO HIS WAIL OF WOE ?
WELL, I'VE HEARD HIM BAWL, BUT I THOUGHT IT WAS A COLIC HE WAS EXPERIENCING -
IT WAS A MORE SERIOUS AFFLICTION - MOUSE.
HE LOOKS HEALTHY.
IT'S THE SOUL OF HIM THAT ACHES - HIS EGO, HIS PRIDE, HIS SENSE OF COSMOS - A HUNDRED BRUISES CRY OUT IN HIM WITH THE SALT OF OPPRESSION IN EVERY WOUND.
HE TOOK THE SWEETNIN' OUT OF MY SUGAR-BOWL - BURIED ALL MY HAPPY HOPES AND TOOK AWAY THE HOLE - HE TAKES TWO FIVES FOR EVERY TEN I EARN
OLE SIR TAXY WAXY - HE SHO' DO MAKE ME BURN.
HAVE YOU EVER HEARD A MOAN MORE MAD - A SOB MORE SAD ?
I STILL SAY THAT CASTOR OIL WOULD EASE IT -
AND IT IS WE WHO MUST HEAL THOSE HURTS, WE WHO MUST FILL THAT GANT AND WILTED SHELL -
Y'MEAN US - KOP ? ME, TOO ? WHAT FOR ?
Y-Y-YOU ICE-HEARTED WRETCH - - I-I-I'LL SLAP YOU DOWN SO FAR YOU'LL BE SIX TIMES UNDER YOURSELF - I'M HERE TO TELL YOU THAT COCONINO COUNTY STANDS READY TO DEAL A DOLE TO THE CRUSHED HEARTS WHO CROON THE HYMN OF THE DOWNTRODDEN.
OH -
THE BANNER
IN OLDEN TIMES OF FANCY DAYS I WAS A DUMPLING DOUGH-DOUGH - BUT IN THESE DAYS OF TRANCEY DAZE I'M JUST A CRUMBLING DO-DO.
THE BANNER
WHO TAXED MY PRIVATE PIVOT TOOTH? WHAT GOUGING VAGABOND UNCOUTH MADE ME ON ASHES LIE ? WHO TOOK FROM ME, MY LAST RUPPEE AND FROM MY HEAD MY BEST TOUPEE - AND WITH MY PRIDE MADE WILD WHOOPEE? - THAT OLE SIR TAXY WAXY GUY - THEN HE UPS TO ME, AND TAKES MY SAKI YUKI
OLE SIR TAXY WAXY
8-22
© 1936, King Features Syndicate, Inc., World rights reserved.

August 22nd, 1936.

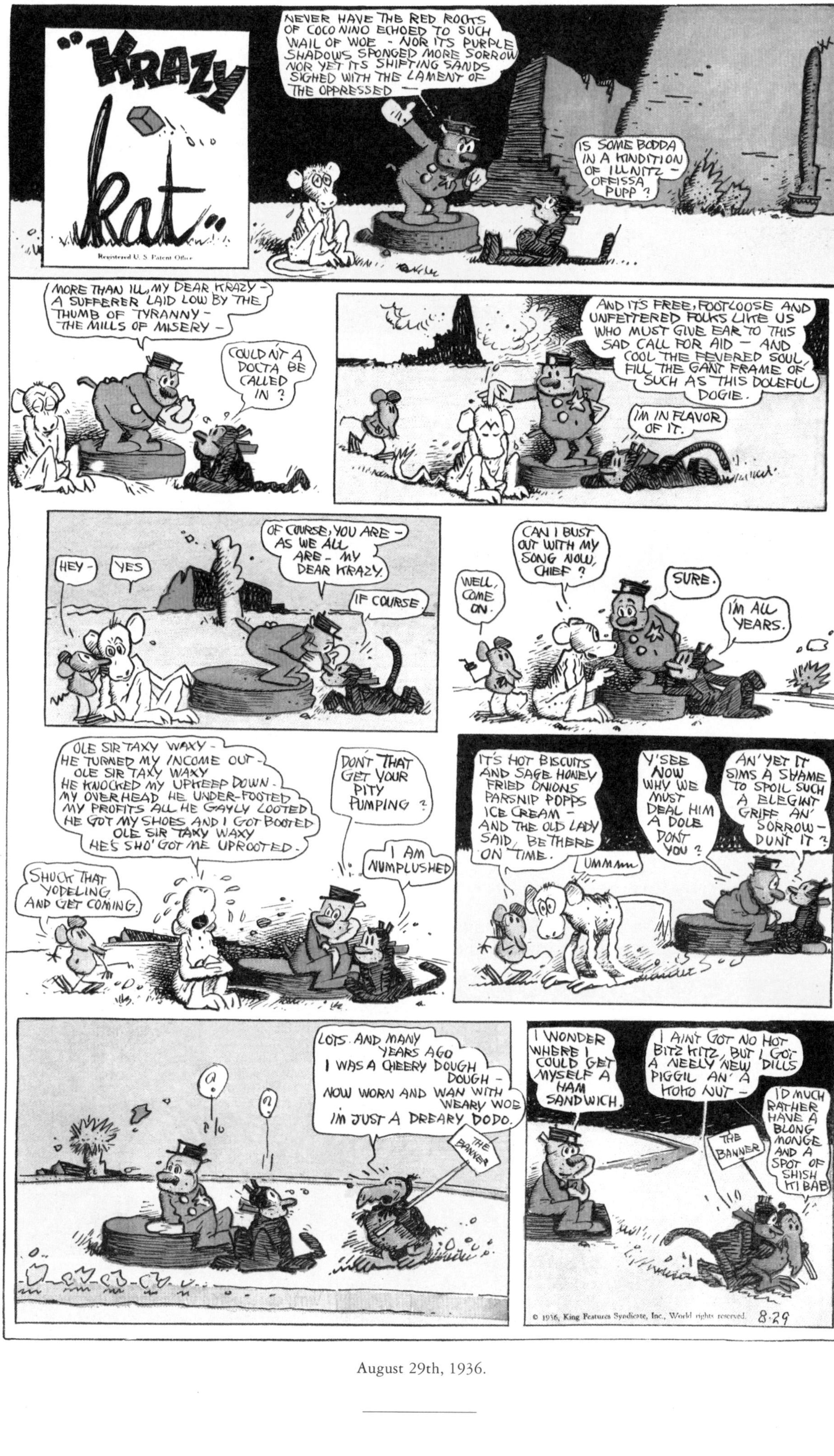
"Krazy Kat"
Registered U. S. Patent Office
NEVER HAVE THE RED ROCKS OF COCONINO ECHOED TO SUCH WAIL OF WOE - NOR ITS PURPLE SHADOWS SPONGED MORE SORROW NOR YET ITS SHIFTING SANDS SIGHED WITH THE LAMENT OF THE OPPRESSED —
IS SOME BODDA IN A KINDITION OF ILLNITZ - OFFISSA PUPP ?
MORE THAN ILL, MY DEAR KRAZY - A SUFFERER LAID LOW BY THE THUMB OF TYRANNY - THE MILLS OF MISERY -
COULDN'T A DOCTA BE CALLED IN ?
AND ITS FREE, FOOTLOOSE AND UNFETTERED FOLKS LIKE US WHO MUST GIVE EAR TO THIS SAD CALL FOR AID - AND COOL THE FEVERED SOUL, FILL THE GANT FRAME OF SUCH AS THIS DOLEFUL DOGIE.
I'M IN FLAVOR OF IT.
HEY -
YES
OF COURSE, YOU ARE - AS WE ALL ARE - MY DEAR KRAZY.
IF COURSE.
CAN I BUST OUT WITH MY SONG NOW, CHIEF ?
WELL, COME ON.
SURE.
I'M ALL YEARS.
OLE SIR TAXY WAXY - HE TURNED MY INCOME OUT - OLE SIR TAXY WAXY HE KNOCKED MY UPKEEP DOWN - MY OVERHEAD HE UNDER-FOOTED MY PROFITS ALL HE GAYLY LOOTED HE GOT MY SHOES AND I GOT BOOTED OLE SIR TAXY WAXY HE'S SHO' GOT ME UPROOTED -
DON'T THAT GET YOUR PITY PUMPING ?
I AM NUMPLUSHED
SHUCK THAT YODELING AND GET COMING.
IT'S HOT BISCUITS AND SAGE HONEY FRIED ONIONS PARSNIP POPPS ICE CREAM - AND THE OLD LADY SAID, BE THERE ON TIME.
UMMAM
Y'SEE NOW WHY WE MUST DEAL HIM A DOLE DON'T YOU ?
AN' YET IT SIMS A SHAME TO SPOIL SUCH A ELEGINT GRIFF AN' SORROW - DUNT IT ?
LOTS AND MANY YEARS AGO I WAS A CHEERY DOUGH DOUGH - NOW WORN AND WAN WITH WEARY WOE I'M JUST A DREARY DODO.
THE BANNER
I WONDER WHERE I COULD GET MYSELF A HAM SANDWICH.
I AIN'T GOT NO HOT BITZ KITZ, BUT I GOT A NEELY NEW DILLS PIGGIL AN' A KOKO NUT -
I'D MUCH RATHER HAVE A BLONG MONGE AND A SPOT OF SHISH KI BAB
THE BANNER
© 1936, King Features Syndicate, Inc., World rights reserved. 8-29

August 29th, 1936.

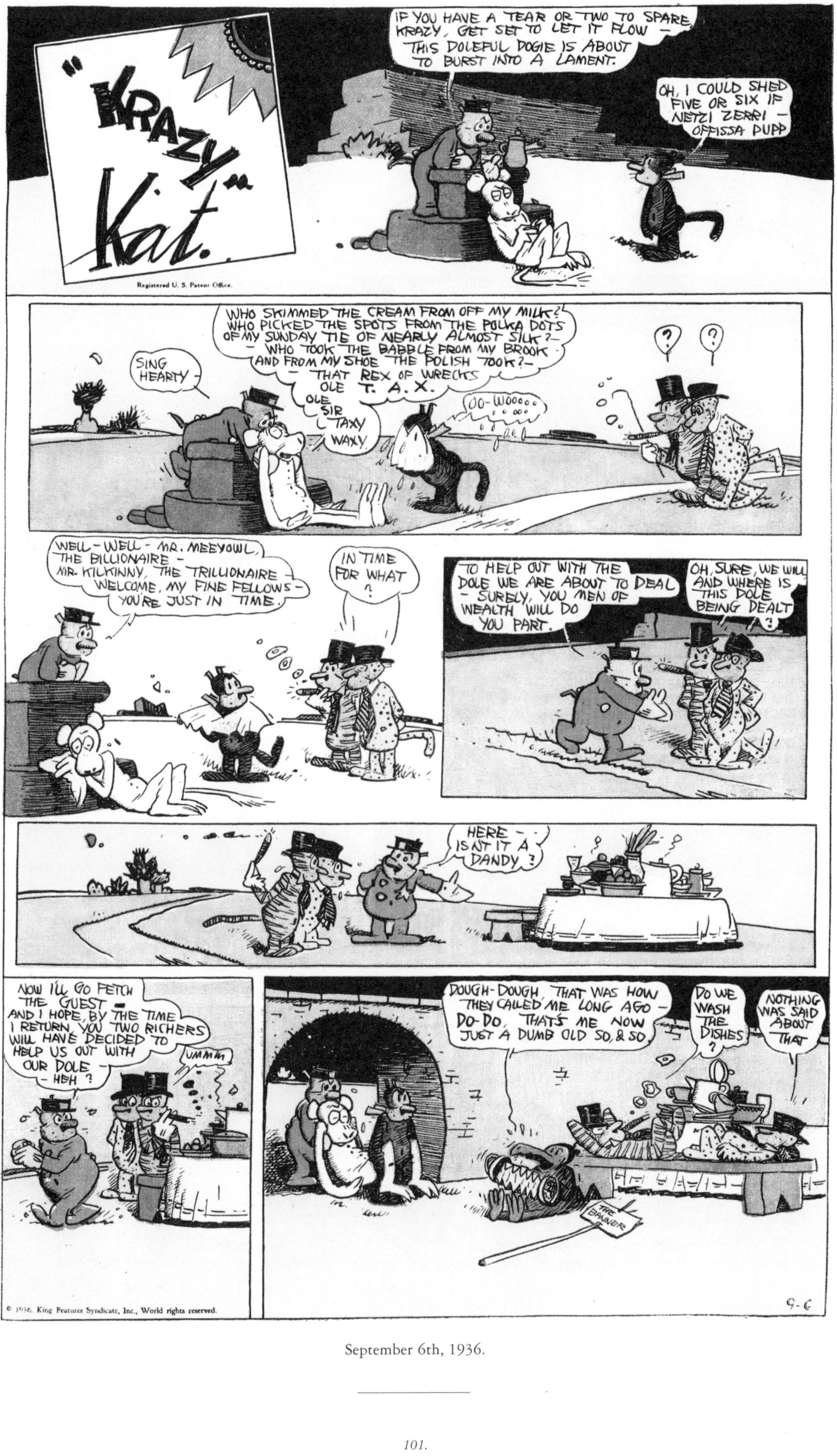
"KRAZY" Kat.
Registered U. S. Patent Office.
IF YOU HAVE A TEAR OR TWO TO SPARE, KRAZY, GET SET TO LET IT FLOW — THIS DOLEFUL DOGIE IS ABOUT TO BURST INTO A LAMENT.
OH, I COULD SHED FIVE OR SIX IF NETZI ZERRI — OFFISSA PUPP
SING HEARTY —
WHO SKIMMED THE CREAM FROM OFF MY MILK? WHO PICKED THE SPOTS FROM THE POLKA DOTS OF MY SUNDAY TIE OF NEARLY ALMOST SILK? — WHO TOOK THE BABBLE FROM MY BROOK AND FROM MY SHOE THE POLISH TOOK? — THAT REX OF WRECKS OLE T. A. X.
OLE SIR TAXY WAXY.
OO-WOOooo
WELL-WELL - MR. MEEYOWL, THE BILLIONAIRE — MR. KILKINNY, THE TRILLIONAIRE — WELCOME, MY FINE FELLOWS — YOU'RE JUST IN TIME.
IN TIME FOR WHAT ?
TO HELP OUT WITH THE DOLE WE ARE ABOUT TO DEAL — SURELY, YOU MEN OF WEALTH WILL DO YOU PART.
OH, SURE, WE WILL AND WHERE IS THIS DOLE BEING DEALT ?
HERE — IS'NT IT A DANDY ?
NOW I'LL GO FETCH THE GUEST — AND I HOPE, BY THE TIME I RETURN, YOU TWO RICHERS WILL HAVE DECIDED TO HELP US OUT WITH OUR DOLE — HEH ?
UMMM
DOUGH-DOUGH, THAT WAS HOW THEY CALLED ME LONG AGO — DO-DO, THAT'S ME NOW JUST A DUMB OLD SO, & SO.
DO WE WASH THE DISHES ?
NOTHING WAS SAID ABOUT THAT
THE BANNER
9-6
© 1936, King Features Syndicate, Inc., World rights reserved.

September 6th, 1936.

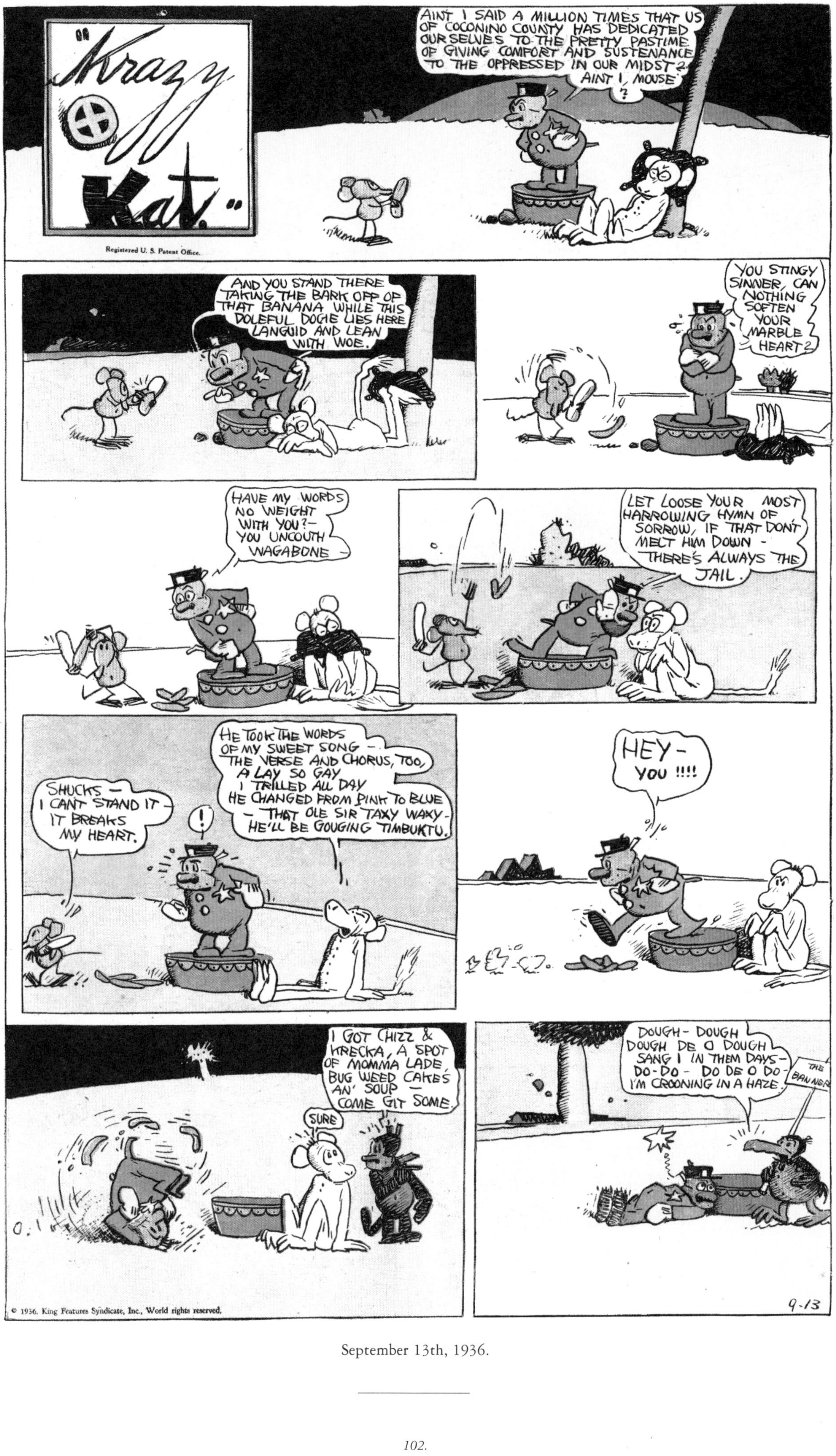
"Krazy Kat."
Registered U. S. Patent Office.
AINT I SAID A MILLION TIMES THAT US OF COCONINO COUNTY HAS DEDICATED OURSELVES TO THE PRETTY PASTIME OF GIVING COMFORT AND SUSTENANCE TO THE OPPRESSED IN OUR MIDST? AINT I, MOUSE ?
AND YOU STAND THERE TAKING THE BARK OFF OF THAT BANANA WHILE THIS DOLEFUL DOGIE LIES HERE LANGUID AND LEAN WITH WOE.
YOU STINGY SINNER, CAN NOTHING SOFTEN YOUR MARBLE HEART?
HAVE MY WORDS NO WEIGHT WITH YOU? - YOU UNCOUTH WAGABONE -
LET LOOSE YOUR MOST HARROWING HYMN OF SORROW, IF THAT DON'T MELT HIM DOWN - THERE'S ALWAYS THE JAIL.
HE TOOK THE WORDS OF MY SWEET SONG - THE VERSE AND CHORUS, TOO, A LAY SO GAY I TRILLED ALL DAY HE CHANGED FROM PINK TO BLUE - THAT OLE SIR TAXY WAXY - HE'LL BE GOUGING TIMBUKTU.
SHUCKS - I CANT STAND IT - IT BREAKS MY HEART.
!
HEY - YOU !!!!
I GOT CHIZZ & KRECKA, A SPOT OF MOMMA LADE, BUG WEED CAKES AN' SOUP - COME GIT SOME
SURE
DOUGH - DOUGH DOUGH DE O DOUGH SANG I IN THEM DAYS - DO-DO - DO DE O DO - I'M CROONING IN A HAZE.
THE BANNER
© 1936, King Features Syndicate, Inc., World rights reserved.
9-13

September 13th, 1936.

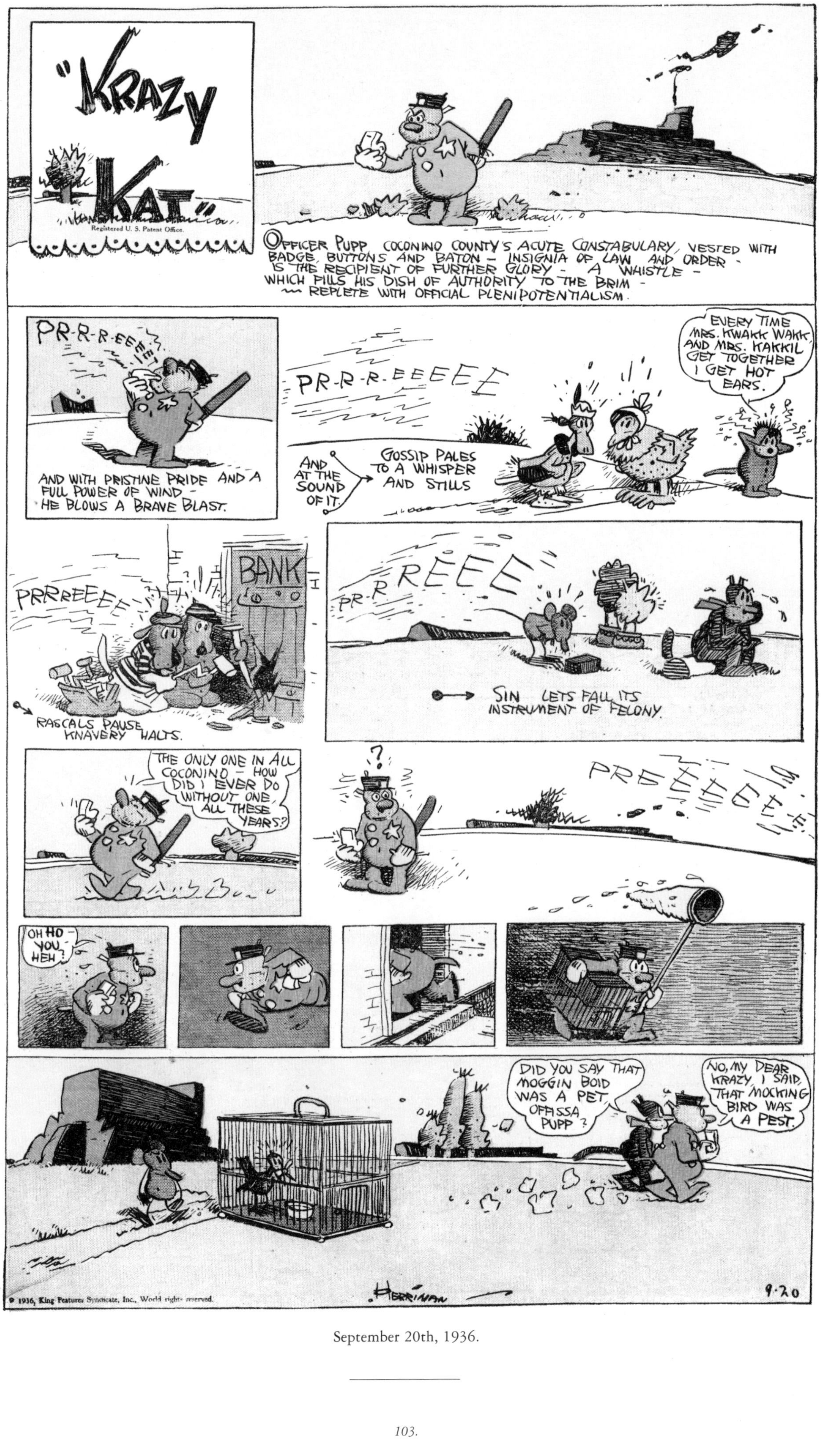
"KRAZY KAT"
Registered U. S. Patent Office.
OFFICER PUPP COCONINO COUNTY'S ACUTE CONSTABULARY, VESTED WITH BADGE, BUTTONS AND BATON - INSIGNIA OF LAW AND ORDER - IS THE RECIPIENT OF FURTHER GLORY - A WHISTLE - WHICH FILLS HIS DISH OF AUTHORITY TO THE BRIM - REPLETE WITH OFFICIAL PLENIPOTENTIALISM.
PR-R-R-EEEE!
AND WITH PRISTINE PRIDE AND A FULL POWER OF WIND - HE BLOWS A BRAVE BLAST.
PR-R-R-EEEEEE
EVERY TIME MRS. KWAKK WAKK AND MRS. KAKKIL GET TOGETHER I GET HOT EARS.
AND AT THE SOUND OF IT.
GOSSIP PALES TO A WHISPER AND STILLS
PRRREEEEE
BANK
RASCALS PAUSE KNAVERY HALTS.
PR-R REEE
SIN LETS FALL ITS INSTRUMENT OF FELONY.
THE ONLY ONE IN ALL COCONINO - HOW DID I EVER DO WITHOUT ONE ALL THESE YEARS?
?
PREEEEE
OH HO - YOU, HEH!
DID YOU SAY THAT MOGGIN BOID WAS A PET, OFFISSA PUPP?
NO, MY DEAR KRAZY, I SAID THAT MOCKING BIRD WAS A PEST.
© 1936, King Features Syndicate, Inc., World rights reserved.
HERRIMAN
9·20

September 20th, 1936.

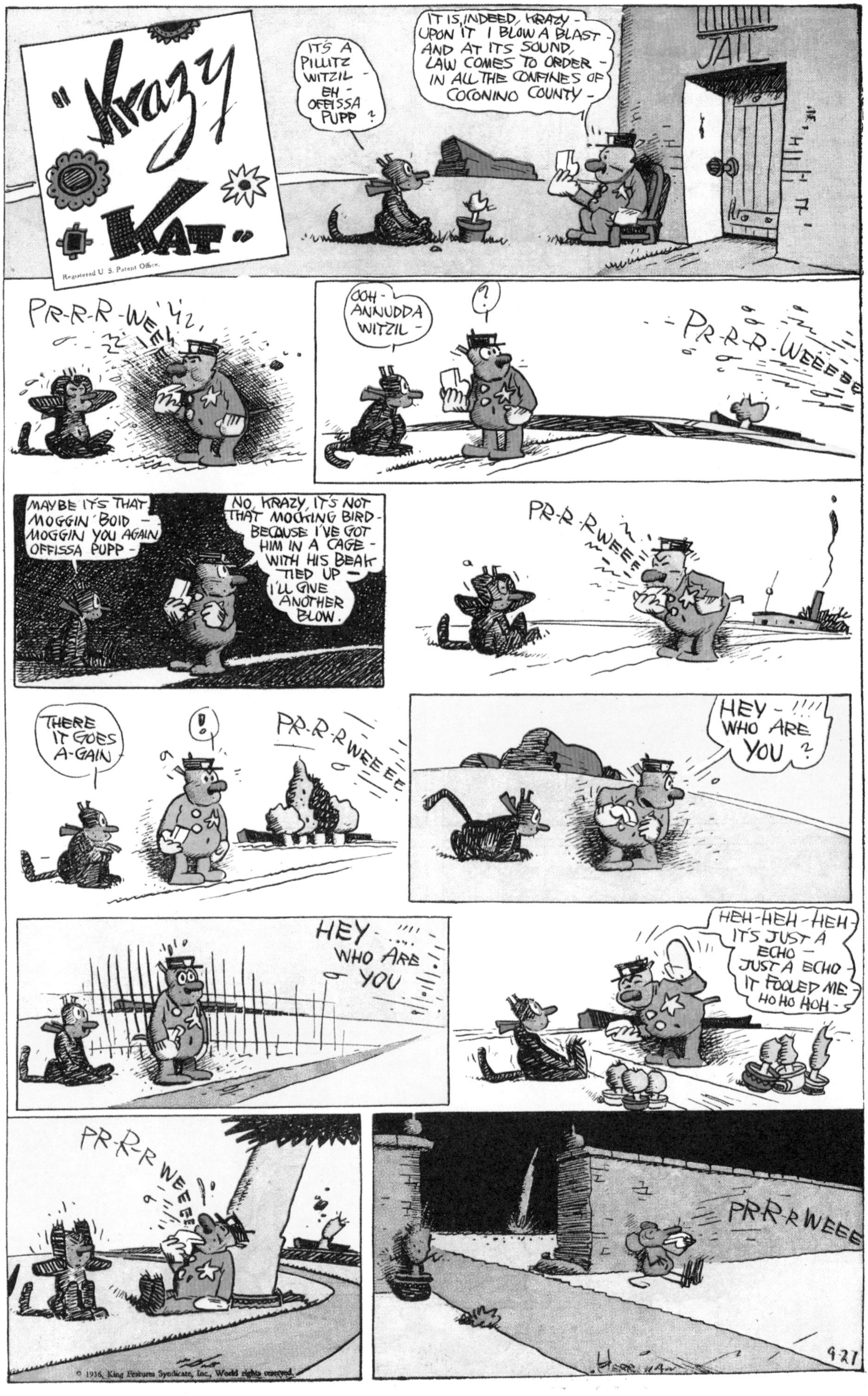
"Krazy Kat"
Registered U. S. Patent Office.
IT'S A PILLITZ WITZIL - EH - OFFISSA PUPP ?
IT IS, INDEED, KRAZY - UPON IT I BLOW A BLAST - AND AT ITS SOUND, LAW COMES TO ORDER - IN ALL THE CONFINES OF COCONINO COUNTY -
JAIL
PR-R-R-WEEEE
OOH - ANNUDDA WITZIL -
PR-R-R-WEEEEEE
MAYBE IT'S THAT MOGGIN' BOID - MOGGIN YOU AGAIN OFFISSA PUPP -
NO, KRAZY, IT'S NOT THAT MOCKING BIRD - BECAUSE I'VE GOT HIM IN A CAGE - WITH HIS BEAK TIED UP - I'LL GIVE ANOTHER BLOW.
PR-R-RWEEE
THERE IT GOES A-GAIN
PR-R-RWEEEEE
HEY - !!!! WHO ARE YOU ?
HEY ..... WHO ARE YOU
HEH-HEH-HEH - IT'S JUST A ECHO - JUST A ECHO - IT FOOLED ME - HO HO HOH -
PR-R-R WEEEE
PR-R-R WEEE
© 1936, King Features Syndicate, Inc., World rights reserved.
9-27

September 27th, 1936.

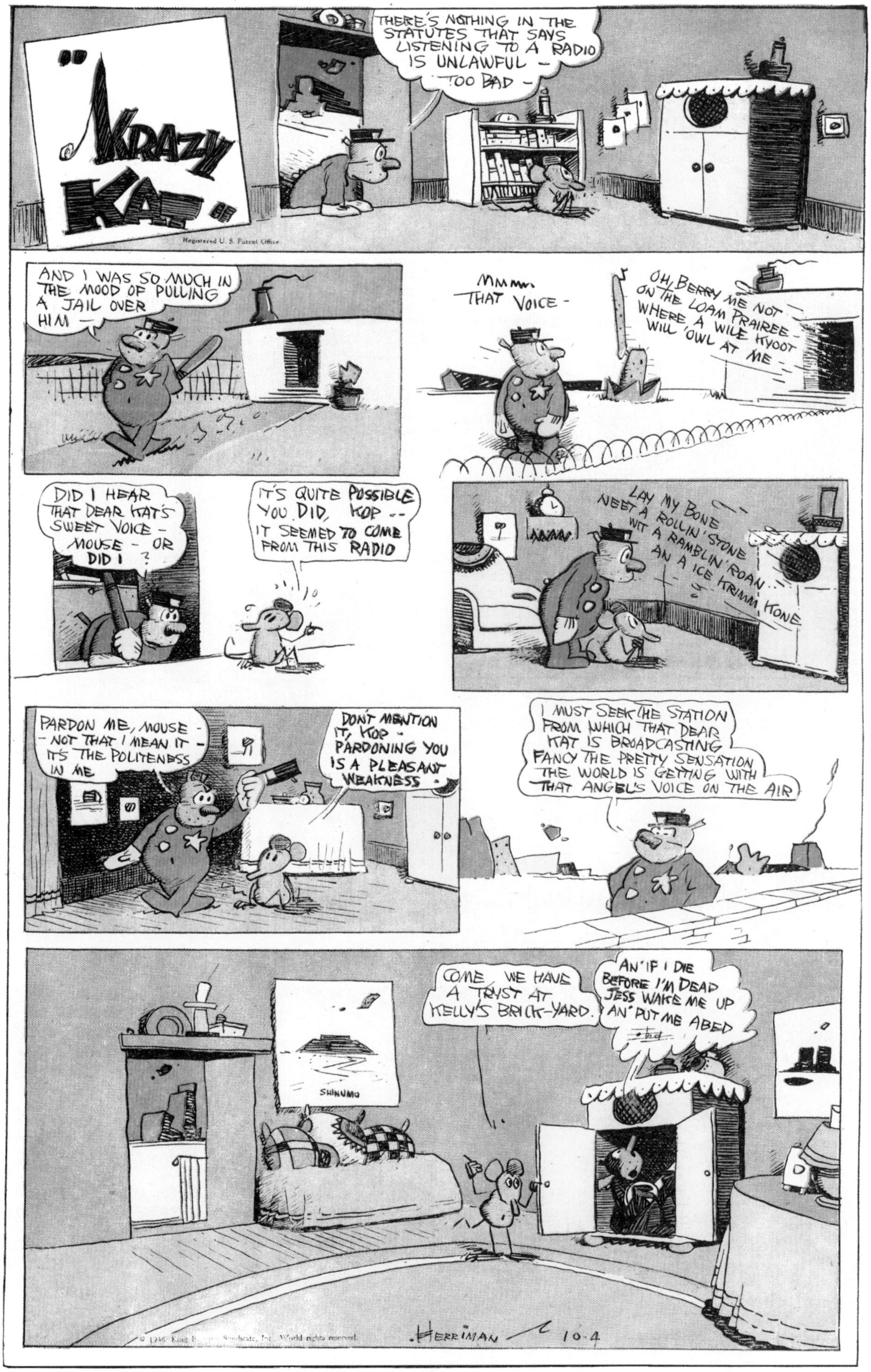

"KRAZY KAT"
Registered U. S. Patent Office
THERE'S NOTHING IN THE STATUTES THAT SAYS LISTENING TO A RADIO IS UNLAWFUL - TOO BAD -
AND I WAS SO MUCH IN THE MOOD OF PULLING A JAIL OVER HIM -
MMMM THAT VOICE -
OH, BERRY ME NOT ON THE LOAM PRAIREE WHERE A WILE KYOOT WILL 'OWL AT ME -
DID I HEAR THAT DEAR KAT'S SWEET VOICE - MOUSE - OR DID I ?
IT'S QUITE POSSIBLE YOU DID, KOP - - IT SEEMED TO COME FROM THIS RADIO
LAY MY BONE NEET A ROLLIN' STONE WIT A RAMBLIN' ROAN AN A ICE KRIMM KONE
PARDON ME, MOUSE - NOT THAT I MEAN IT - IT'S THE POLITENESS IN ME
DON'T MENTION IT, KOP - PARDONING YOU IS A PLEASANT WEAKNESS.
I MUST SEEK THE STATION FROM WHICH THAT DEAR KAT IS BROADCASTING FANCY THE PRETTY SENSATION THE WORLD IS GETTING WITH THAT ANGEL'S VOICE ON THE AIR
COME WE HAVE A TRYST AT KELLY'S BRICK-YARD.
AN' IF I DIE BEFORE I'M DEAD JESS WAKE ME UP AN' PUT ME ABED
SHINUMO
HERRIMAN 10-4

October 4th, 1936.

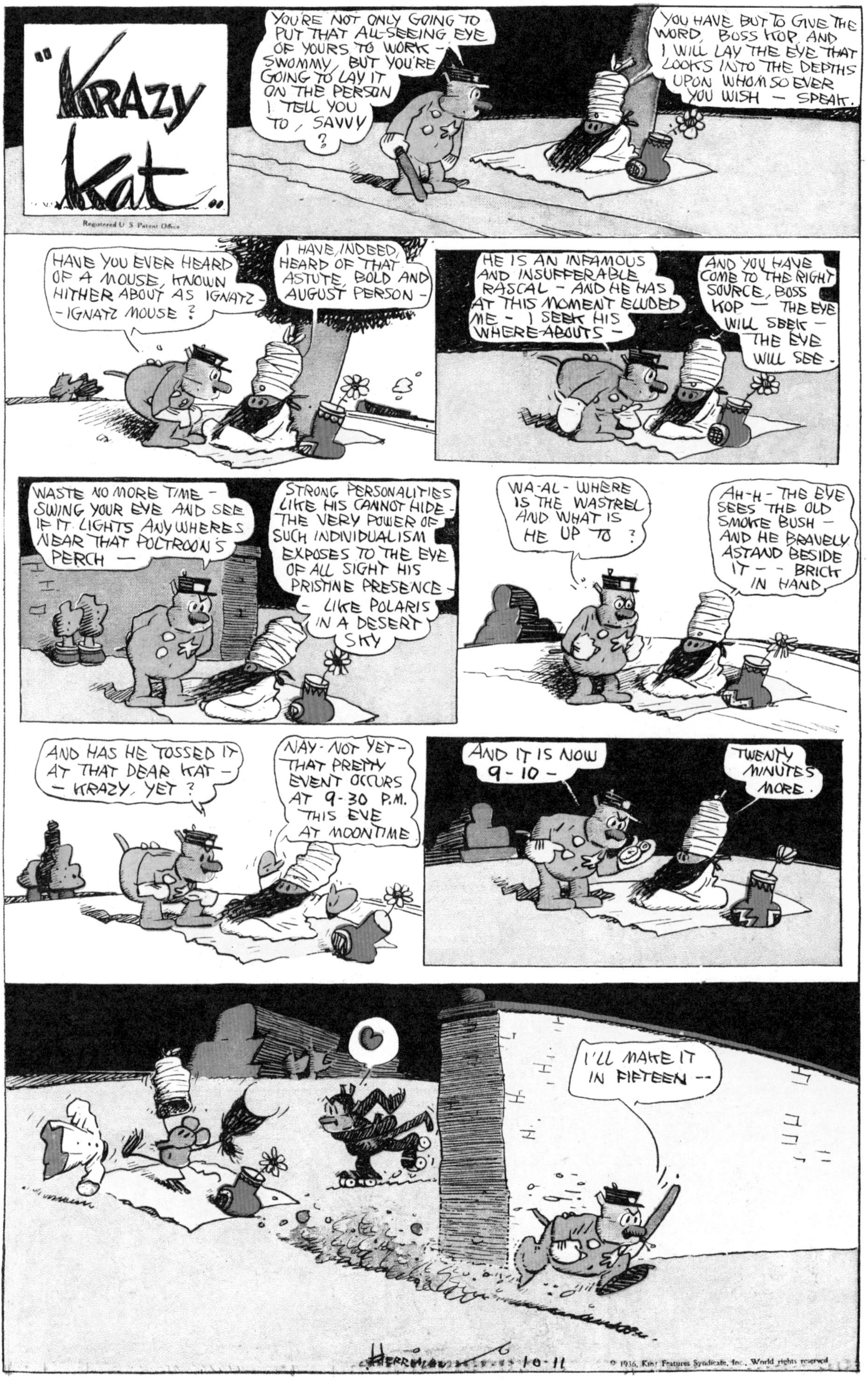
"Krazy Kat"
Registered U.S. Patent Office
YOU'RE NOT ONLY GOING TO PUT THAT ALL-SEEING EYE OF YOURS TO WORK - SWOMMY, BUT YOU'RE GOING TO LAY IT ON THE PERSON I TELL YOU TO, SAVVY ?
YOU HAVE BUT TO GIVE THE WORD, BOSS KOP, AND I WILL LAY THE EYE THAT LOOKS INTO THE DEPTHS UPON WHOM SO EVER YOU WISH - SPEAK.
HAVE YOU EVER HEARD OF A MOUSE, KNOWN HITHER ABOUT AS IGNATZ - IGNATZ MOUSE ?
I HAVE, INDEED, HEARD OF THAT ASTUTE, BOLD AND AUGUST PERSON -
HE IS AN INFAMOUS AND INSUFFERABLE RASCAL - AND HE HAS AT THIS MOMENT ELUDED ME - I SEEK HIS WHERE-ABOUTS -
AND YOU HAVE COME TO THE RIGHT SOURCE, BOSS KOP - THE EYE WILL SEEK - THE EYE WILL SEE.
WASTE NO MORE TIME - SWING YOUR EYE AND SEE IF IT LIGHTS ANYWHERES NEAR THAT POLTROON'S PERCH -
STRONG PERSONALITIES LIKE HIS CANNOT HIDE - THE VERY POWER OF SUCH INDIVIDUALISM EXPOSES TO THE EYE OF ALL SIGHT HIS PRISTINE PRESENCE - LIKE POLARIS IN A DESERT SKY
WA-AL- WHERE IS THE WASTREL AND WHAT IS HE UP TO ?
AH-H - THE EYE SEES THE OLD SMOKE BUSH - AND HE BRAVELY ASTAND BESIDE IT - - BRICK IN HAND
AND HAS HE TOSSED IT AT THAT DEAR KAT - KRAZY, YET ?
NAY - NOT YET - THAT PRETTY EVENT OCCURS AT 9-30 P.M. THIS EVE AT MOONTIME
AND IT IS NOW 9-10 -
TWENTY MINUTES MORE.
I'LL MAKE IT IN FIFTEEN --
HERRIMAN 10-11
© 1936, King Features Syndicate, Inc., World rights reserved

October 11th, 1936.

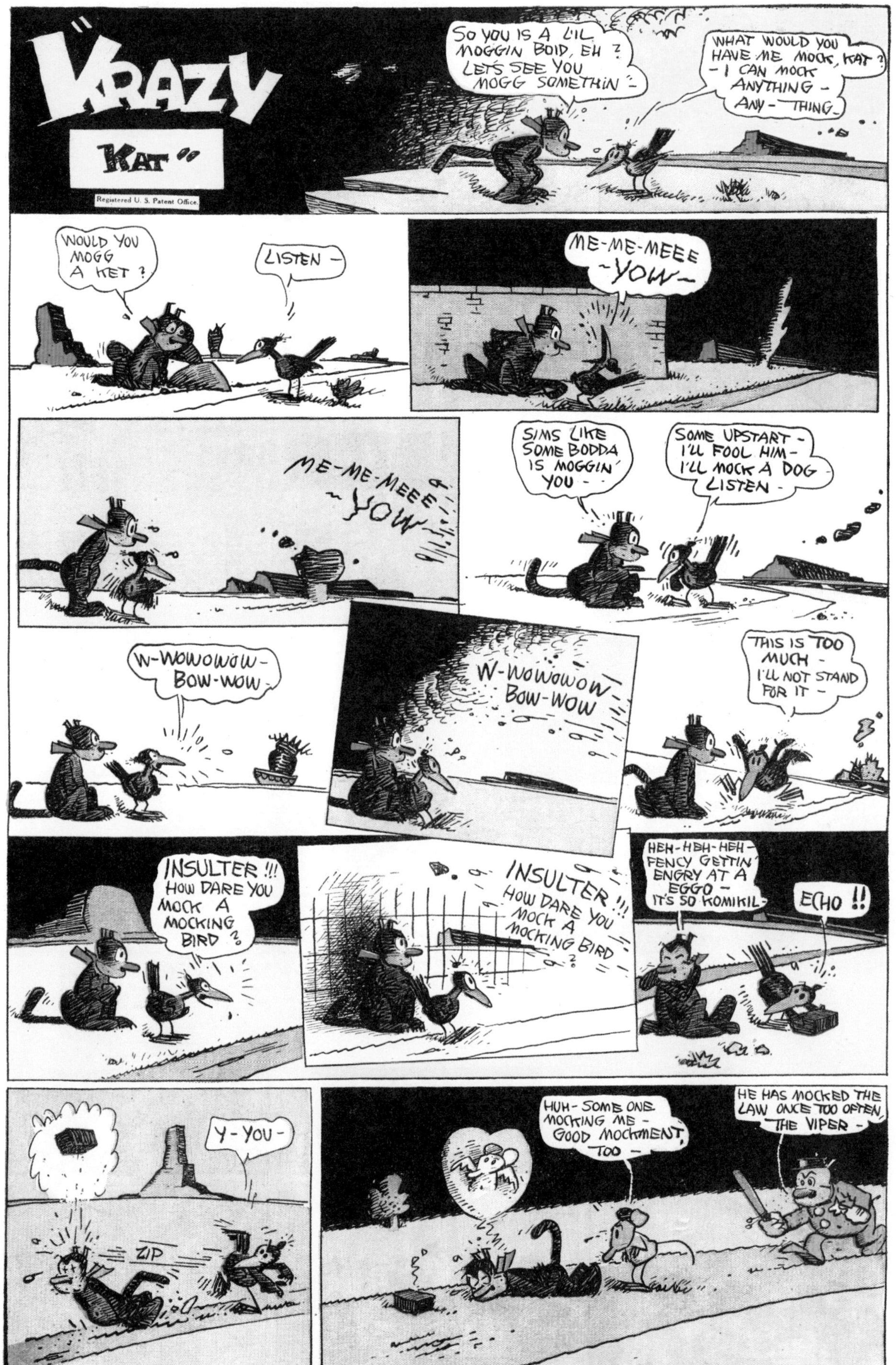
"KRAZY KAT"
Registered U. S. Patent Office.
SO YOU IS A L'IL MOGGIN BOID, EH ? LET'S SEE YOU MOGG SOMETHIN -
WHAT WOULD YOU HAVE ME MOCK, KAT ? - I CAN MOCK ANYTHING - ANY - THING -
WOULD YOU MOGG A KET ?
LISTEN -
ME-ME-MEEE ~YOW~
ME-ME-MEEE ~YOW
SIMS LIKE SOME BODDA IS MOGGIN' YOU -
SOME UPSTART - I'LL FOOL HIM - I'LL MOCK A DOG LISTEN -
W-WOWOWOW - BOW-WOW -
W-WOWOWOW BOW-WOW
THIS IS TOO MUCH - I'LL NOT STAND FOR IT -
INSULTER !!! HOW DARE YOU MOCK A MOCKING BIRD ?
INSULTER !!! HOW DARE YOU MOCK A MOCKING BIRD ?
HEH-HEH-HEH FENCY GETTIN' ENGRY AT A EGGO - IT'S SO KOMIKIL
ECHO !!
Y-YOU-
ZIP
HUH- SOME ONE MOCKING ME - GOOD MOCKMENT, TOO -
HE HAS MOCKED THE LAW ONCE TOO OFTEN, THE VIPER -
© 1936, King Features Syndicate, Inc., World rights reserved.
HERRIMAN
10-18

October 18th, 1936.

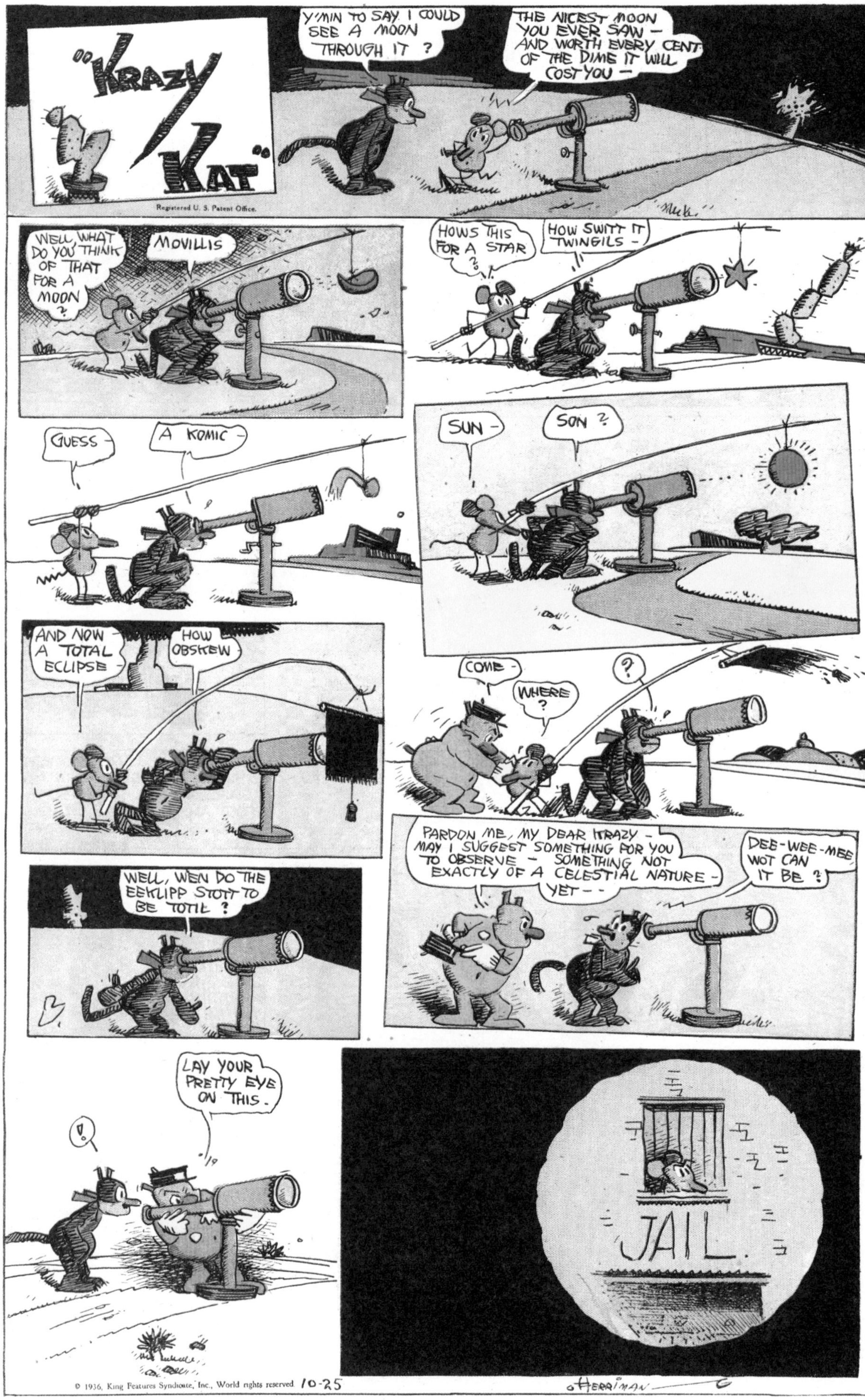
"Krazy Kat"
Registered U. S. Patent Office.
Y'MIN TO SAY I COULD SEE A MOON THROUGH IT ?
THE NICEST MOON YOU EVER SAW – AND WORTH EVERY CENT OF THE DIME IT WILL COST YOU –
WELL, WHAT DO YOU THINK OF THAT FOR A MOON ?
MOVILLIS
HOWS THIS FOR A STAR ?
HOW SWITT IT TWINGILS –
GUESS –
A KOMIC –
SUN –
SON ?
AND NOW A TOTAL ECLIPSE –
HOW OBSKEW –
COME –
WHERE ?
?
WELL, WEN DO THE EEKLIPP STOTT TO BE TOTIL ?
PARDON ME, MY DEAR KRAZY – MAY I SUGGEST SOMETHING FOR YOU TO OBSERVE – SOMETHING NOT EXACTLY OF A CELESTIAL NATURE – YET – –
DEE-WEE-MEE WOT CAN IT BE ?
LAY YOUR PRETTY EYE ON THIS –
!
JAIL
© 1936, King Features Syndicate, Inc., World rights reserved 10-25
Herriman

October 25th, 1936.

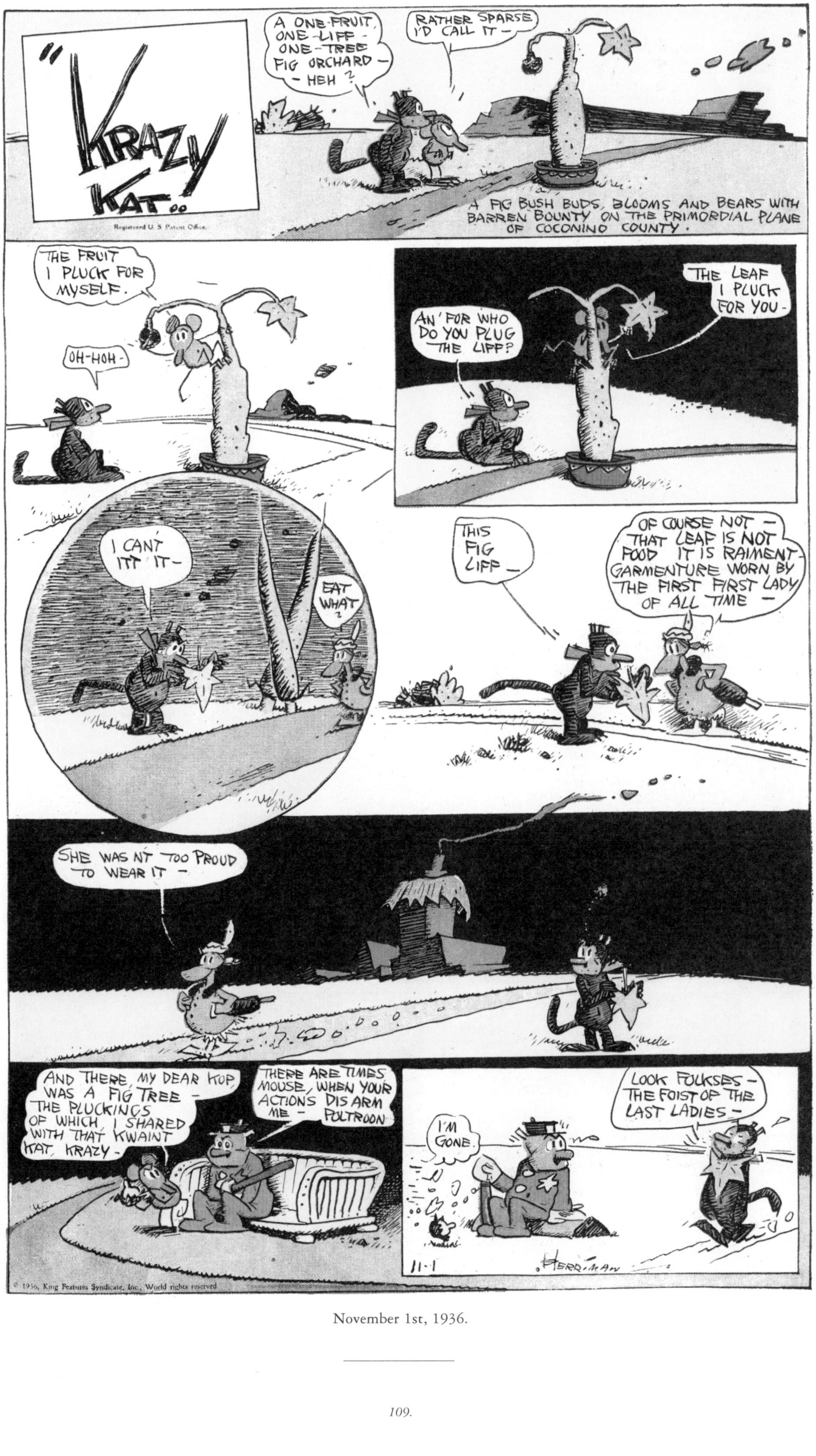
"KRAZY KAT"
Registered U. S. Patent Office.
A ONE-FRUIT, ONE-LIFF - ONE-TREE FIG ORCHARD - HEH ?
RATHER SPARSE I'D CALL IT -
A FIG BUSH BUDS, BLOOMS AND BEARS WITH BARREN BOUNTY ON THE PRIMORDIAL PLANE OF COCONINO COUNTY.
THE FRUIT I PLUCK FOR MYSELF.
OH-HOH -
AN' FOR WHO DO YOU PLUG THE LIFF?
THE LEAF I PLUCK FOR YOU -
I CAN'T ITT IT -
EAT WHAT ?
THIS FIG LIFF -
OF COURSE NOT - THAT LEAF IS NOT FOOD IT IS RAIMENT - GARMENTURE WORN BY THE FIRST FIRST LADY OF ALL TIME -
SHE WAS N'T TOO PROUD TO WEAR IT -
AND THERE, MY DEAR KOP WAS A FIG TREE - THE PLUCKINGS OF WHICH, I SHARED WITH THAT KWAINT KAT, KRAZY -
THERE ARE TIMES MOUSE, WHEN YOUR ACTIONS DIS ARM ME - POLTROON
I'M GONE.
LOOK FOLKSES - THE FOIST OF THE LAST LADIES -
11-1
HERRIMAN
© 1936, King Features Syndicate, Inc., World rights reserved.

November 1st, 1936.

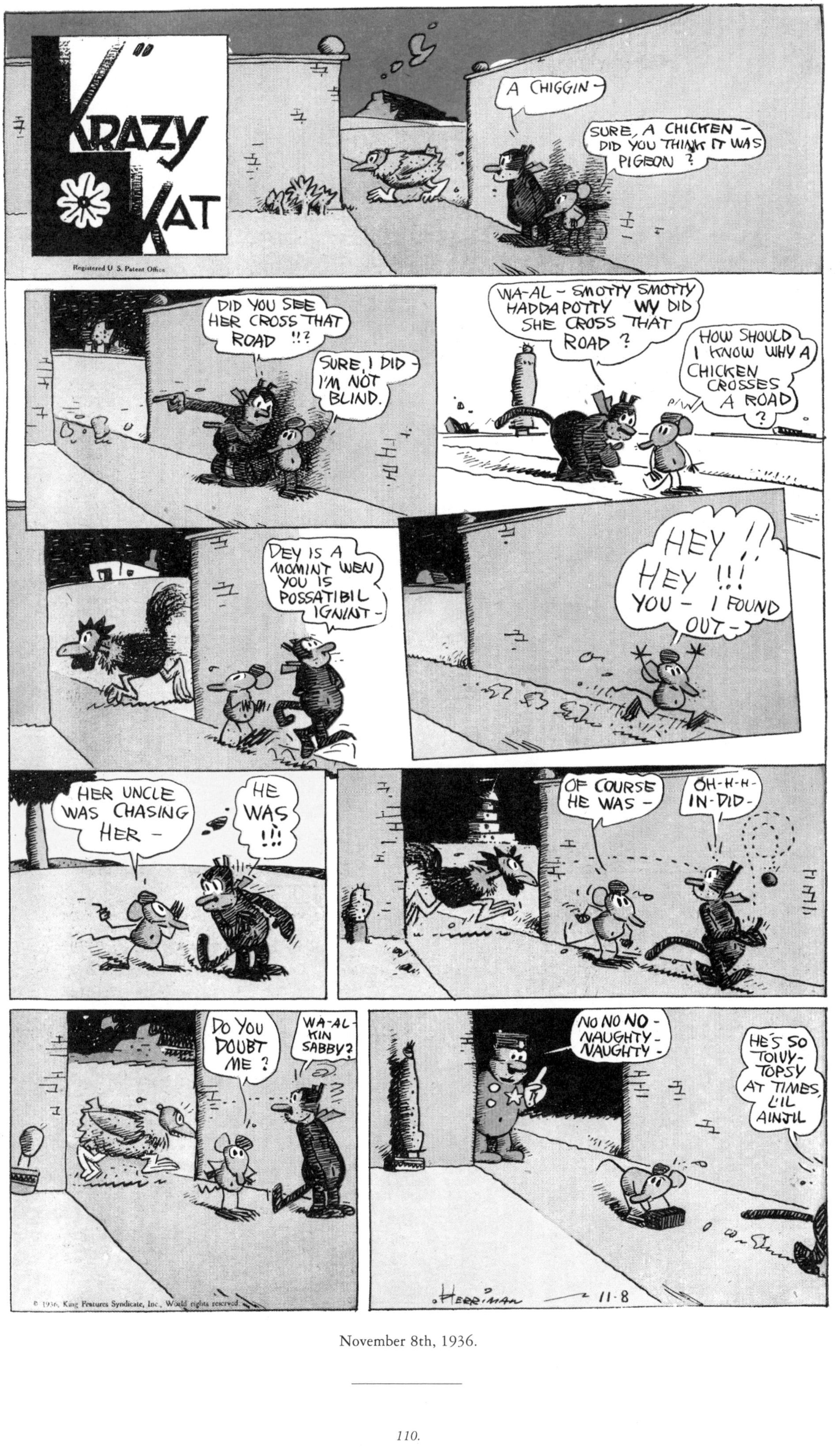

Krazy Kat
Registered U. S. Patent Office
A CHIGGIN -
SURE, A CHICKEN - DID YOU THINK IT WAS PIGEON ?
DID YOU SEE HER CROSS THAT ROAD !!?
SURE, I DID - I'M NOT BLIND.
WA-AL - SMOTTY SMOTTY HADDAPOTTY WY DID SHE CROSS THAT ROAD ?
HOW SHOULD I KNOW WHY A CHICKEN CROSSES A ROAD ?
DEY IS A MOMINT WEN YOU IS POSSATIBIL IGNINT -
HEY !!
HEY !!!
YOU - I FOUND OUT -
HER UNCLE WAS CHASING HER -
HE WAS !!!
OF COURSE HE WAS -
OH-H-H IN-DID -
Do YOU DOUBT ME ?
WA-AL KIN SABBY ?
NO NO NO - NAUGHTY - NAUGHTY -
HE'S SO TOIVY-TOPSY AT TIMES, L'IL AINJIL
HERRIMAN 11-8
© 1936, King Features Syndicate, Inc., World rights reserved.

November 8th, 1936.

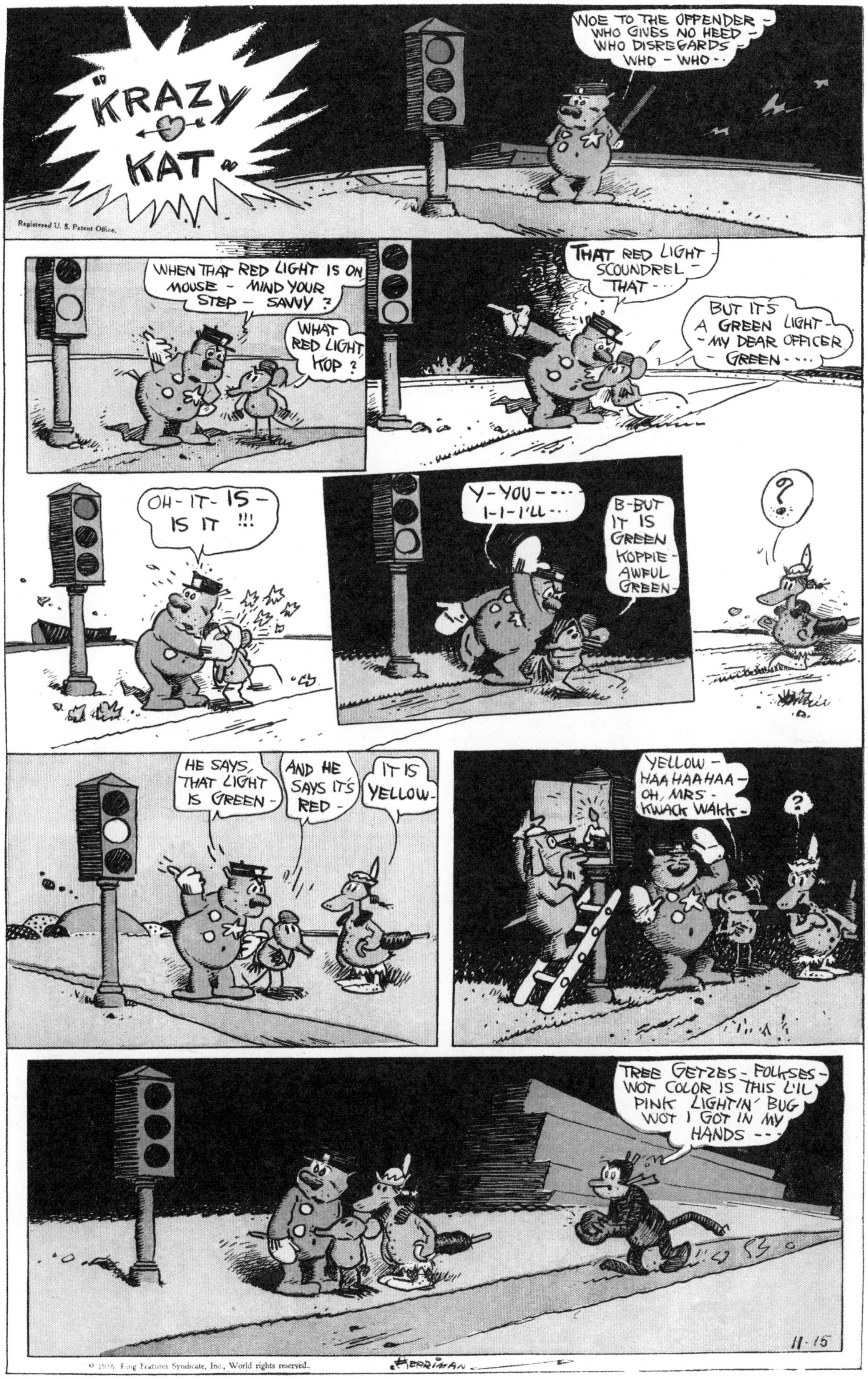
KRAZY KAT
Registered U. S. Patent Office.
WOE TO THE OFFENDER - WHO GIVES NO HEED - WHO DISREGARDS - WHO - WHO - -
WHEN THAT RED LIGHT IS ON MOUSE - MIND YOUR STEP - SAVVY ?
WHAT RED LIGHT, KOP ?
THAT RED LIGHT - SCOUNDREL - THAT - - -
BUT IT'S A GREEN LIGHT - - MY DEAR OFFICER - GREEN - - - -
OH - IT - IS - IS IT !!!
Y - YOU - - - - I - I - I'LL - - -
B-BUT IT IS GREEN KOPPIE - AWFUL GREEN -
?
HE SAYS, THAT LIGHT IS GREEN -
AND HE SAYS IT'S RED -
IT IS YELLOW -
YELLOW - HAA HAA HAA - OH, MRS - KWACK WAKK -
?
TREE GETZES - FOLKSES - WOT COLOR IS THIS L'IL PINK LIGHT'N' BUG WOT I GOT IN MY HANDS - - -
11 - 15
© 1936, King Features Syndicate, Inc., World rights reserved.
HERRIMAN

November 15th, 1936.

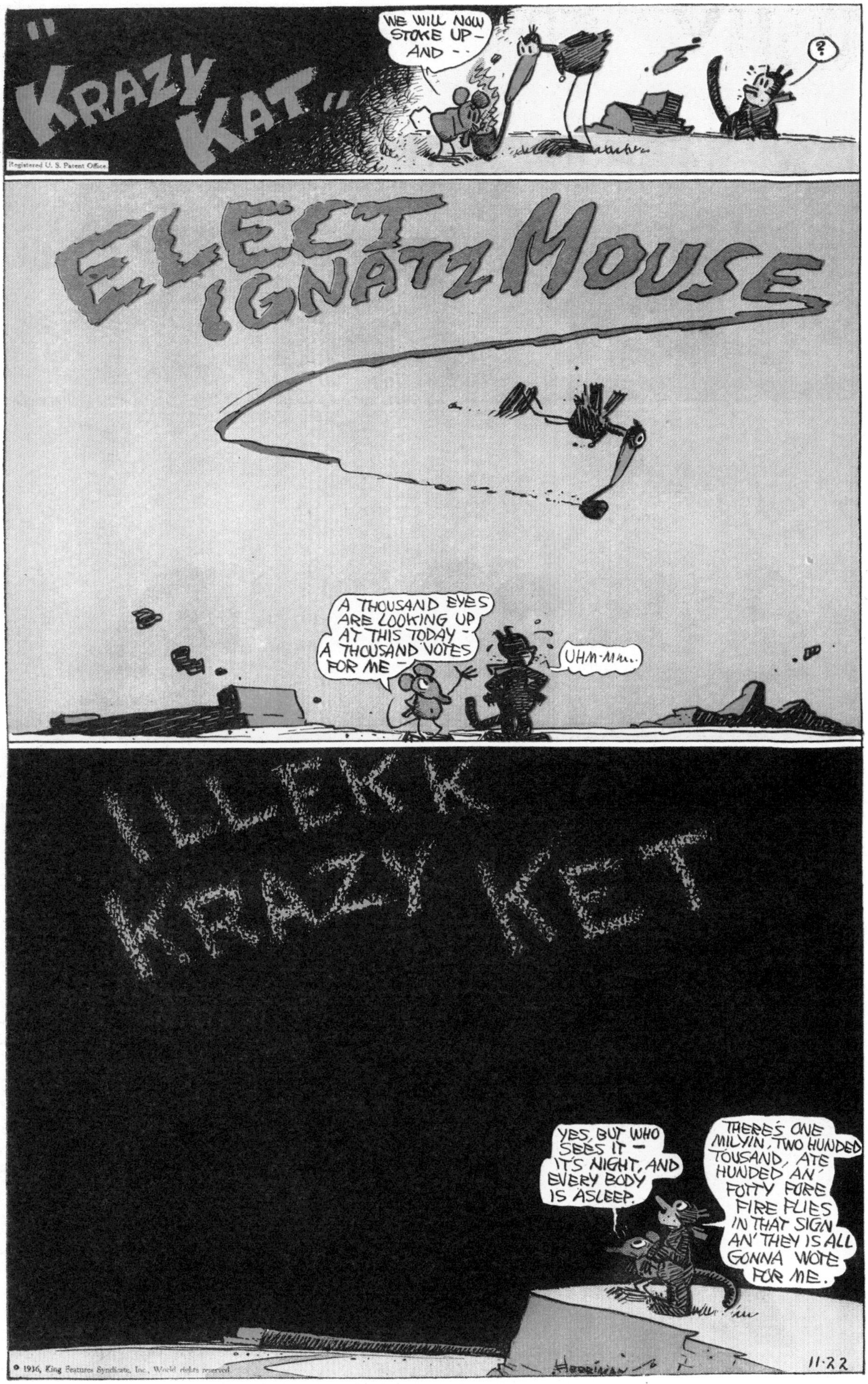
"KRAZY KAT"
Registered U. S. Patent Office.
WE WILL NOW STOKE UP - AND - -
?
ELECT IGNATZ MOUSE
A THOUSAND EYES ARE LOOKING UP AT THIS TODAY - A THOUSAND VOTES FOR ME -
UHM-MM...
ILLEKK KRAZY KET
YES, BUT WHO SEES IT - IT'S NIGHT, AND EVERY BODY IS ASLEEP.
THERE'S ONE MILYIN, TWO HUNDED TOUSAND, ATE HUNDED AN' FOTTY FORE FIRE FLIES IN THAT SIGN AN' THEY IS ALL GONNA WOTE FOR ME.
© 1936, King Features Syndicate, Inc., World rights reserved.
HERRIMAN
11-22

November 22nd, 1936.

"KRAZY KAT"
Registered U. S. Patent Office
I'M GOING TO GIVE A LOOK-SEE AT A WOLCANO —
A VOLCANO - SURELY, KRAZY, YOU JEST - AND WHERE CAN THIS VOLCANO BE ?
OVA BY THE BLUE BIN BUTCH -
I'VE NEVER SEEN ANY VOLCANO BY THE BLUE BEAN BUSH -
BUT IT MUST BE THERE - IGNATZ MICE SAID IT WAS —
OH-HOH-H-H...
I GO -
I GO, TOO -
THIS MUST BE IT -
IT'S THE RIGHT SHAPE, BUT FROM PICTURES I'VE SEEN IT SHOULD BE PUFFING OUT A SNORT OF SMOKE —
IT PUFFED -
S-SURE DID -
ALL WAYS HE TELLS THE TRUE - L'IL DOLLIN - HE'S SO UNFIBBIN -
MOVILLIS
KOFF KOFF KOFF KOFF
DO YOU HAPPEN TO HEAR SOME ONE COUGHING BACK OF YON WALL ?
I DO INDID
I WONDER WHO IT WAS
SOME BODDA WIT'A BRONNIKIL ILLMINT NO DOT —
© 1936, King Features Syndicate, Inc., World rights reserved.
11-29
HERRIMAN

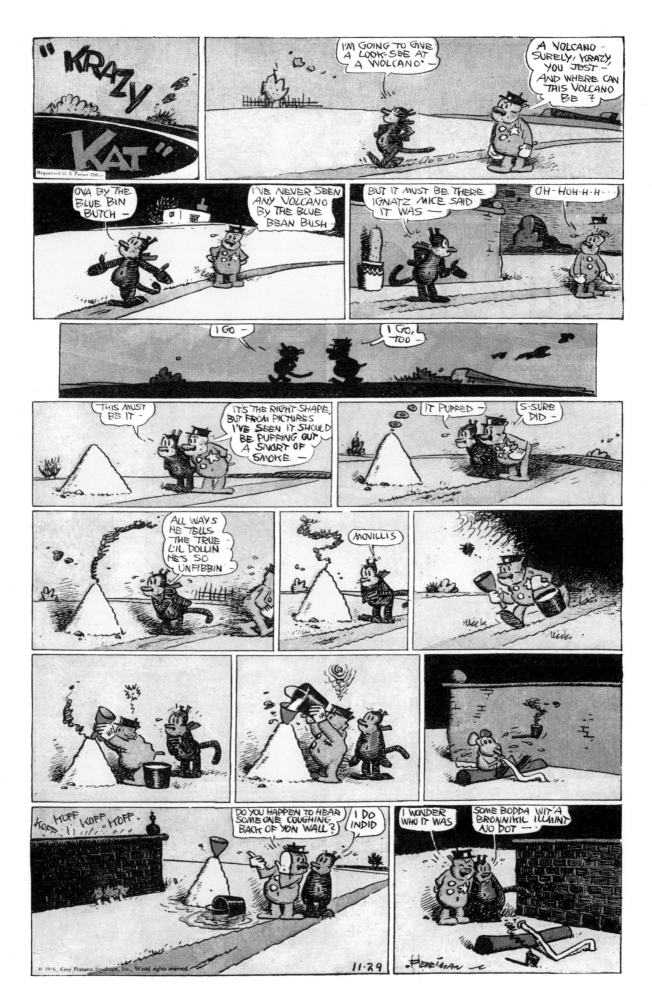

November 29th, 1936.

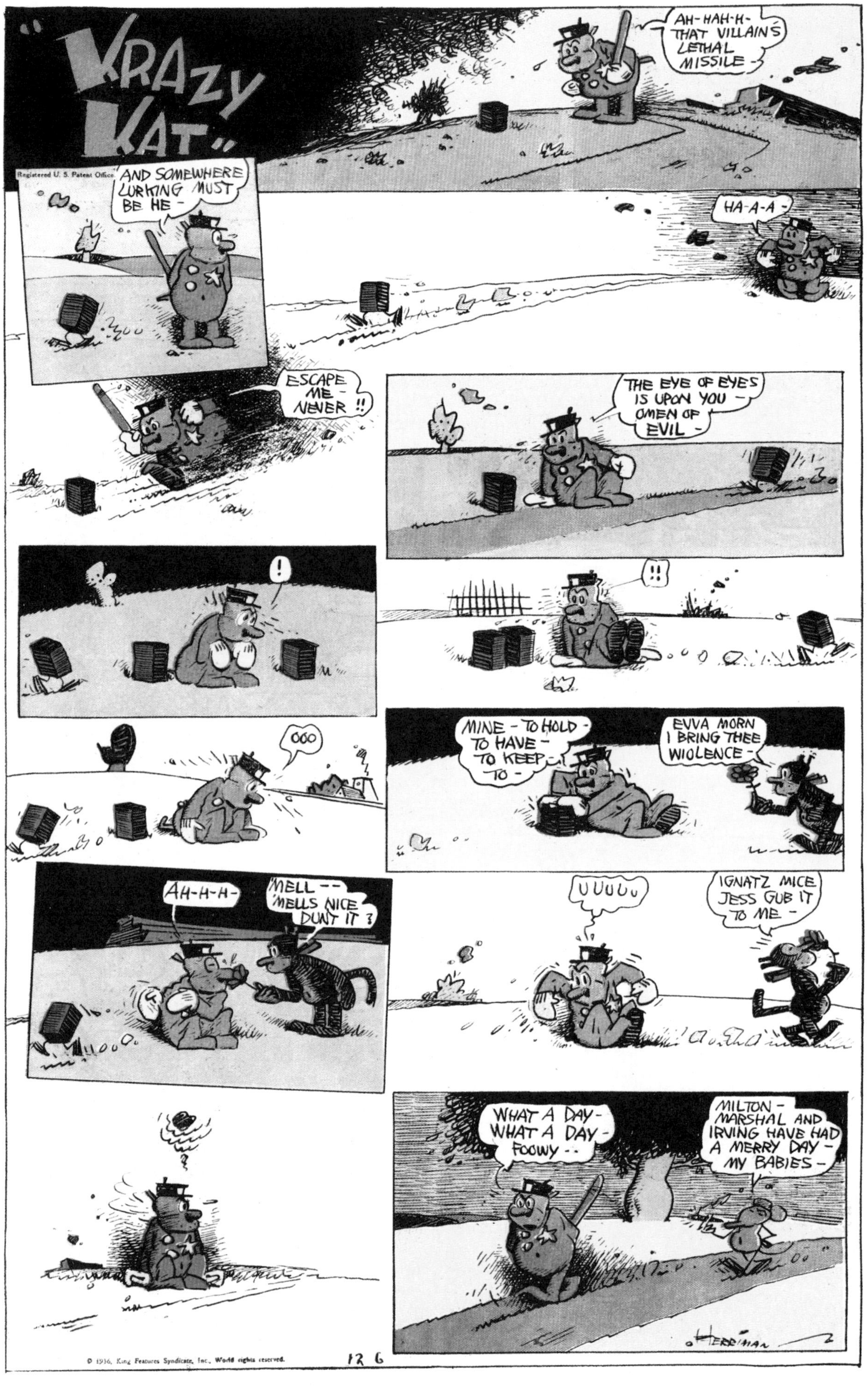
"KRAZY KAT"
Registered U. S. Patent Office
AH-HAH-H- THAT VILLAINS LETHAL MISSILE -
AND SOMEWHERE LURKING MUST BE HE -
HA-A-A -
ESCAPE ME NEVER !!
THE EYE OF EYES IS UPON YOU - OMEN OF EVIL -
!
!!
OOO
MINE - TO HOLD - TO HAVE - TO KEEP - TO -
EVVA MORN I BRING THEE WIOLENCE -
AH-H-H-
'MELL -- 'MELLS NICE DUNT IT ?
UUUUU
IGNATZ MICE JESS GUB IT TO ME -
WHAT A DAY - WHAT A DAY - FOOWY --
MILTON - MARSHAL AND IRVING HAVE HAD A MERRY DAY - MY BABIES -
HERRIMAN
© 1936, King Features Syndicate, Inc., World rights reserved.
12 6

December 6th, 1936.

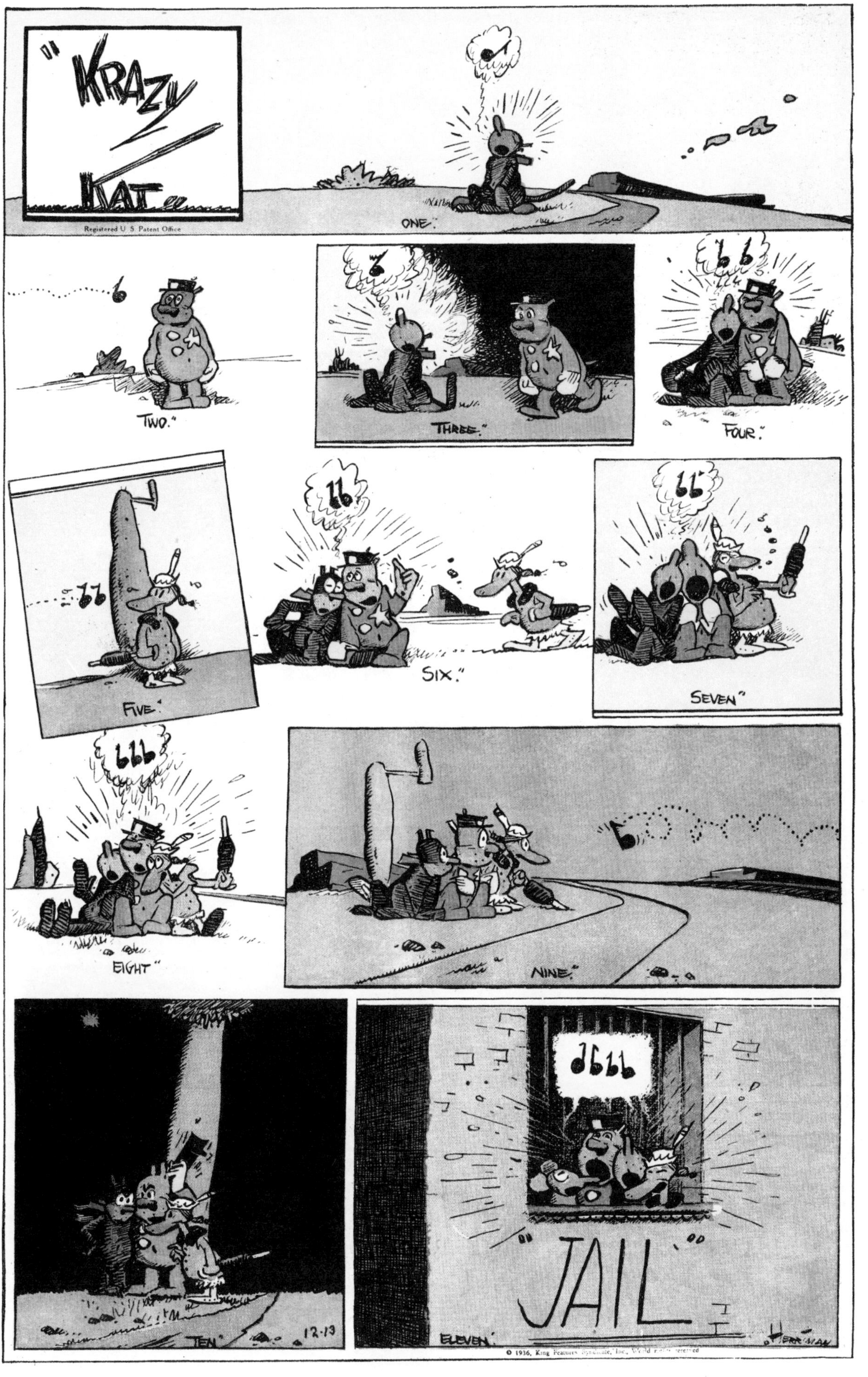
"KRAZY KAT"
Registered U. S. Patent Office
ONE."
TWO."
THREE."
FOUR."
FIVE."
SIX."
SEVEN"
EIGHT"
NINE."
TEN"
12-13
ELEVEN."
"JAIL"
HERRIMAN

December 13th, 1936.

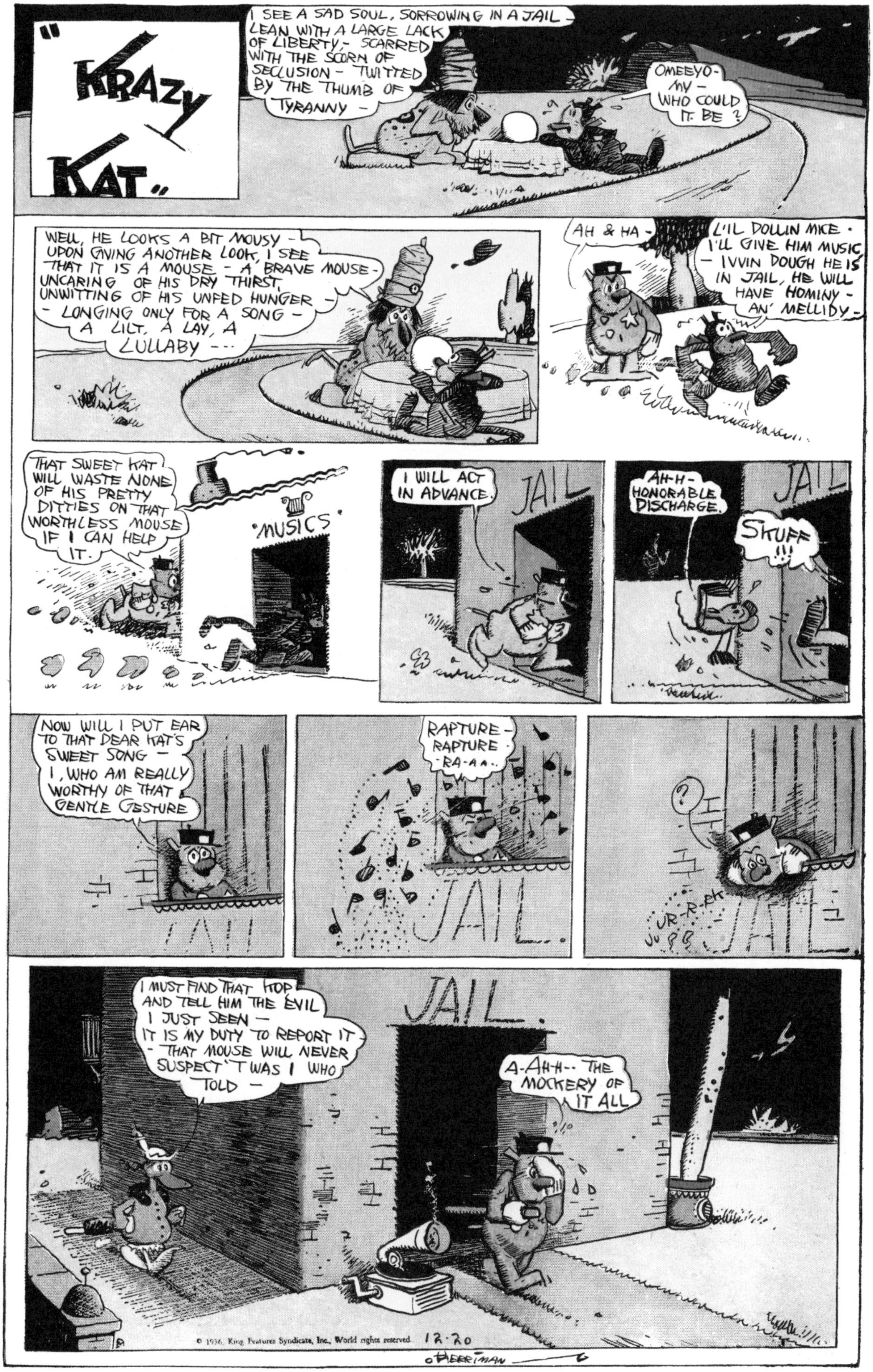
"KRAZY KAT"
I SEE A SAD SOUL, SORROWING IN A JAIL-LEAN WITH A LARGE LACK OF LIBERTY,- SCARRED WITH THE SCORN OF SECLUSION- TWITTED BY THE THUMB OF TYRANNY -
OMEEYO-MY - WHO COULD IT BE ?
WELL, HE LOOKS A BIT MOUSY - UPON GIVING ANOTHER LOOK, I SEE THAT IT IS A MOUSE - A BRAVE MOUSE - UNCARING OF HIS DRY THIRST, UNWITTING OF HIS UNFED HUNGER - - LONGING ONLY FOR A SONG - A LILT, A LAY, A LULLABY ---
AH & HA -
L'IL DOLLIN MICE - I'LL GIVE HIM MUSIC - IVVIN DOUGH HE IS IN JAIL, HE WILL HAVE HOMINY - AN' MELLIDY -
THAT SWEET KAT WILL WASTE NONE OF HIS PRETTY DITTIES ON THAT WORTHLESS MOUSE IF I CAN HELP IT.
"MUSICS"
I WILL ACT IN ADVANCE.
JAIL
AH-H- HONORABLE DISCHARGE.
JAIL
SKUFF !!!
NOW WILL I PUT EAR TO THAT DEAR KAT'S SWEET SONG - I, WHO AM REALLY WORTHY OF THAT GENTLE GESTURE
JAIL
RAPTURE - RAPTURE - RA-A-A-
JAIL
?
UR-R-RK
JAIL
JAIL
I MUST FIND THAT KOP AND TELL HIM THE EVIL I JUST SEEN - IT IS MY DUTY TO REPORT IT - THAT MOUSE WILL NEVER SUSPECT 'T WAS I WHO TOLD -
A-AH-H-- THE MOCKERY OF IT ALL
© 1936, King Features Syndicate, Inc., World rights reserved.
12-20
HERRIMAN

December 20th, 1936.

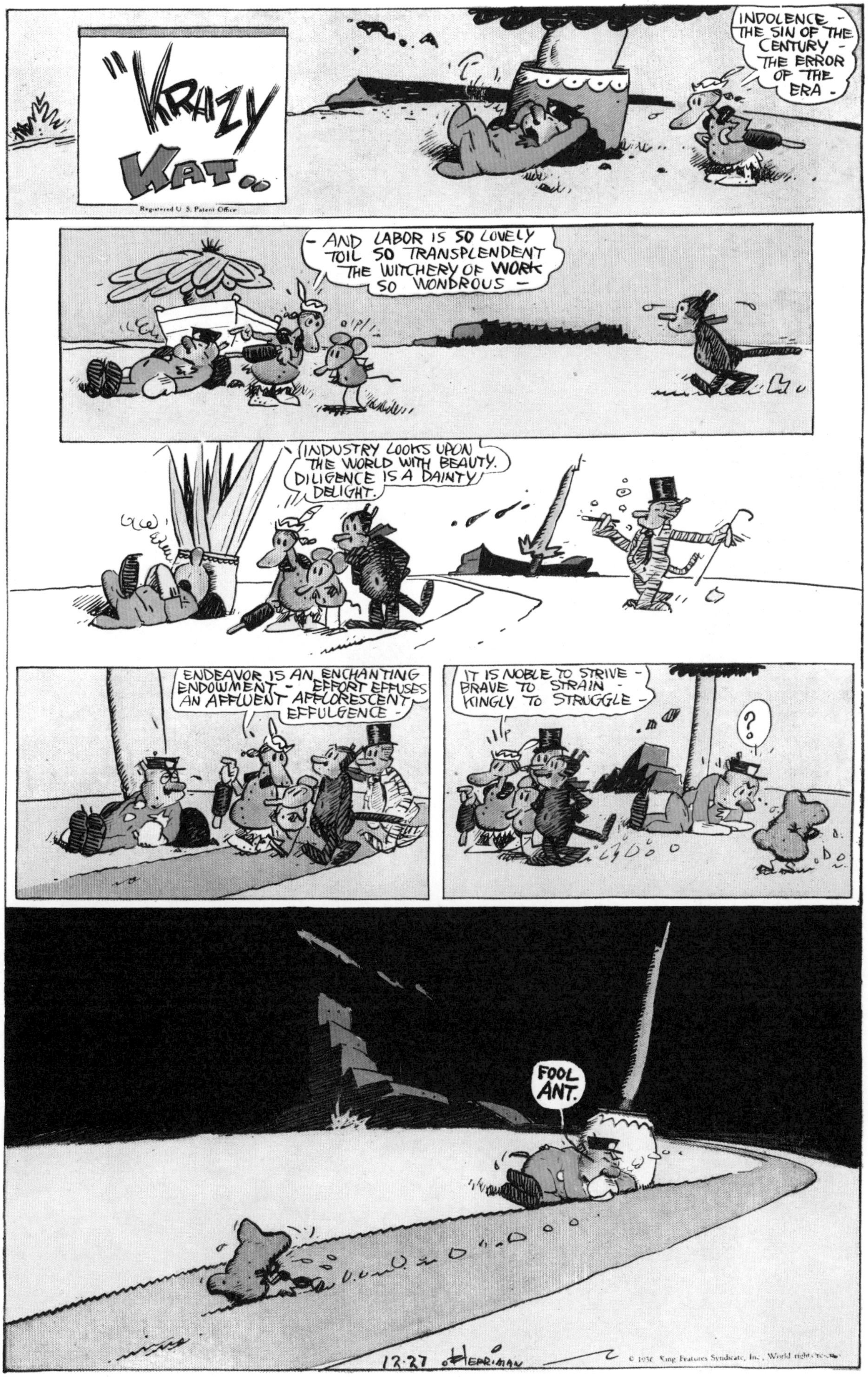
"KRAZY KAT"
Registered U. S. Patent Office
INDOLENCE - THE SIN OF THE CENTURY - THE ERROR OF THE ERA -
- AND LABOR IS SO LOVELY TOIL SO TRANSPLENDENT THE WITCHERY OF WORK SO WONDROUS -
INDUSTRY LOOKS UPON THE WORLD WITH BEAUTY. DILIGENCE IS A DAINTY DELIGHT.
ENDEAVOR IS AN ENCHANTING ENDOWMENT - EFFORT EFFUSES AN AFFLUENT AFFLORESCENT EFFULGENCE -
IT IS NOBLE TO STRIVE - BRAVE TO STRAIN - KINGLY TO STRUGGLE -
?
FOOL ANT.
12·27 Herriman

December 27th, 1936.

The IGNATZ MOUSE DEBAFFLER PAGE.

6/1/35: The Growler was a new character in the KK epic, taking his bow with the first published page of the new color strip.

3/29/36: Why the grimly limned skulking of Offisa Pupp prior to his picking a stogie from inside his cap for a nicotine puff? Certainly such was neither illegal or anti-social in Coconino County, being indulged openly by cop and citizen alike frequently and openly in the strip, often in the introduction of exploding cigars at opportune moments. In this odd instance the Debaffler confesses itself baffled.

4/4/36: Here it would appear that while Coconino County mammalia can conduct romantic pursuits ardently in the instances of kats, pupps, and mice, avians such as ducks must seek mates solely among other ducks; thus only bachelor birds of a feather need duck out at news of Mrs. Kwakk Wakk's marital pursuits.

4/25/36: A Hit Parade ditty of the period beleaguered the radio networks with a refrain that told rapt listeners that "Oh, the music goes 'round and 'round...and it comes out here!"

6/6/36: Mr. Ignatz Mouse's triumphant outburst — "Keno" — reflects the cries of movie theatre audience winners of an inter-feature number matching game in the mid-thirties called — yea — Keno.

6/13/36: The King Features komic strip kolorists, usually deft and diligent at their rainbow palettes, goofed ever so insignificantly here in omitting the otherwise uniform blue of Offisa Pupp's regalia from its left sleeve in not one but two far right panels of this episode. The Fantagraphics Daub Squad have korrected these lapses in the main text of this volume, but have preserved one of them on this Debaffler page for the record.

7/25/36: History buffs who want a reference-by-reference and quote-by quote translation of Krazy's and Offisa Pupp's erudite commentary in this episode — as dreamed up by Offisa Pupp in this episode after a sturdy sip of Tiger Tea — will have to supply their own: Fantagraphics can't afford the budget-busting typography involved. Sheesh! What a deluge of name drops! (And all ending superbly with a classic limning of the old Zip! POW! two-step.)

8/8/36-9/15/36: Poetic political ribbing runs rampant in these six remarkable episodes featuring a dogie and a dodo. Those who are interested can diligently delve for klews to Garge's politix, the rest of us can only gape agog at the master's superbly sustained poetry and graphic delights.

10/11/36: Even Homer nods: there is an odd absence of brick from the celebratory last panel here despite its immediate need.

In the late nineteen-teens the
Averill Company, "in arrangement
with Geo. Herriman," produced this
Krazy Kay stuffed doll, and, judging
from the number of them still extant, it
must have been at least moderately popular. (A similar toy, possibly a prototype,
is seen on Herriman's desk in the photograph at the start of this volume, as well as
in the family portrait reprinted in one of the
Kitchen Sink color volumes 15 years ago.)
Sewn from felt and tightly stuffed with sawdust
(or some other unhuggable material) over a vague-
ly posable wire armature, it is a little over 12" tall.
(A "negative image" version of the doll was also produced, in orange felt with black footpads and ribbon.)

The novelty pinback buttons at right (enlarged here for
clarity) produced for the New York *Evening Journal* and
Tokio cigarettes date respectively from probably the 1930s
and the 1910s. One has to wonder, though — what's so
wrong with being a "Krazy Kat"?
Collection of C. Ware.

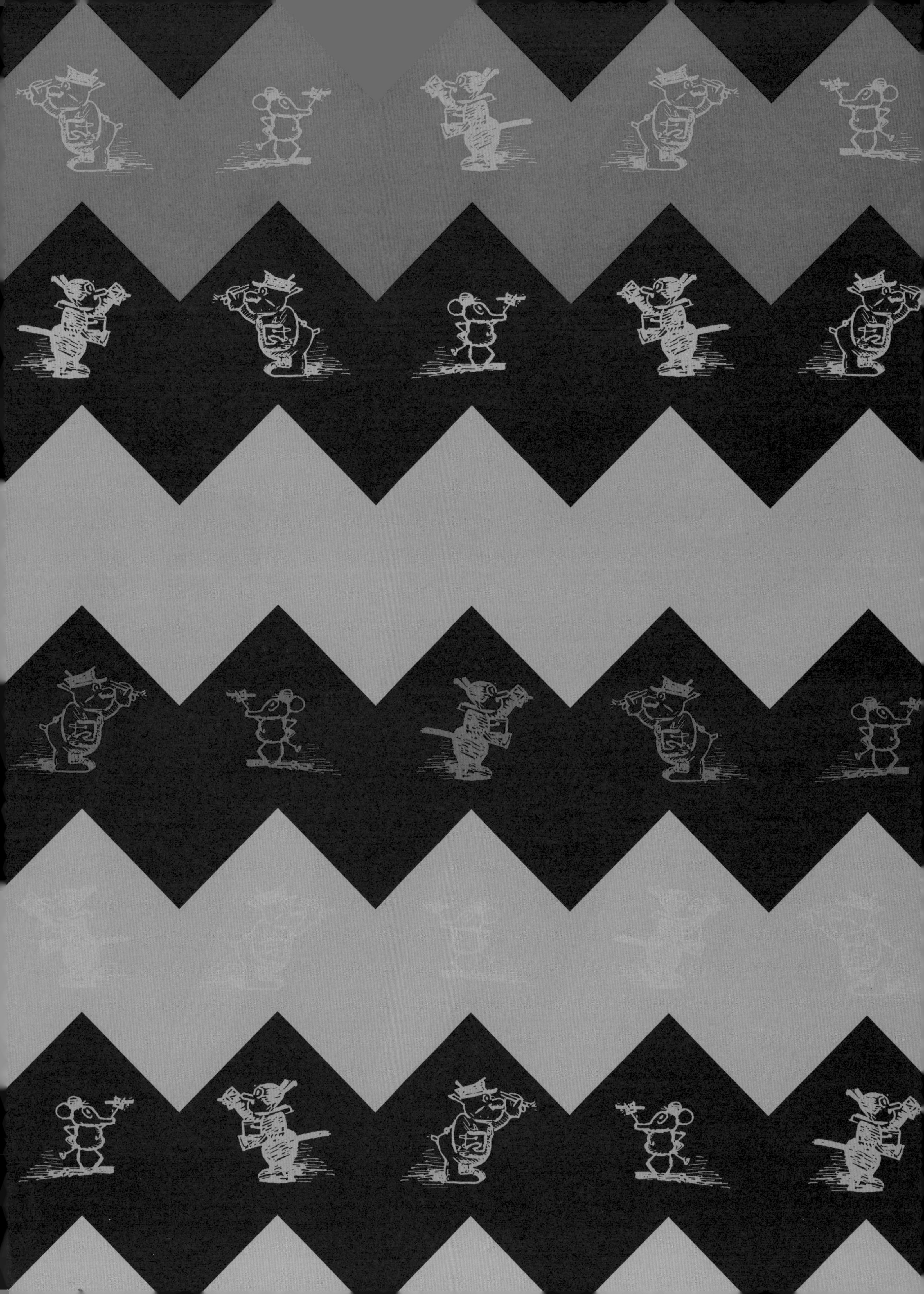